CRISIS!

The patrol's mission was to seize prisoners and remain in the houses the following day to observe German movements.

The parachutists had just entered the woods when a trooper set off a trip flare. It shot into the air, illuminating the area. The men froze in place, hardly daring to breathe. Suddenly, a frightening noise: the revving of a tank or a self-propelled gun motor. Moments later, swissshh—CRACK! A shell exploded among the paratroopers.

Navas led a rush toward the dark farmhouses and the flame-spitting enemy gun. Almost immediately there was another explosion under the lieutenant's feet. He fell to the ground, writhing in agony. He had run into a minefield. . . .

AGONY
AT ANZIO

THE ALLIES'
MOST CONTROVERSIAL
AND BIZARRE OPERATION
OF WORLD WAR II

WILLIAM B. BREUER

AGONY AT ANZIO

A Jove Book / published by arrangement with
the author

PRINTING HISTORY
Zeus Publishers edition published 1985
Jove edition / January 1990

ISBN: 0-515-10211-3

Jove Books are published by The Berkley Publishing Group,
200 Madison Avenue, New York, New York 10016.
The name "JOVE" and the "J" logo
are trademarks belonging to Jove Publications, Inc.

10 9 8 7 6 5 4 3 2 1

Dedicated to the Memory of the
SIX WOMEN NURSES
of the U.S. Army Medical Corps
who were
Killed in Action
during the bloody struggle
at Anzio.
They and 200 other women nurses
shared the suffering and the peril
in equal measure
and with equal fortitude

CONTENTS

INTRODUCTION

As December 1943 approached, a suffocating pall of gloom and discouragement hovered over those in the Allied camp knowledgeable of the military situation in bleak, mountainous Italy. Only 11 weeks before, Anglo-American forces had stormed ashore along 30 miles of the beautiful Gulf of Salerno, about one-quarter of the way up the boot of Italy, and after a bloody two-week struggle, drove north to capture the major port of Naples.

The main strategic objectives of the Anglo-American campaign in Italy were to bleed the German army and to lure enemy divisions away from the Russian front and from France where the Allies planned to launch a massive cross-Channel attack from England in the Spring. That invasion would be code-named Overlord, an all-out effort to knife into the heart of the Third Reich and destroy the German Wehrmacht (armed forces).

Meanwhile, Adolf Hitler, warlord of the Third Reich, was conferring with his two top commanders in Italy, Field Marshals Albrecht Kesselring and Erwin Rommel, the latter having gained world fame as the Desert Fox. A dispute erupted over the best strategy to be followed in Italy. Kesselring held it advisable to keep the Allies as far from Germany as possible, to contest the invaders every yard of the way south of Rome.

Rommel disagreed. He saw no strategic importance in

holding onto the Italian capital and brushed off references to its political significance. He proposed conceding Rome to the Anglo-Americans and establishing a defense in depth along the towering peaks of the Alps in the north.

Hitler solved the impasse by shifting Rommel to France where he would be charged with defending the Atlantic Wall against an impending cross-Channel attack by the Allies and bestowing upon Kesselring, recognized by his foes as among the ablest of German tacticians, full command of the Wehrmacht in the Mediterranean.

The fuehrer at the same time issued a stern order to Field Marshal Kesselring: hold Rome and central Italy at all costs.

The energetic Kesselring—known to the Allies as "Smiling Al"—plunged into his task and ordered engineers to begin feverishly constructing a defensive position running diagonally across the full width of Italy known as the Gustav Line, some 90 miles south of Rome. Utilizing natural terrain features such as towering mountains and swift-flowing streams, the Gustav Line stretched from Gaeta on the west coast to a point near Ortona on the Adriatic Sea, on the east.

With U.S. Lieutenant General Mark W. Clark's Fifth Army on the left and British General Bernard L. Montgomery's seasoned Eighth Army on the right, the Allies attacked northward with high hopes early in October. The road to Rome appeared open. A sprinkling of Allied optimists had even launched a new battle cry—"Rome by Christmas!"

The two Allied armies were attacking over some of the world's most rugged terrain. The towering Apennines ran generally north and south down the center of the peninsula, furnishing a formidable barrier between the U.S. Fifth and the British Eighth armies. In General Clark's zone of advance along the west coast toward Rome the Lepini and Aurunci mountain ranges had to be confronted.

It was terrain ideally suited for the defense. Entrenched on mountain peaks, a handful of Germans with a few machine guns and mortars could stall an entire attacking battalion for days, exacting a heavy toll, then falling back to the next mountain where the bloody process would have to be repeated again.

General Clark's Fifth Army on the west coast had to attack along Route 6, which ran from Naples to Rome through the

Liri Valley, a gap five to seven miles wide between the
Apennines in central Italy and the Lepini and Aurunci moun-
tain ranges near the Tyrrhenian Sea. The fact that the Ameri-
cans would have to attack through the Liri Valley gap to reach
Rome was obvious to the commander of the German Tenth
Army, General of Panzer Troops Heinrich von Vietinghoff.

If the Liri Valley was the gateway to Rome, von Vietinghoff
knew that a 1,600-foot elevation named Monte Cassino was the
key to the gate. From the heights of Monte Cassino and its
ancient monastery, German observers could gain a sweeping
panoramic view of Route 6 and the Liri Valley. Lofty Monte
Cassino would be, in effect, a giant eye in the sky from where
devastating artillery and mortar fire could rain down on any
American force seeking passage up the valley.

As the purpose of the Italian campaign was to lure German
divisions away from France and from the Russian front, Allied
commanders knew the only way to accomplish that mission
was to "attack and keep attacking." The Allies did, and the
peaks and valleys ran red with American and British blood.

General Dwight D. Eisenhower, the Kansas farm boy who
was Allied Supreme Commander in the Mediterranean, set the
Italian campaign in perspective with a signal to the Anglo-
American Combined Chiefs of Staff: "If we can keep the
German on his heels (in Italy) until early Spring, then the more
divisions (the Germans) use in a counteroffensive against us
the better it will be for Overlord."

Eisenhower concluded his signal on an ominous note: "Then
it makes little difference what happens to us (in Italy)."

It was a starkly realistic military appraisal of the situation in
freezing, bloody Italy: the Allied campaign there was a
sacrifice upon the altar of Overlord.

As a cold and rainy autumn in Italy turned into a biting,
miserable winter, the German Tenth Army halted its steady
fighting withdrawal from southern Italy and dug in along the
prepared fortifications of the Gustav Line. There the Allied
advance slowed to a crawl and finally halted entirely.

Major General Lucian K. Truscott, commander of the U.S.
3rd Infantry Division which was hammering its head against
the Gustav Line in the vicinity of Venafro, briefed war
correspondents at his headquarters in the shell-torn town:
"This is by far the strongest defense we've run into so far in

Italy. The Krauts have the mountaintops fortified with pill-boxes blasted out of rock and reinforced with concrete. Along the lower features, the Germans have very deep entrenchments, wired in, and extensive mine fields. In a great many places they have machine gun nests in concrete bunkers."

Truscott went on to paint a gloomy picture of what American infantrymen had run up against in efforts to crack the Gustav Line—miserable weather conditions, including heavy rains, snow, fog, sleet, gusty winds on the peaks and extremely cold weather. There were oceans of gummy, freezing mud that bogged down trucks, halftracks, tanks and artillery which made it a major task simply to move up supplies and reinforcements.

Truck convoys and troop formations had to move largely by night due to highly accurate and heavy German mortar and artillery fire directed by enemy observers on the heights. Even at night movement in the valley was highly perilous as the enemy had zeroed in roads, defiles and other approaches used by the Americans.

All of these negative factors would result in the gains, if any, measured in yards.

The Italian campaign to bleed German reserves and lure Wehrmacht divisions from France and from in front of the Russians had bogged down in a sea of mud before the mighty Gustav Line. Cynics were conjecturing whether it was the Germans or the Anglo-Americans who were being bled to death among the towering, frigid peaks of the ominous Italian mountains.

PART ONE

Clawing Out
A Beachhead

1

"A Pistol's Pointed at My Head!"

Winston Churchill was at his eloquent best. Jabbing the air for emphasis with a long black cigar, the British Bulldog was regaling a glittering galaxy of top Allied brass in the Mediterranean with tales of military wonders to accrue from taking advantage of Anglo-American naval superiority to launch an amphibious landing far behind the Germans' Gustav Line. This would cause the foe to panic and withdraw from his apparently impregnable winter defensive positions and "leave the road to Rome wide open."

Short in physical stature, rotund and with the flabby jowls and stern facial features commonly associated with the tenacious member of the animal kingdom known as the bulldog, the 69-year-old Churchill had been stricken with pneumonia while on his way home from summit conferences on global strategy with U.S. President Franklin D. Roosevelt and Russian Premier Josef Stalin at Cairo and Teheran.

At the Cairo conference Churchill, despite his customary eloquence, had been shot down by Roosevelt and Stalin in the Briton's proposal to "continue to set the Mediterranean ablaze" with diversionary operations and to resume the Italian offensive in order to capture Rome, 100 miles north of the stalled Anglo-American armies, even if it meant weakening or postponing Overlord, the massive Allied cross-Channel assault from England against German-held Northwest France slated for May 1944.

The Americans, joined by Stalin, had rejected this British strategic concept. "I am strongly opposed to interminable operations in the black hole of the Mediterranean," General George C. Marshall, the low-key U.S. Army Chief of Staff, had stressed forcefully. The Americans held that the quickest way to successfully conclude the war was by mustering all available Anglo-American resources for Overlord to engage the powerful German *Wehrmacht* in massive land battles and knife into the heart of Adolf Hitler's Third Reich.

Stalin was suspicious that Churchill and the British were merely paying lip service to Overlord and intended to nibble away at the fringes of the Third Reich until the Red Army had been bled white. The Russian dictator had joined with Roosevelt and General Marshall in vigorously opposing expanded Mediterranean operations.

Typical of his tenacious nature, Winston Churchill refused to take "no" as an answer. While still recovering from his bout with pneumonia, the prime minister assuming the mantle of a sort of super supreme commander in the Mediterranean, had summoned the top Allied brass to appear before him. In the interest of maintaining Anglo-American harmony, the duly-appointed supreme commander in the Mediterranean, General Dwight D. Eisenhower, and other top American and British commanders heeded Churchill's call.

Now, on Christmas Day 1943, Eisenhower and high-ranking generals and admirals were dutifully arrayed before Churchill in a huge drawing room in the stately mansion in Tunis, North Africa, which was being used as an impromptu convalescent center for the prime minister. Answering the summons of The Prime, as he was privately termed by American commanders, in addition to Eisenhower were British General Harold R.L.G. Alexander, leader of 15th Army Group, British General Henry Maitland Wilson, known as Jumbo due to his ponderous bulk, who would soon be Eisenhower's successor in the Mediterranean, and Admiral John Cunningham and Air Marshal Arthur Tedder, the latter pair also British.

Churchill's reason for summoning the Mediterranean brass was due to his increasing concern with the bogged-down Anglo-American armies before the Gustav Line. The entire

Italian campaign had been The Prime's "baby"—the Americans had gone along with the invasion in return for Churchill's pledge to mount Overlord the following Spring.

Since Naples had been secured three months previously, Generals Eisenhower and Alexander, and U.S. Lieutenant General Mark W. Clark, the 47-year-old commander of Fifth Army, a mixture of American, British, French, Polish and New Zealand forces, had been thinking about an amphibious "end run" behind German lines south of Rome. But any such audacious action would depend upon one key factor: the main body of Mark Clark's Fifth Army would have to be in a position where it could quickly break through to link up with the landing behind enemy lines.

Now, clad in pajamas, bathrobe and slippers, his ashen face reflecting his bout with pneumonia and the smoking cigar in his hand defying the stern edict of his personal physician Lord Moran to abandon the Havana coronas until he had fully recovered from his lung ailment, Winston Churchill was ready to spring a pet military scheme upon his eager-eared but leery American and British commanders.

The Prime's timing was perfect: how could the gathered Allied brass take vehement issue with a sick man?

Assuming the role as chairman of the conference, Churchill declared, "It would be folly to invade France in the spring with Rome still in German hands. The Italian campaign must not be allowed to languish." He puffed on his cigar momentarily to allow the audience to digest his opening words, then added solemnly, "He who holds Rome, holds the title deeds to Italy!"

Americans in the room, long fearful that the British were seeking to continue a campaign of peripheral warfare in lieu of a cross-Channel attack, now had their latent suspicions aroused once again when the prime minister observed, "Overlord remains on top of the bill, of course, but it should not be such a tyrant as to rule out every other activity in the Mediterranean."

The Americans shifted nervously in their chairs. The Prime drew thoughtfully on his Havana corona.

Now the portly, keen-witted Churchill, relishing his assumed role as chief military strategist in the Mediterranean, unfurled his proposal for breaking the stalemate in front of the Gustav Line and promptly seizing Rome. His plan was to land a force of at least two divisions at a small Tyrrhenian port known as Anzio, some 60 miles behind German lines and only 30 miles south of Rome, the Eternal City.

The Prime declared that the amphibious landing deep in his rear would cause the enemy to panic and withdraw from the Gustav Line, leaving the door to Rome wide open.

Waving his cigar about, Churchill enthused, "We will be hurling a raging wildcat onto the beaches to rip the bowels out of the Boches!"

Hearing Churchill out, General Eisenhower, who would be shifted from the Mediterranean in days to command Overlord, immediately protested, foreseeing the Anzio venture as a continuing drain on manpower, shipping and other resources which should be husbanded for the cross-Channel assault.

Eisenhower, who stressed that he was acting only as an advisor due to his imminent departure from Mediterranean command, was especially concerned with "dangerous presumptions" on which the "left hook" code-named Operation Shingle would be based. Ike, as he was known to his friends, doubted if the Germans would make a precipitate withdrawal from the Gustav Line but would fight it out there while trying to contain an Anzio bridgehead. The supreme commander's prophetic words were quickly overriden by Churchill.

General Alexander deferred to his boss, the prime minister, but other British commanders and all Americans present protested Shingle in one way or the other.

Churchill continued to speak out forcefully for the Anzio operation, and succeeded, as usual, in gaining his will over others. Come hell or high water, an Anglo-American amphibious force would be hurled onto a strip of beach far to the German rear. Anzio would become Winston Churchill's particular "baby."

Once the decision had been made at the Christmas Day conference, The Prime turned to Brigadier Kenneth Strong, the tall, black-haired Briton who was chief intelligence officer in the Mediterranean—literally as an afterthought. "Now, we'll hear the seamy side of the question," Churchill observed, tugging on the sash of his bathrobe and lighting his fourth "prohibited" cigar.

Brigadier Strong was skeptical of the advisability of the Anzio operation. He pointed out that Rome was of the utmost political significance to Adolf Hitler, that the German dictator could not afford to let the capital of his recently defected Italian partners fall into Allied hands. Strong pointed out that many German divisions were lying idle in France and in Yugoslavia which could be rushed to Italy, and other strong Wehrmacht formations were available even closer, in northern Italy.

All of these factors added up to a perilous venture, Strong summarized. Churchill listened quietly, then brushed off the intelligence chief's arguments. The hazards at Anzio would have to be accepted as a calculated risk due to the prize to be gained—Rome.

Indeed it was a calculated risk. If the Anzio operation were successful, the Allies, hopelessly bogged down in front of the mighty Gustav Line and suffering heavy casualties daily, would soon be in Rome, 90 miles to the north. If Anzio proved to be a hard nut to crack and the Germans reacted energetically and swiftly, then the Anglo-Americans would have a large amphibious force marooned south of Rome, like a great whale floundering and thrashing helplessly on the beach.

An Allied disaster at Anzio would have an impact transcending the Italian campaign. General Jumbo Wilson, soon to succeed Eisenhower in the Mediterranean, would point out, "The (Allied) force would have to be withdrawn with total loss of equipment, some loss of personnel and serious risk to landing craft needed for the later assault in France." Overlord would have to be postponed, perhaps even cancelled.

Having emerged the victor in the strategy skirmish at Tunis, Prime Minister Churchill immediately set about consolidating the hard-earned position. He signaled President Roosevelt in Washington: "Unanimous agreement has been reached on Shingle (Anzio) and everyone is in good heart."

Actually, this was almost totally opposite the facts. Churchill, who had an uncanny talent for forcing his will on others, had won out over the generals and admirals, nearly all of whom had severe reservations about the "left hook" gamble.

Next, to cement Shingle, The Prime insisted on the immediate appointment of principal commanders for the operation. General Mark Clark named Major General John P. Lucas, who had taken over command of VI Corps on the Salerno bridgehead, to lead ground forces. Rear Admiral Frank J. Lowry had previously been designated naval commander. Both Lucas and

Lowry were Americans, but their commands would be mixtures of American and British.

No one had any way of knowing it at the time, but the appointment of General Lucas to command an operation which would require nerves of steel and an audacious spirit would be a tragic one. Mild-mannered and white-haired, his pleasant blue eyes shielded by rimless glasses, Lucas was seldom found without his corncob pipe. He had demonstrated on the touch-and-go Salerno killing grounds that he was cool, if not audacious, and capable. He was considered a candidate to take over General Clark's job at Fifth Army when Clark would move up to army group command.

Known to his troops as Foxy Grandpa or Uncle Luke, John Lucas was almost universally admired in the United States Army. He was intelligent, conscientious and had a deeply compassionate concern for the men his profession required him to send into battle, to be wounded and to die. Despite Lucas' wealth of attributes, he was not an inspirational leader, and his penchant for bundling up in a wool-lined trenchcoat and heavy scarf when the weather was relatively mild hardly projected the image of a two-fisted, fire-breathing fighting man.

In reality, General Lucas, at 54 years of age, was a troubled man, physically and emotionally exhausted. It constantly preyed on his being that he was in a calling where the flower of American youth were sent to their deaths at his command. "I am far too tenderhearted ever to be a success at my chosen profession," he would confide to his diary.

Foxy Grandpa doubted the wisdom of the Anzio operation from the outset. As commander of VI Corps, Lucas would be sent ashore with an initial assault force of only 40,000 men—about half of what General Mark Clark had at his disposal when he hit Salerno in a similar operation and was nearly driven back into the sea.

Mark Clark, at 47 one of the army's youngest three-star generals, while beset with many doubts, approved Shingle on condition that it was undertaken with sufficient strength. What strength would be needed would revolve around an unknown equation: how soon would the Germans react at Anzio and in what force?

General Clark, more than any other one man, fully understood what Fifth Army was facing as it banged its head up against the highly formidable defenses of the Gustav Line. It was Clark who was responsible for seizing the prize of Rome, and as his men inched forward against the outposts of the Gustav Line, he continually exposed himself in forward positions to urge his men onward under the most trying of

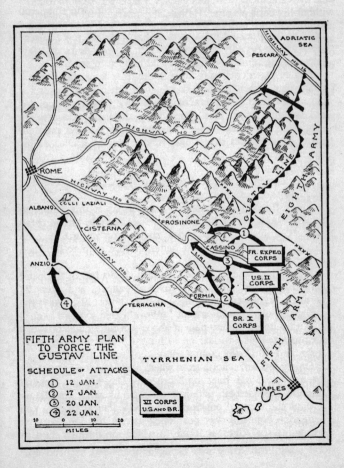

FIFTH ARMY PLAN
TO FORCE THE
GUSTAV LINE

SCHEDULE OF ATTACKS

1. 12 JAN.
2. 17 JAN.
3. 20 JAN.
4. 22 JAN.

10 0 10 20
MILES

circumstances. The angular Clark knew, firsthand, the brutal ordeal his troops were undergoing.

Consequently, Shingle appeared to offer a reasonable hope for extracting his men from the blood and mud of the Germans' winter line.

On Christmas Day, while Prime Minister Churchill was mesmerizing high Allied commanders in the mild climate of Tunis, General Clark, his jeep, boots and uniform splattered with mud—cold, gummy, oozing mud—was touring the front lines in the freezing mountains of Italy. He offered a cheery word here, a friendly pat on the back there, now and then a few encouraging remarks—if any would happen to apply.

At one ice-encrusted foxhole in the front lines, the 6 foot 3 Clark came upon a small-sized young private, his overcoat caked with mud and several days' growth of beard adorning his red weather-beaten face. The young rifleman, conversation disclosed, had been fighting in the sleet, rain and mud for many days without shoes; only rubber overshoes encased his freezing feet.

"Why don't you have shoes?" Clark inquired.

"Because my feet are too small, sir. They said they couldn't find any shoes in my size."

The Fifth Army commander was furious at this failure to provide footwear for the diminutive soldier. He turned to an aide: "Get this man some shoes, right away, and get them up to him. Somebody back there better produce or there'll be hell to pay."

Mark Clark's anger was dramatized by his use of the word hell. He cursed only under extreme anger, and then he normally exploded with an expletive "Ybsob!" Only the initiated knew "Ybsob" meant "yellow bellied son of a bitch."

Within hours, a new pair of shoes—in the young private's precise size—was rushed up to him. A "Christmas present" from the Fifth Army commander.

Only a few miles north from where Mark Clark was trekking through the front lines on Christmas Day, Major General Fridolin von Senger und Etterlin was likewise circulating through the forward positions of his XIV Panzer Corps. Von Senger's command was positioned astride the *Via Casilina* (known to the Allies as Route 6) which ran through the Liri Valley gap between Rome and Naples. It was von Senger's mission to halt the northward thrust of General Clark's Fifth Army toward Monte Cassino and beyond to Rome.

Fridolin von Senger was not cast in the mold of the popular conception of a Prussian general. He was a devout Catholic and scion of an old-line, wealthy family from Baden, in southwest Germany. He was a Rhodes Scholar at Oxford University in England just prior to the First World War. Von Senger's low opinion of the Nazi regime was known to Adolf Hitler and his subalterns, but the panzer leader had performed so well in fierce battles in Russia and in Sicily that he was given a key command in Italy.

Concluding his front-line visits in the freezing mud of towering mountains, General von Senger ordered his chauffeur to head for the centuries-old Abbey of Monte Cassino perched majestically on the mountaintop standing sentinel-like above the Liri Valley and Naples-to-Rome Route 6. Ascending Monte Cassino along the double-bends and horseshoe curves of the steep incline, von Senger gained a sweeping view of the broad expanse of the Liri Valley.

He noted with a mixture of astonishment and admiration how the entire width of the defile was being plastered with almost continual American artillery fire. The bombardment unrolling before his eyes far below dramatized the fierceness of the bitter fight for the Liri Valley, the Gateway to Rome.

Climbing out of his staff car, von Senger entered the ancient monastery and attended Christmas Day Mass in the crypt. The corps commander was careful not to be seen from the abbey, for he had issued orders that no German soldier was to enter the monastery. An armed sentinel had been placed at the door to enforce the ruling.

Von Senger had no way of knowing that in the near future a worldwide controversy would rage as to whether German troops strictly obeyed the corps edict.

The day after Christmas, General Harold Alexander, commander of 15th Army Group which controlled Clark's Fifth and Montgomery's Eighth armies, was standing in quiet reflection before a huge situation map in the war room of his headquarters, located in the sumptuous Royal Palace in Caserta. At the doors to the war room stood sharp-eyed sentries with orders not to permit unauthorized visitors. Only a handful of officers in all the Allied forces in Italy were authorized to enter.

On the map and several other wall-maps, General Alexander was viewing a precise and exhaustive display of up-to-the-minute German unit positions on the Italian battlefront, the movement and routes of enemy formations being brought to the vicinity of the Gustav Line from as far away as France and the Balkans, and a reconstruction of the enemy's view of the Allied order of battle.

Alexander, suave, friendly, intelligent, would stroll into the war room several times each day, as the data on the maps was being constantly updated around-the-clock. Now the Army Group commander moved over to a file marked "U" where the officer in charge of the facility, Captain Judy Hutchinson, removed a sheaf of papers marked "Ultra" and handed them to Alexander. There were translations of German wireless signals which had been intercepted and decoded since General Alexander's last visit to the war room.

Had the Allied ground commander in Italy been invited to inspect German army headquarters in Italy and the *Oberkommando der Wehrmacht* (armed forces high command) in Berlin, it is doubtful if he could have been better informed on the German army in Italy, its plans, aspirations and the attitudes of its leaders.

This special intelligence furnished General Alexander, and a handful of other top Anglo-American commanders and staff officers in Italy, was code-named Ultra. Its existence was one of the most profoundly guarded secrets of the war.

In 1939, just before the outbreak of hostilities, British intelligence had stolen a precise copy of the highly secret and complex German coding machine code-named Enigma. So ingenious was the enciphering Enigma machine that Adolf Hitler and the Wehrmacht considered its code "unbreakable."

A team of Great Britain's leading scientific brains, working under intensely secret conditions, months later solved the "unbreakable" Enigma code with the aid of another highly sophisticated British machine. Since the outbreak of war, Ultra had intercepted top-secret German signals, decoded them and rushed the messages on to Allied commanders and selected governmental officials.

Now in the super-secret war room, General Alexander handed the sheaf of Ultra messages back to Captain Hutchinson, who promptly destroyed them. No one—not even the

Allied Supreme Commander, General Eisenhower—could keep or even make a copy of Ultra messages. Once they were read by authorized officers, the deciphered German signals were elaborately shredded, then burned in an incinerator.

General Alexander walked down the hall to the ornate dining room of the Royal Palace. There, with key members of his staff, he joined in a belated Christmas dinner. The atmosphere was subdued. In the back of each officer's mind was the haunting specter of the menacing Gustav Line with its towering peaks, swift-flowing rivers, concrete bunkers with their bristling machine guns, extensive mine fields, mortars and artillery.

Soon after New Year's Day 1944 fearfully edged onto the scene and prudently disappeared as rapidly as possible, General Mark Clark received a secret signal from his chief of staff, Major General Alfred M. Gruenther, who at 44, was one of the army's youngest two-star officers. The contents of the message sent alarm bells ringing in the Fifth Army commander's nimble brain:

> According to information here (Allied Force Headquarters for the Mediterranean), the Anzio force must land with eight days supplies, but with no expectation of further supplies by water.

A troubled Mark Clark probed deeper into the significance of this startling revelation and learned that nearly all the large, multi-purpose LST's (landing ship-tanks), which were vital to take troops, vehicles and guns ashore and resupply the Anzio beachhead, would be ordered to proceed to England no later than February 2. There they would be prepared for use in the Allies' maximum effort—Overlord.

As D-Day for Anzio had been tentatively set for January 22, 1944, the loss of all the LST's in 10 days or less would mean one of two things: General Lucas' assaulting VI Corps would have to establish a solid beachhead and fight its way across 30 miles of rugged terrain and reach Rome, or break out of the beachhead toward the southeast and link up with the main body of Fifth Army, now 60 miles from Anzio and bogged-down in front of the Gustav Line—all in 10 days or less.

Otherwise, General Lucas' force would be marooned in the

Anzio region with its only possible source of resupply by air. And it was doubtful if the entire fleet of C-47 transport planes in the Mediterranean region would be sufficient to resupply such a large force on a continuing basis.

Mark Clark's early cautious optimism that Shingle would life his stalled army out of the mire of the Gustav Line and catapult it all the way to Rome now began to pale.

Clark was in a serious dilemma. He had been ordered by higher echelons to make an end run to Anzio, but now was told that it would have to be done without sufficient craft and that virtually all those vessels would be withdrawn shortly after two divisions hit the beach.

"I feel that I have a pistol pointed at my head!" a dejected and deeply worried Mark Clark remarked to confidants on his staff.

Now confusion had set in among the Allied high command—including Winston Churchill—and the situation in Italy in general and the Anzio operation in particular became more muddled each day. But time for planning and rehearsing Anzio was getting short, and Fifth Army staff work proceeded full steam.

At a staff conference at Caserta on January 4, General Clark stated in a mixture of deep concern and contrived optimism: "We are supposed to go up there (to Anzio), dump two divisions ashore without resupply or reinforcement, and wait for the rest of Fifth Army to join up. I am trying to find ways to do it, and I am not looking for ways in which we cannot do it. We are going to do it successfully."

As the conference broke up and Clark was leaving the room, an aide sidled up to the Fifth Army commander and softly inquired, "How *are* you going to do it, General?"

Clark replied, "At this time, I don't know how."

Later that afternoon, the Allied ground force commander in Italy, General Harold Alexander, arrived at Clark's head-quarters. Clark, now thoroughly angry, frustrated and even confused by developments, poured out his candid views to his superior. He spoke out bluntly because he felt that the Tunis conference decision on Anzio rammed through by Prime Minister Churchill had been made carelessly and without the participants in the meeting understanding the requisites for a successful amphibious operation.

Churchill, General Clark believed, in his anxiety to seize Rome from Hitler, had compounded the Allied confusion by assuming that the Anzio assault could make use of a large number of American landing craft, which were not subject to the prime minister's control.

Clark's blunt views on the looming Anzio operation left little doubt as to who he considered the chief culprit in the muddled Allied situation—Winston Churchill. General Alexander, caught in the middle of a delicate situation, promptly fired off a cable to The Prime in Marrakech, where Churchill had proceeded in his convalescent trip back to England. Alexander supported the shipping concerns outlined by Clark. Now the ball was in Churchill's court.

Four days later, General Clark opened a top-secret signal and issued a sigh of relief. Using his uncanny powers of persuasion, Churchill had intervened with President Roosevelt to secure enough craft for resupply and to bring in reinforcements at Anzio. Roosevelt made this assurance even though it might mean a postponement of Overlord, the cross-Channel assault against Northwest France.

"If Winny (Churchill) ever loses his job as prime minister, he could always make a hell of a fine living as a con man!" a wag in Clark's headquarters observed.

2

A Carload of Allied Spies

Johnny Lucas, the mild-mannered general who had fallen heir to the risky Anzio assignment, walked out of 15th Army Group headquarters in the lavish palace at Caserta, some 20 miles north of Naples, on the afternoon of January 9. He was barely able to conceal his emotions.

The Shingle planning session from which he had just emerged plunged him into an even deeper mood of despair. Instead of receiving the word he had hoped for—a strengthening of his force and shipping for the Anzio assault—it was confirmed by General Harold Alexander that Lucas would hit the beach with a bare 40,000 men.

In the gathering twilight of a bitter wintry night, Lucas went alone to his room at VI Corps headquarters and penned in his diary: "I feel like a lamb being led to the slaughter. The whole affair has a strong odor of Gallipoli and apparently the same amateur (is) still on the coach's bench."

The "coach" was General Eisenhower, the "amateur" was Winston Churchill, and Gallipoli had been a military scheme of the prime minister when he was First Lord of the Admiralty in World War I. It had ended in disaster when a force of British, French, Australian and New Zealand troops was routed in an amphibious assault on Turkey in 1915.

Gallipoli. That's what Anzio would be, Lucas was convinced. Another Gallipoli! And the same "coach" had called the plays for both bloody catastrophies, one historical, the other looming.

Meanwhile the Allied supreme commander for Overlord, Dwight Eisenhower, was furtively slinking around Washington D.C. like a fugitive with a price on his head. As German spies might be lurking around the nation's capital, Eisenhower had removed the stars from his uniform and gave the appearance of an aging private wearing an officer's uniform. Or perhaps a Red Cross field worker. A soldier in plain clothes drove the supreme commander in an unmarked Chevrolet.

Eisenhower had secretly returned to Washington for a round of conferences and a few days of vacation with wife Mamie before taking up his burdensome new assignment in London as commander-in-chief of Allied forces for the cross-Channel assault.

The plain-clothes driver tooled up before the massive, even awe-inspiring new Pentagon building where Eisenhower hopped out of the Chevrolet and was led through a secret passage to the office of Secretary of War Henry L. Stimson, the alert, 75-year old lawyer who many felt was one of Washington's shrewdest minds.

Gathered in Stimson's office was an impressive array of generals, leading scientists and top governmental officials. The subject of Italy was broached, and Eisenhower told the assemblage what was already vividly evident: the Germans were resisting ferociously.

Eisenhower gave a rundown on the forthcoming Anzio operation, and told of Winston Churchill's dominant, even dictatorial, role.

Secretary Stimson observed, "He is dead set on making this offensive for political reasons." Later Stimson added, "Of course, Churchill is banking on pulling off this operation quickly" so that the landing craft involved could be released for the cross-Channel attack.

None of the Pentagon generals endorsed Anzio. They considered it merely an infuriating "sideshow" to sop up manpower, landing craft and resources for the "main event"— Overlord.

As Allied generals and heads of state jockeyed for position among themselves in the high-level Italian sweepstakes, a brutal, no-holds-barred war had been raging relentlessly on the

freezing mountains and grim valleys in front of the Gustav
Line. General Mark Clark was seeking to get his force of
mixed nationalities into position to launch the Fifth Army
offensive designed to lure German divisions from the Anzio
beachhead area.

For nearly six weeks the attacking Fifth Army soldier had
been forced to endure a savage ordeal: cold, snow, sleet, rain,
fog and gummy mud, along with incessant poundings from
deadly accurate mortars and artillery and fierce counterattacks
by German infantry. Each new salvo of shells, each vicious
firefight, each passage over thick mine fields brought the Black
Angel of Death hovering over the battlegrounds.

It was war in its most primitive form—vicious, savage, even
obscene.

As the middle of January approached, the six-week offensive had gained a miniscule total of eight miles—each yard
paid for in Allied blood. But Mark Clark's men had chipped
chunks out of the "impregnable" Gustav Line and reached
heights overlooking the swift-flowing Rapido River, the Gari
River and the Garigliano River, all formidable components of
the German's winter defensive positions.

Allied casualties in the 42-day advance into the teeth of
enemy fortifications had been heavy: 8,841 for the Americans,
3,132 for the British, 3,305 for the French, and 586 for the
Italians—a total of 15,864.

The high casualty rate and the snail-like progress in penetrating the Gustav Line infused planning for Anzio with an
increasing sense of urgency. But the directives issued for what
the Allies now termed The Battle for Rome further muddled the
Anzio operation. Suddenly the little, unpretentious port of
Anzio loomed gigantic in Allied global strategy.

Anzio in peacetime had been a pleasant resort of great
popularity, only an hour's drive from the Eternal City, where
Romans flocked for holidays by the blue Tyrrhenian Sea. The
town was built on a small promontory and on each side were
sandy beaches. Holiday villas snuggled in the pine woods
behind the white shoreline.

Only a mile south of Anzio was the smaller old town of
Nettuno. Beneath its ancient cobble-stoned streets was a maze
of catacombs and tunnels used by the natives as cellars for
ripening local wine.

Inland and north of Anzio, guarding Rome less than 10 miles south of the capital, were the Alban Hills. Around the foot of these hills and in the valleys ran the key highway and railroad between Naples and Rome.

The Alban Hills were clearly the crucial topographic feature in the Anzio region. Whoever occupied those elevations could view the entire sweep of coastline and terrain around Anzio, then look over their shoulder for a bird's-eye view of Rome.

Alban Hills. Those two words would haunt the sleep and give waking nightmares to top Allied leaders in the weeks ahead. Already great confusion had centered around those hills.

In his directive to General Clark, 15th Army Group commander Harold Alexander ordered Fifth Army to assault the Gustav Line by forcing crossings over the Rapido and Garigliano rivers, luring German reserve divisions positioned in the Rome area to its front. When intelligence had established that these Wehrmacht reserves had been committed along the Gustav Line, Clark was to land General Lucas' VI Corps, an Anglo-American force, at Anzio. Lucas' corps was to bolt inland and seize the key Alban Hills, and Fifth Army's main body was to break through the Gustav Line and join up with the Anzio formations for the drive on Rome.

But Clark was skeptical of Alexander's directive. It was only too fresh in the mind of the angular American general how his assault force at Salerno beachhead, much stronger than the one General Lucas would have at Anzio, was nearly driven into the Tyrrhenian by early powerful German counterattacks. No, Clark believed, the first order of business when VI Corps stormed ashore at Anzio on January 22 would be to quickly establish a firm beachhead, then dig in to ward off a certain Wehrmacht counterattack.

Consequently, in his orders to General Lucas, Clark ordered VI Corps to secure a beachhead and advance on the Alban Hills as soon as Lucas felt his invasion force was able to do so.

Alexander's and Clark's directives were consistent with each other except for the semantics of three words—Alexander had ordered VI Corps to *seize* the Alban Hills and Clark had directed an *advance on* the key terrain feature. New fuel had been added to the already muddled saga of Anzio—and not a shot had as yet been fired.

General Lucas' plan for the amphibious assault called for the British 1st Division and Commando formations to land on Peter Beach, code-name for a three-mile strip of shoreline stretching north from Anzio. At the same time, the U.S. 3rd Infantry Division, veterans of North Africa and Sicily, was to storm ashore about three miles to the south of Anzio. As these landings to the north and south were taking place, a force of veteran American Rangers and the battle-tested 509th Parachute Infantry Battalion, the first airborne outfit to make a combat jump during the war, would assault the town of Anzio itself.

These coordinated landings were to take place in the early-morning hours of darkness on the twenty-second. The veteran 504th Parachute Infantry Regiment of the 82nd Airborne Division would reinforce the on-shore units after daybreak, and later a regiment of the U.S. 45th Infantry Division and elements of the U.S. 1st Armored Division, both experienced fighting formations, would be landed to beef up VI Corps.

As time neared for D-Day, General Lucas became increasingly concerned—even despondent—over the entire Anzio venture. He wrote in his diary: "I have a bare minimum of ships and craft. The force that can be gotten ashore in a hurry is a weak one."

An increasing aura of doom for the Anzio operation was not confined to General Lucas alone. General Lucian Truscott was also deeply concerned. A tough, resourceful and bold commander, Truscott had told his assembled division over a bullhorn just before its baptism of fire in Sicily the previous July: "Let the Boche know you're there—cut your name in his goddamned face!"

Truscott was 49 years of age, a forthright officer who shunned personal publicity. He always wore a leather battle jacket, a steel helmet with two shiny stars, and knee-high patent-leather boots. His personal courage had become a byword in the 3rd "Rock of the Marne" Division.

No one ever questioned Lucian Truscott's fighting spirit. Yet, shortly before the Anzio assault, he wrote his superior officer, General Clark:

"If this (Anzio) is to be a 'forlorn hope' or a 'suicide sashay,' then all I want to know is that fact. I will carry out my duty."

Word of the disaster awaiting the Allied force at Anzio had reached the ears of Lieutenant General George S. Patton, the tactical genius who had been in General Eisenhower's doghouse since slapping a private in Sicily a few months before while in an emotionally disturbed mood from viewing badly mutilated patients at a field hospital.

Although diametrically opposite the reserved, mild-mannered Lucas in temperament and mannerisms, Patton sincerely liked Foxy Grandpa Lucas, so much so that he flew from Sicily to VI Corps headquarters to cheer up his long-time friend.

In typical fashion, General Patton had a somewhat peculiar method for "cheering up" his fellow generals. Addressing Lucas in his high-pitched voice, the armored leader bellowed, "John, there's no one in the army that I'd hate to see get killed as much as you, but you can't get out of this thing alive!"

Patton allowed those words to sink in as he fondled his ivory-handled pistol, then added, "Of course, you might only get wounded. No one ever blames a wounded general."

Turning aside to one of Lucas' aides, Patton suggested, "If things get too bad at Anzio, shoot the Old Man in the ass. But be sure not to kill him, only wound him."

Having "cheered up" General Lucas and his staff, Patton bid his farewells and left the headquarters to wing back to Sicily where he would strain at the leash in the solitary splendor of an ornate castle until summoned out of the doghouse and to a leading role in Overlord.

It was pitch black on the night of January 20, two days before the Anzio assault, as two swift torpedo boats knifed through the murky waters of the Tyrrhenian, bound from the island of Corsica to a point 55 miles north of German-occupied Rome. Huddled in the cramped cabins below deck were 11 men and women—Allied spies. They were being planted behind German lines to aid the Anzio operation.

Most of the spies were grim-faced and silent—except for one. Peter Tompkins, 24 but looking older due to the heavy beard which fringed his intent face. He was exuberant at the thought of returning to his beloved Rome to play a role in ejecting the hated Nazis.

Tompkins' mother, a painter, and father, a sculptor, both Americans, had settled down in Rome when Peter was an infant, and while attending school in England young Tompkins spent his vacations roaming about Rome. When America entered the war, Peter Tompkins, who spoke Italian like a native, was recruited into the fledgling cloak-and-dagger organization, the Office of Strategic Services (OSS). Tompkins thrilled in his role as a spy.

Tompkins' mission was a totally impossible one. Yet he plunged into it with great vigor, strengthened by his deep-rooted Fabian socialist ideology. When Italy was liberated he hoped to help establish what he termed a democratic government to replace the monarchy.

Major General William "Wild Bill" Donovan, the World War I hero and prominent New York attorney who founded and headed the infant OSS, had ordered Tompkins to infiltrate Rome, set up an intelligence and sabotage network, and prevent a disastrous civil war among warring Italian underground factions when the Germans were about to evacuate the Eternal City and flee northward—presumably within hours after the Anglo-Americans stormed ashore at Anzio on Rome's front porch. This task would have to be carried out in only a few days, but Tompkins was determined to achieve it.

Now the hearts of the men and women Allied spies in the pair of motor torpedo boats suddenly quickened. The engines had been shut off, and the craft were drifting silently in the blackness just off shore. Who would be the welcoming party on land—Italian partisans or armed Germans?

Minutes later a green light winked through the darkness from on land and Tompkins and the other spies slipped into a rubber boat and silently paddled for the shore. There a number of ghostly figures were standing—Allied spies who would climb into the rubber craft and be taken south to report on their findings behind German lines on virtually the eve of the Anzio operation.

As Peter Tompkins, feeling an intoxication from his role as spy, and the others peered intently into the blackness of night, a native appeared with a horse and cart and took the just-landed agents to a nearby farmhouse. There a group of sullen-faced Italians were idly drinking coffee. They stared in silence and suspicion at the young American stranger and his companions. In wartime Italy, *no one* could be trusted.

Tompkins' efforts to coerce the coffee-drinking Italian "patriots" to drive him and others into Rome proved of no avail—until the OSS agent offered a hefty sum of money. Five of the spies crowded into a batterd old limousine with the pair of strangers, and the vehicle, loaded with guns, bombs, ammunition and explosives, sped down the highway toward the dark, tightly-guarded Eternal City. Time was short; the Anglo-Americans would storm ashore at the pleasant resort of Anzio in 30 hours.

As the seven persons drove along in the darkness, Tompkins peered intently at the pair of strangers. Were these Gestapo men, or paid agents of the dreaded German police organization? Was their mission to infiltrate and break up Allied espionage groups in the Rome region? Would they drive right up to Gestapo headquarters in Rome with their captive bag of Allied agents? Tompkins refused to dwell on such unthinkable thoughts—yet they returned time and again.

As the old vehicle raced along the main highway on the outskirts of the Eternal City, the young American spy felt a sudden chill surge through his being. A short distance to the front two red lanterns were swinging in the center of the road, lanterns held by two members of the German Wehrmacht. This would be the end of his spy career—and his life—Tompkins thought. In fleeting seconds he could visualize being tortured in Gestapo dungeons before being placed against a wall and shot.

But the driver and his Italian companion showed no sign of slowing down at the German checkpoint. Instead, the speed was increased and the ancient limousine crashed through the wooden barrier across the road, sending the pair of sentries leaping for safety. Other Germans poured out of a nearby guardhouse as the racing car with its seven Allied spies was swallowed up by the night. Not a shot had been fired.

Two miles farther down the road, at the Rome city limits, another roadblock was encountered. This one was of cement; there was no way to charge through it. The driver screeched to a halt as several Germans, Schmeisser automatic pistols slung across their shoulders, emerged from a tiny building to intercept them.

The Italian driver got out of the vehicle, showed his forged identity papers to one sentry. Another helmeted German walked over to the vehicle and shined his flashlight inside, slowly moving the bright beam from face to face. When the glow reached Tompkins' features, it seemed to linger. The American could feel his heart thumping furiously and was fearful its beating would give him away.

Satisfied that the occupants were genuine Italians returning from a visit in the country, the German shut off the flashlight and walked away. Tompkins, perspiration on his forehead and palms and a sickening churning in his stomach, instinctively cast a quick glance down to the floorboard by his feet. There was piled an assortment of handguns, ammunition and explosives. Had the German turned his flashlight beam only a few inches downward, the seven spies would by now be on their way to the Gestapo chambers in the Eternal City.

The German sentries, having looked at the papers of each occupant and satisfied with their authenticity—even though all documents were forged—waved the car onward. "Push on the gas pedal! Push on the gas pedal!" Peter Tompkins wanted to cry out. "Let's get the hell out of here!" he felt like shouting.

But before the driver could put the vehicle in gear, a voice called out from the dark back seat, "Wait a minute." One of the spies climbed out of the old car and with the German sentries standing about, calmly urinated alongside the road.

3

A River Runs Red

Lanky Staff Sergeant Bill Kirby, a 22-year-old machine-gun section leader from Gatesville, Texas, was arduously picking his way through the thick fog and darkness across the marshy flatland which reached out for more than a mile on the southern approaches to the Rapido River. Kirby might have thought he was advancing alone toward German positions on the far bank of the stream, which formed a natural barrier in the Wehrmacht's formidable Gustav Line, had it not been for the labored breathing and muffled curses of his comrades on all sides. Visibility was only a few yards.

It was 8 p.m. on January 20. Unknown to the sergeant and his 36th Infantry Division comrades in the attack, the assault to seize crossings on the far side of the Rapido was a crucial preliminary to the Anzio landing, which would unfold in only 30 hours. Neither Kirby nor his fellow infantrymen in the Texas National Guard outfit were aware of their role in what American fighting men called The Big Picture.

The Rapido River was not impressive looking, running between banks some four feet high, the stream was only 30 to 55 feet wide. But it was swift-moving, 12 feet deep and the water was ice cold. As part of the Gustav Line defenses, the Germans had cut down all trees on both sides of the river, which would require attackers to move across a mile of flat marshland without a trace of cover or concealment.

On the few patches of solid ground and among the reeds and scrub-brush on the American side of the Rapido, the Germans had sewn thick minefields. That same evening after dark the enemy had infiltrated patrols across the stream under cover of the murky fog to plant additional mines in anticipation of an American assault.

On the German side of the Rapido the defenses were fiendish. Deep dugouts, concrete bunkers and foxholes, protected by heavy strands of barbed wire interspersed with mines and booby-traps, ran a twisted course which would permit machine gunners to pour fire frontally and into the flanks of any American force which might make it across the fast-moving and treacherous Rapido.

The battered little town of Sant Angelo, long before pulverized by Allied bombing attacks, was perched on a bluff 50 feet above the river. Dug in among the stone ruins of Sant Angelo, German riflemen and machine gunners could pour withering blasts of fire into an advancing enemy.

The attack across the Rapido River had been ordered by General Mark Clark, Fifth Army commander, in compliance with the directive he had received from Fifteenth Army Group: "Make as strong a thrust as possible toward Cassino and Frosinone shortly prior to the (Anzio) assault landing to draw in enemy reserves (near Rome) which might be employed against the landing forces, and then create a breach in (the enemy) front through which every opportunity should be taken to link up rapidly with the seaborne operation."

There was no question in Mark Clark's mind—nor in that of any other top Allied commander—that blood was going to be spilled. The decision had been made to spill most of that blood along the Gustav Line in order to draw off the three German reserve divisions near Rome and maximize the chances for a successful landing at Anzio.

As infantrymen of the 36th Division edged across the ominous flat marshlands toward the Germans dug in on the far bank of the Rapido, General Clark wrote in his personal diary: "I maintain that it is essential that I make the attack (across the Rapido), fully expecting heavy losses . . . thereby clearing the way for Shingle (the Anzio landing)."

Earlier that evening of the twentieth, as his men were advancing into position to attack the German defenses along the Rapido, a concerned Major General Fred L. Walker, was also scribbling a passage in his diary. The 56-year old, silver-haired Walker, a transplanted Ohioan and World War I infantry lieutenant who commanded the division of largely Texas fighting men, was deeply pessimistic—a dangerous frame of mind for a commander. He wrote:

"The (Rapido) River is the principal obstacle of the German main line of resistance. I do not know a single case in military history where an attempt to cross a river that is incorporated into the main line of resistance has succeeded."[*]

General Walker added ominously: "I am prepared for defeat."

The 36th Infantry Division's commanding general's pessimism may have been deepened by a factor known to all military men: a night crossing of a heavily defended river is the most difficult infantry operation in warfare.

Yet, had the Texans been sent into the attack in broad daylight across a mile of floodplain into the teeth of German automatic weapons, artillery and mortar fire, the chances for a successful crossing would have been virtually nil.

General Walker's plan of attack was an assault by two regiments, each with some 3,000 men. The 141st Infantry would cross the Rapido upstream, to the north, of Sant Angelo and the 143rd Infantry would force a crossing south of the pulverized town perched on the knoll overlooking the river. After establishing bridgeheads, the two infantry regiments were to converge beyond Sant Angelo, trapping German defenders in the town.

Now, on the night of January 20, the strategic planning had been concluded and the ultimate burden for forcing a crossing of the Rapido shifted to the shoulders of Sergeant Billy Kirby and hundreds of fellow infantrymen trudging through the choking blanket of fog toward German positions overlooking the river. The dark night was eerie—even ghost-like. Not a weapon was being fired up and down the wide sweep of the Rapido front. Crickets could be heard merrily chirping as the heavily-loaded infantrymen from Texas plodded ahead, drag-

---

[*]Many military commanders and historians did not agree with this assertion, including General Mark Clark.

ging one foot after the other, which gave off sucking noises much like a cow pulling its feet out of barnyard slime.

Bayonets were fixed, as Germans might pop up in the fog at any moment during the attack. Groups of men were lugging 12-man wooden assault boats weighing more than 420 pounds which were more than 13 feet long, bulky and difficult to carry. Others carried easier to handle 24-man rubber rafts.

Out in front of the attacking 36th Division infantrymen were combat engineers who the night before had performed the perilous and laborious task of clearing paths through mine fields and marking them with white tape. Now the engineers were serving as guides to the river.

It was cold, but the men's palms and foreheads were damp with perspiration. Stomachs churned. Hearts beat faster. There was not a man in the 6,000-member attacking force who did not know that they were trekking into a lethal buzzsaw. Earlier in the day after learning of the attack, Sergeant Kirby had remarked to comrades, "Hell, we ain't even sent a patrol down to the river but what it got the hell shot out of it!"

Suddenly the stillness of the dark night was shattered. The advancing dogfaces heard the familiar rustling noise of enemy shells heading their way and moments later explosives sent orange flashes into the sky all around them. Somehow the Germans, although three-quarters of a mile away along the far side of the Rapido, knew the Americans were coming. Perhaps the enemy had slipped small patrols across the swift-flowing stream to give advance warning of an assault.

The Texans dropped their rafts and assault boats and flopped face downward. They clung desperately to the ground as the deadly accurate fire caused the earth to pitch and shake all around them. Screams pierced the fog as men were hacked apart by shell fragments. One infantry company had 30 men killed or wounded by one salvo. The company commander was among those killed. He was replaced by a second-in-command who was wounded minutes later.

Shell fragments ripped open the rubber rafts and ground the wooden boats into splinters. White tape that lined safe routes through the minefields was torn out by the heavy barrage or buried in the mud. Now chaos set in among the American attackers, yet somehow they crawled and scrambled forward. But the paths through the minefields had been obliterated and the engineer guides lost their way, leading the following infantrymen into forests of mines. Bodies were blown into the sky, came to the earth and blocked the cleared routes through the hidden explosive devices.

Onward pushed the Americans through the rain of explosives, the darkness and the fog. The 141st Regiment reached the Rapido River bank where it was raked with automatic weapons concealed in the blackness of the far shore. Left behind along the mile of shell-racked marshland were more than one-third of the assault boats, damaged or abandoned.

Now it was time for the engineers to install four footbridges. But one which reached the river's edge was found to be defective, another had been destroyed by mines in the advance, and the remaining two were torn to pieces by German shells as they were being put into place.

Under intense automatic weapons and mortar fire, the boats reaching the river were launched. But some had unseen holes and sank in the deep, swift-flowing stream, and others, loaded with infantrymen, were swept out of control down the river.

Chaos erupted.

Some men in boats deliberately leaped into the water; others refused to climb into the wooden or rubber craft and instead clung stubbornly to the ground. Still others, many replacements and under fire for the first time, were paralyzed with fear and could not budge. Urged on by junior officers and noncoms, individually and in tiny groups the 36th Division men scrambled up the far shore and by 3 a.m. nearly 1,000 of them were on the German side of the bloody Rapido.

Using parts salvaged from the wrecked footbridges, 36th Division engineers installed one crossing, and another 325 infantrymen edged on over the river. As the first twinges of daylight creeped over the Rapido River, the German artillery fire increased in fury, and the one footbridge and remaining boats were knocked out. Telephone wires leading back over the Rapido were destroyed and radios refused to function. The battered men of the 141st Infantry were isolated on the far shore, and the Germans began to close in to wipe out the entire force.

Meanwhile, downstream from Sant Angelo, the 143rd Infantry had pushed one battalion and part of another, totaling some 1,000 men, over the Rapido. But after dawn German artillery observers, stationed on the high ground overlooking the river, brought devastating fire down onto the trapped elements of the 143rd Regiment. Major David M. Frazior, a battalion commander whose battery-powered radios were functioning, knew his men were in a hopeless situation. German tanks and self-propelled guns had ringed his position along the heights and were pouring flat-trajectory rounds into the Americans.

Major Frazior asked for permission to withdraw his battered elements across the Rapido, a request which was granted. By 10 a.m. on January 21, only 14 hours after the attack had jumped off, those Americans who could scurried back over the river.

The horror that was the Rapido had not been concluded. Late that same afternoon, the 143rd Infantry Regiment received orders from II Corps to again assault the river barrier. The dogfaces jumped off and headed for the stream as German artillery fire pounded them every step of the way. Soon Sergeant Bill Kirby, the lanky machine gunner from Texas, found himself crossing the Rapido in a rubber raft with three separate compartments. An enemy bullet deflated one compartment, but the other two held as Kirby and others scrambled up onto the far shore in the face of withering machine gun fire.

Kirby had already been through many battles in Italy, but the scene that greeted him on the enemy side of the river was the only one that reminded him of the war movies he had seen back home.

He had never seen so many dead bodies in one place— American bodies. So intense was the German machine gun fire that even the dead were being raked by bullets. Kirby looked on in horror and fascination as one youthful comrade was struck down by enemy automatic weapons bursts, then bounced along like a tin can as the enemy continued to pour fire into his lifeless body.

Kirby and his company crawled forward under constant fire, passed through numerous barbed wire entanglements and reached a point in the gathering darkness where they could hear Germans talking excitedly among themselves. Now units on the enemy shore lost track of each other.

With shells crashing about them, Sergeant Kirby's company commander ordered him to "crawl over to the right and establish contact with whoever is there." It was now dark. Kirby edged off on his mission, snaking through a barbed wire strand and disappearing into the blackness. Moments later a shell screamed into his company position, killing the unit commander who had just dispatched the sergeant to locate the neighboring company.

Kirby was crawling around in the darkness trying to find someone—anyone—when he felt a heavy blow on his shoulder. It was as though a giant figure had struck him with a huge sledgehammer. When blood began streaming down his combat jacket he knew he had been hit. His head was spinning and he feared he would pass out. But a soldier helped him to the river, found a rubber raft and paddled the wounded Kirby back across the Rapido.

Meanwhile, members of Kirby's company were being raked by machine gun fire from concrete bunkers as they clung to the ground. Cries repeatedly rang out in the darkness as bullets found their marks. Platoon Sergeant Charles R. Rummel, a Texan from Waco and a close friend of Kirby's, was struck in both legs at the same time by German automatic weapons fire. Curiously, he felt no pain, but deep-seated fear surged through his being. Two comrades offered to carry Rummel back to the river, but the firing was so intense he knew they would never make it. "Get the hell out of here any way you can," he told them.

Knowing that he was seriously wounded and could receive no immediate medical attention, Sergeant Rummel knew blood poisoning might set in. So he began arduously crawling around in the pitch-black night and removing sulfa tablets from those who would no longer need them—his dead comrades.

Each time Rummel moved he could hear the bones cracking in his legs. One leg was so badly mangled that he could not get his boot off; the boot was pointing backward, to the rear. Now intense pain started to knife through his body. His eyes became glazed and the loss of much blood increasingly weakened him. He did not call out for a medic, for he knew there was no medic to attend to him. Minutes later he lost consciousness.

All through the night the Germans kept pouring artillery, mortar and machine gun fire into the rapidly thinning ranks of the Americans clinging to the enemy side of the Rapido. One battalion of the 36th Division had all of its company commanders cut down. Within a four-hour time period, another battalion lost three commanders, two wounded and one killed. Major Milton J. Landry, a battalion commander in the 141st Regiment, was hit three times in less than a half hour.

The Rapido River ran red with blood—American blood. But already German reserves near Rome had been alerted by Field Marshal Albrecht Kesselring and were racing south to the Gustav Line to help block the threat posed by the 36th Infantry Division along the Rapido River and the 10 battalions of the British X Corps which had forced a crossing over the Garigliano River the day previously on the Americans' left flank. Only one German battalion was left behind south of Rome, in the vicinity of Anzio.

As the din of ferocious battle echoed among the mountains along the Rapido River, a crescendo of radio traffic was filling the airwaves out of advance headquarters of the U.S. VI Corps on the Mediterranean island of Corsica, west of Rome. Army engineers on Corsica had constructed ammunition dumps, and harbors and inlets on the island were filled with landing craft.

All of this feverish activity—corps headquarters, shipping and installations—were fake, part of an elaborate cover plan for the Anzio landing designed to make the Germans believe that the Allies in Italy would attack Leghorn late in January, diverting Wehrmacht attention from the true objective. Leghorn was an Italian port some 200 miles north of Rome on the Ligurian Sea.

"Inside information" was leaked from Fifth Army headquarters at Caserta that General Mark Clark's command was exhausted and would take no offensive action for several weeks. Instead, the "leaks" indicated, fresh troops were being funneled into General Bernard Montgomery's British Eighth Army on the east for an attack up the Adriatic coast.

On the night of January 21, only hours before General John Lucas' VI Corps was to storm ashore at the seaside resort of Anzio, a British cruiser and two destroyers bombarded the northern Italy coastal town of Civitavecchia at the time six cruisers and destroyers anchored off Terracina sent many salvos into that town. All this extensive naval activity was part of Shingle's cover plan, to convince the German high command that Leghorn was the impending Allied amphibious target.

Forty miles north of London at Bletchley, known as Station X, the Ultra facility that intercepted and decoded top-secret messages, technicians were intently monitoring enemy wireless traffic to and from Kesselring's headquarters at Monte Soratte near Rome for any indication of German reaction to this extensive cover plan. There was none.

The wily Kesselring, who had learned to fly and joined the Luftwaffe after 19 years as an artilleryman, had long recognized the possibility of an Allied amphibious landing deep behind his lines in Italy. He had many divisions in northern Italy and others available in France and Germany. Plans had been drafted to rush reserves to the scene if the Allies would land at Leghorn, Genoa, Ravenna, Isria or Anzio. A simple code-word would set defensive measures into action at any one of these locales, so Kesselring bided his time until the Allies struck.

As D-Day for Anzio inched ever closer, Anglo-American air forces accelerated efforts to "seal off" the Anzio beachhead, a strategic term Allied planners loved to bandy about. Bombers and fighter-bombers hammered German airfields around Rome and struck at other airdromes and railroad bridges and marshaling yards as far north as Florence and southern France.

On January 21, the Allied air forces declared that "all communications from northern Italy to the Rome region have been cut" and the Anzio area was "isolated." This proved to be far from the truth. German engineers rapidly filled in bomb-pocked airstrips. Air photos of the vast carnage inflicted upon enemy marshaling yards made impressive viewing, but the Germans overnight got at least one track repaired—enough to allow troop trains and others carrying vital military supplies to proceed southward.

If the Anzio area were to be "sealed off," it would not be by the Americans but by the Germans after General Lucas' VI Corps had landed.

In German-infested Rome on the morning of January 21, some 18 hours before the Allied landing at Anzio, Peter Tompkins, the young Fabian Socialist who was a spy for General Wild Bill Donovan's OSS, was deep in sleep in an armchair at the home of an Italian partisan. Tompkins, who had been landed north of the Eternal City by motor-torpedo boat the night before to set up an intelligence and sabotage network to aid the Anzio landing, suddenly awakened from his exhausted slumber.

A surge of fear flowed through his being as standing in front of him was an Italian police lieutenant, a revolver in hip holster. The policeman stared at Tompkins whose face had instantly turned ashen. This is the end, he was convinced. Visions of Gestapo torture chambers danced in his head.

"Don't be alarmed!" he heard a woman's voice call out. "He's one of us." It was the wife of the partisan who lived in the "safe house."

The young American glanced about the room and saw four Italians who were introduced as agents of the OSS. They had been infiltrated into Rome several weeks before with a radio transmitter code-named Vittoria. Tompkins would send information over Vittoria to Allied intelligence after the Anglo-American landing at Anzio, 30 miles to the south, the following day.

The radio-team agents had not been informed of the precise locale and time of impending Allied amphibious operations. The bearded Tompkins instinctively did not like the appearance or actions of two of the four men, so he would only tell them that "the Allies will land along the coast soon."

After the four men had departed, Tompkins was beset by a new fear. He began to doubt if the Anglo-Americans *really* planned to land at Anzio. He was conversant with the devious devices employed by sophisticated intelligence services to confound and confuse the enemy—and all agents were considered expendable.

Tompkins almost convinced himself that the OSS had "planted" him in Rome with the knowledge that he would be captured, tortured and forced to reveal Anzio as the site of the Allied landing. The amphibious attack would actually strike at another locale. "No," he finally rationalized, "the OSS wouldn't do that to me . . . or would they?"

At Monte Soratte, headquarters for the Wehrmacht in the Mediterranean, on January 21, the eve of the Anzio assault, Albrecht Kesselring was conferring with a visitor from Berlin. Wearing the gold braid of a full admiral in the Kriegsmarine, the outsider was a small, nervous man with a slight lisp and an intense disposition. He had a shock of white hair and when contemplating a matter paced about in a slight stoop with hands clasped behind his back.

He was 57-year-old Admiral Wilhelm Canaris, Germany's Master Spy and long head of the Third Reich's secret intelligence agency, the Abwehr.

Canaris, brilliant, courteous, tough-minded, was such a powerful—though shadowy—figure in Hitler's Nazi government that Wehrmacht commanders invariably felt uneasy when around the mysterious admiral. They would have been more uneasy had they known a monumental secret: Canaris was a leading figure in the Schwarze Kapelle (Black Orchestra), a small but highly influential group of top German military governmental officials who were conspiring to overthrow Adolf Hitler and his cronies.

The German Spy Master had for three years been flirting with sudden personal disaster in plotting to rid the nation of the menace of Hitler and Nazism—he had been feeding Great Britain's top-secret intelligence agency, MI-6, with a stream of reports on the political and military situation in Germany.

Now, at his office at Monte Soratte, the imperturbable Kesselring was showing Admiral Canaris recent evidence which indicated that an Allied amphibious landing was imminent—at Civitavecchia, a coastal town north of Rome.

During the past 24 hours, the phantom U.S. VI Corps headquarters on Corsica had been filling the airwaves with messages to phony Italian resistance forces, using a cipher the Allies knew the Germans could decode. The "secret" broadcasts warned natives to leave the coast around Civitavecchia for their "personal safety."

Donning his horn-rimmed spectacles, Admiral Canaris closely examined the "evidence" and proclaimed Abwehr's view on the military situation in Italy: there was no need for the Wehrmacht to fear a new Allied landing in the near future.

One hour later Canaris departed for Berlin—even as American and British assault troops were boarding vessels less than 100 miles to the south.

In the higher levels of the Allied command on D-Day Minus 1 the customary gnawing concerns of security leaks racked the generals. Always there was the question: have the Germans discovered our intentions and will they be lying in wait?

What had happened to the team of Allied naval officers that

had slipped ashore at Anzio in rubber boats several nights
before to test the texture of the beaches? These men had never
returned, simply vanished. The Germans had means to make
prisoners talk.

An Allied officer had attended the final briefing and was on
the way to rejoin his assault unit. He dropped a notebook filled
with his instructions in a muddy street in Naples. There it lay
for hours. Finally an Italian civilian spotted the notebook,
turned it over to a British corporal who gave it to his company
commander.

Had the Italian read the top-secret Allied instructions? If so,
did he understand them? Had he shown the notebook to some
other unauthorized person who did read and comprehend the
crucial data inside? If so, would word of the notebook's
contents be shuttled on to a German spy in Naples?

Tormented Allied security officers would not have the
answers to these crucial questions until assault waves hit the
Anzio beaches. The time to make changes in Operation Shingle
had long since passed.

Now it was time for Anglo-American assault troops—some
36,000 of them—to board vessels in the Naples region. Loaded
with them were scores of artillery pieces, tanks and supplies.
Among the latter, labeled as urgently needed by the assault
troops, were nearly 500 hymn books which, through clerical
error, would accompany the fighting men ashore.

A festive air surrounded embarkation. As the men who
would hit the beaches at Anzio in a few hours swung down
from the hills to march up gangplanks of designated ships,
wildly cheering Neapolitans lined the streets. At Castellam-
mare, proud members of the Irish Guards marched along in
precise parade-ground formation behind their band blaring out
the regimental march. Colonel Andrew Scott of the Irish Guard
stood erect on the pedestal of a statue and took the salute as his
fighting men moved past.

It was a scene reminiscent of a Hollywood World War I
movie.

Grim-faced yet projecting their customary cocky air, baggy-
panted members of the crack American 504th Parachute
Infantry Regiment scrambled into a tiny flotilla of LST's
(landing ship, tank). Many of the veteran paratroopers won-
dered why they had been left behind to fight as straight infantry

in savage battles in Italy when the main body of the 82nd Airborne Division had gone to England to prepare for the mammoth cross-Channel attack in the Spring.

For that they could thank (or blame) the British Bulldog, Winston Churchill. The prime minister had long been infatuated by paratroopers, and in his self-appointed role as a sort of super supreme commander for the Mediterranean had projected a bold drop by the American parachutists to seize the Alban Hills in front of seaborne invaders.

Churchill, in fact, had appealed to General George Marshall, the U.S. Army Chief of Staff, for the 504th Parachute Infantry Regiment to spearhead his tactical concept for Anzio. Marshall agreed to leave the paratroop regiment behind in Italy as the rest of the division sailed off for Great Britain.

General Clark, General Lucas and other Allied planners were far from enthralled by Churchill's concept for dropping the lightly-armed parachute regiment far from the Anzio beaches. There was serious doubt at the top whether Anglo-American seaborne forces would be strong enough to make a dash for the Alban Hills to link up with the parachutists.

But now that the rugged fighting men of the 504th were available, General Clark decided to use the adaptable paratroopers in the seaborne assault.

As General Truscott, smartly attired in his customary highly-glossed cavalry boots and battle jacket, stepped aboard the USS *Biscayne*, his 3rd Infantry Division band, backed by the throaty chorus of 200 of his men, broke out with the rousing music and words of the veteran fighting outfit's theme song, "The Dogface Soldier," which began:

I wouldn't give a bean, to be a fancy assed Marine,
I'd rather be a dogface soldier like I am.
I wouldn't trade my old ODs for all the Navy's dungarees,
For I'm the walking pride of Uncle Sam.

As the battle-tested 509th Parachute Infantry Battalion, a close-knit independent formation, moved toward the HMS *Winchester Castle* the unit's dashing bachelor surgeon, Captain Carlos C. Alden, was being needled by his comrades. Alden had just learned that, without his knowledge, the highly protective mother of one of the many attractive young

Neapolitan ladies he had been squiring had published banns in her parish church announcing the forthcoming marriage of Alden and the daughter.

On the eve of battle, the customarily unflappable Captain Alden took the shocking news in stride. "Hell, there's still hope," he observed with a straight face. "I might get killed at Anzio."

4

Landing at an Old Pirates' Lair

In perfect weather on the twenty-first, the great Allied fleet set sail from the Bay of Naples under a heavy cloud of barrage balloons. Mild breezes barely ruffled a calm sea, and the sun shone in cheerful fashion through stratocumulus clouds, warming the bodies and spirits of thousands of grim-faced American and British assault troops.

There were 374 craft in all, stretching for as far as the eye could see—210 British, 157 American, 4 Greek, 2 Dutch and 1 Polish.

It was an assorted group of ships and boats. Cruisers and destroyers, gunboats and minesweepers, tugs and trawlers, antiaircraft and headquarters vessels, submarines and hospital ships, motor launches and scout craft, and a variety of landing craft for infantry, tanks and vehicles.

In the midst of the vast armanda, mild-mannered and scholarly General Lucas—Foxy Grandpa—had settled aboard his command ship, the *Biscayne*. Lucas was not feeling well and his mood remained a pessimistic one. He penned in his diary:

"My subordinates do all of the work and most of the thinking. I must keep from thinking of the fact that my order will send these men into a desperate attack."

Leaving the Bay of Naples, the fleet sailed south in order to deceive Axis agents on shore and Luftwaffe reconnaissance planes. The convoy plowed through the Tyrrhenian Sea in the direction of North Africa, and as darkness enveloped the Mediterranean the ships remained on a southernly course. Suddenly, all vessels reversed direction and began steaming north toward Anzio.

Throughout the hours of daylight, at dusk and now in the blackness of night, assault troops and naval personnel constantly scanned the skies and cocked ears to detect the almost certain appearance of Luftwaffe fighter-bombers. But the Luftwaffe never arrived. Field Marshal Kesselring only hours before had been assured by Germany's master spy, Admiral Canaris, that no Allied amphibious operation was imminent.

Unseen by the approaching Allied invaders, blacked-out Anzio lay quiet and serene, totally unaware of the holocaust that was about to descend upon it in the days ahead. For centuries ancient Anzio—once known as Antium—had the dubious distinction of serving as one of the Mediterranean's most thriving pirates' lairs. It was cleaned up during the Augustan Era and became a fashionable seaside resort.

The fun-loving Emperor Nero, who later would fiddle while Rome burned, built an ornate palace there, as well as a mole and artificial harbor to be used for his convenience when he moored the imperial barge there. After Nero's death, Anzio rapidly deteriorated and reverted to its former status as a pirates' hangout and stronghold. The harbor silted up and it was not until the seventeenth century that renewed official interest was shown in Anzio. Pope Innocent XII built a new mole east of Nero's and a smaller mole which formed a completely protected small-boat basin. Three centuries later that basin would serve the cause of Anglo-American invaders.

Now, in the twentieth century, a powerful Allied fleet was knifing through the dark waters of the Tyrrhenian Sea toward the once-thriving pirates' lair. At 11:12 P.M. on January 21, Admiral Lowry, an old Sea Dog in command of the Allied naval task force, on his flagship *Biscayne* made radar contact with the Anzio lighthouse, and at 12:05 A.M. on D-Day anchored four miles southeast of the ancient city. All around the *Biscayne,* along the coast off Anzio, hundreds of other vessels quickly slipped into assigned places.

Other than for the clanking of anchor chains, sea and shore were deathly quiet—even eerie, ominous. Was an alerted

Wehrmacht lurking along the shoreline in the darkness, ready to pour withering blasts of fire into the ranks of assault troops when they were debarking tiny craft and wading toward the beaches? Nervous American and British soldiers recalled the Italian vendors back in Naples just before the fleet sailed. They were hawking pictorial postcards to boarding troops and sailors. A beautiful color photograph on the card had been identified as . . . Anzio.

At 1:20 A.M. an ominous call over loudspeakers filtered through the bowels of assault transports: "Troops to your boarding stations!" In several vessels, soldiers heavily burdened with battle gear scrambled up steel ladders to their assigned positions around the rails, just above tiny landing craft which could be heard down below banging gently against the steel hides of mother ships.

Minutes later, on signal, assault troops threw legs over railings and, toting full field packs, personal weapons, machine guns, bazookas and heavy boxes of ammunition, descended expertly down rope ladders and into the tiny Higgins boats still bobbing nervously in the black waters. Now, waiting to cast off and begin the run to the beaches, the first wave of assault soldiers became increasingly tense. Perspiration broke out. Stomachs knotted, breathing became heavy and labored. All tried to part the darkness and peer at the shadowy shore.

Hoping to gain surprise, there was no thunderous naval bombardment of the shoreline and facilities farther inland. As the tiny Higgins boats and LCIs (landing craft, infantry) knifed through the calm water on the way to the sandy beaches, a swishing noise, eerie-sounding yet reassuring to tense assault troops, suddenly erupted.

Rockets would pound the landing beaches for five minutes before the first wave hit the shoreline at 2 A.M.

In the heart of Anzio, Colonel William O. Darby's tough and resourceful 1st and 4th Ranger Battalions landed abreast and began to fan out in and around the resort city. The 31-year-old Darby, thick-chested and tall, was at the head of his troops, barking out orders in his rapid-fire style, urging his men onward.

Resistance in Anzio itself was negligible and by dawn Darby's Rangers had a firm grasp on the town. The only action in the town caused great glee among fighting men on the beachhead. Four German officers, roaring drunk and returning from a gala night in Rome, drove their Volkswagen into the yawning open doors of an American LCI as it was unloading supplies on the beach, thinking they were driving into a garage. Widely grinning Rangers promptly collared the four officers, whose befuddled minds labored mightily to determine how these swarms of American soldiers got into the Anzio "garage."

The British 1st Division, under Major General W. R. C. Penney, landed unopposed on Peter Beach, north of Anzio, and pushed rapidly inland. Three miles south of Anzio, veterans of the U.S. 3rd Infantry Division, commanded by General Truscott, splashed ashore on X-Ray Beach and advanced steadily. The only contact with the enemy occurred when 190 German service troops were captured en masse—caught in bed in their underwear.

Immediately after depositing Colonel Darby's two battalions in Anzio, the assault craft returned to vessels offshore where they picked up the Ranger 3rd Battalion and Lieutenant Colonel William P. Yarborough's veteran 509th Parachute Infantry Battalion and carried them ashore in the town of Anzio. Quickly forming up into march formation in the darkness, the parachutists headed south along the tree-lined coastal road, bound for their immediate objective of Nettuno, one mile away.

As the men of the 509th Parachute Infantry were pacing along the road, a German staff car bearing two officers and a driver was feeling its way through the night toward Nettuno. Unknown to them, they were on a collision course with the American paratroopers.

One of the officers, Lieutenant Siegmund Seiler, a 40-year-old engineer, had arrived in Anzio only two days before to take charge of a detachment of men and destroy the mole, making the port of Anzio useless. Seiler had no illusions as to his fighting ability, considering himself "a civilian wearing an army uniform."

The other officer in the car was the town commandant of Anzio, like Seiler a recent arrival in Anzio.

Shortly before the pair of officers entered the car, they had heard loud explosions in the town which told them an Allied invasion was in progress. The nervous town commandant pointed out to his equally anxious fellow officer that there was a combat unit just south of Nettuno, only some three miles away. They could drive there and find out what was going on in the locale.

Seiler balked at the proposal, but the commandant ordered him to go along. If it were an amphibious assault, plans were for Seiler and his 18 noncombat engineers to take their place in a defensive line.

Seiler turned ashen. He had never as much as seen an enemy soldier, and had had no training for combat.

With the town commandant sitting in the front seat with the sergeant driver, the three Germans headed for Nettuno. But in the darkness and his excitement, the sergeant took a wrong turn and wound around the town for more than 20 minutes before locating the coastal road. Reaching the road, the three Germans promptly spotted members of the 509th Parachute Infantry Battalion heading for Nettuno.

The driver pushed hard on the gas pedal and tried to speed through the paratroopers, but was greeted with heavy bursts of fire. The commandant of Anzio was killed and the driver badly wounded. Lieutenant Seiler escaped unscathed by ducking down behind the front seat as the vehicle plunged into a ditch and came to an abrupt halt.

Slightly dazed, Seiler was aware of someone slowly pulling open a jammed door and found himself staring into the muzzle of a Tommy gun held by an American paratrooper. The war was over for the "civilian wearing an army uniform."

In the darkness of Anzio town, a mild degree of confusion reigned. Lieutenant Louis Martin of the Rangers gripped his carbine and edged through the eerie streets at the head of a column of his men. Suddenly an automatic weapon erupted somewhere off to the right, followed by a loud American roar which carried for great distances in the nighttime air: "Cut it out, you sons of bitches! We ain't Krauts!"

Then all was silent again.

Minutes later there was a heavy outburst of firing in the direction of Nettuno, only a short distance down the beach known as the Riviera di Levante which connected the sister cities. Lieutenant Martin squinted through his spectacles in the direction of the heavy small arms fire. He knew a veteran parachute unit was to seize Nettuno.

"What'n hell do you think that is, Lieutenant?" a Ranger called out.

"Don't know. Might be trouble. But hell, those hopheads of the 509th parachutes would shoot up a storm in any situation. Hell, anyone who would join hands and jump out of airplanes" . . . His voice trailed off as he resumed moving forward.

The Anglo-American assault waves were ashore with virtually no opposition. Total surprise had been achieved. From his vantage point on the *Biscayne* four miles offshore, General Lucas could hardly believe his good fortune. Peering into the darkness toward Anzio, he could neither see nor hear any firing on the beaches except for the short-lived bursts from the 509th Parachute Infantry shooting up a Nettuno void of enemy troops.

Expecting a bloodbath, Lucas' spirits soared. He radioed a coded signal to General Mark Clark, the Fifth Army commander, who was in his command trailer at Caserta anxiously awaiting early reports on the Anzio assault:

"Paris—Bordeaux—Turin—Tangiers—Bari—Albany."

The terse message was filled with meaning: "Weather clear, sea calm, little wind, force's presence not discovered, landings in progress, no reports from landings yet."

A tense Mark Clark read the decoded message and beamed broadly at a few confidants who were maintaining the vigil with their commanding general. So far, so good, Clark told himself. He reached down and patted the head of his pet black cocker spaniel, Pal.

Minutes after Darby's Rangers had splashed ashore in Anzio town, A German corporal in the railway engineers heard a commotion outside his quarters and looked out a window. He was astonished to see rockets exploding along the dockside and shoreline, followed by American soldiers storming ashore.

Frightened on finding himself alone in the center of an American amphibious assault, the German corporal leaped onto his motorcycle and raced out of town toward the north, glancing nervously over his shoulder periodically to ward off a gnawing feeling that someone was chasing him. A few miles up the road, purely by chance, the corporal ran into Lieutenant Helmut Heuritsch of the 200th Panzer Grenadier Regiment and rapidly blurted out all that he knew about the American assault at Anzio.

Heuritsch, with no means for communicating with high headquarters, dashed to the home of the mayor of Albano who, at 4 A.M., telephoned the Wehrmacht command post in Rome.

Minutes later Field Marshal Kesselring was roused from a deep sleep at his headquarters at Monte Soratte near Rome by an aide. He rushed to his office and began poring over a large map of the region the Germans called Nettuno. Major Wolfgang Hagemann, a staff officer who had been summoned by Kesselring, burst into the room.

Without looking up the Wehrmacht commander in the Mediterranean snapped, "Hagemann, where in the hell is Aprilia? I can't find it on the map."

The aide explained that Aprilia was not on the map because it was a new town Benito Mussolini, the recently ousted premier of Italy, had founded near Nettuno.

Kesselring explained that an Anglo-American force had landed near Nettuno only a few hours previously and was reported to have reached Aprilia. "Better pack your bags, Wolfgang," the imperturbable field marshal observed in a calm voice. "We have nothing between Nettuno and Rome."

"The *feldmarschall* is just joshing," Hagemann mused. "Or is he?"

Reports from the field continued to pour into Kesselring's office and by 5 A.M. the Mediterranean commander had determined that Anzio was a full-blooded Allied invasion and not a diversionary raid to mask a major landing elsewhere along the Italian coast. The code-phrase was flashed from Monte Soratte: *Code Richard!* (converge on Anzio).

Kesselring ordered his 4th Parachute Division, positioned just north of Rome, and elements of the elite Hermann Goering Division to block roads between Anzio and the obvious objective of the Anzio seaborne assault—the Alban Hills.

The field marshal contacted the Oberkommando der Wehrmacht in Berlin seeking additional troops, and within hours battle-tested German formations from as far away as France, Yugoslavia and the Third Reich were being rushed to the seaside resort south of Rome. Three hours after the first Allied soldier had stepped ashore in the darkness at Anzio, Kesselring was fashioning an iron noose around the bridgehead.

As a fearful dawn broke over the bleak mountains of Italy, Colonel Reuben H. Tucker, commander of the 504th Parachute Infantry Regiment of the 82nd Airborne Division, was impatiently pacing about one of the 13 LCIs that were standing offshore. Tucker, barrel-chested, deep voiced and relatively short in physical stature, was known as Rube to most fellow officers. He was an aggressive leader and was straining at the leash to get ashore and into the fight.

Eager as he was to join the fray, 31-year-old Rube Tucker was disappointed to be landing by sea. "Hell, we're paratroopers, not sailors!" he had snorted to fellow parachute officers a few days previously. That was when a planned combat jump by the Five-O-Fours had been cancelled and the parachutists ordered to reach Anzio by boat.

Early plans had called for Colonel Tucker and his men to bail out ahead of seaborne landings on the Anzio-Albano road about 10 miles north of Anzio and just short of the key Alban Hills. Some British commanders had objected to the proposed drop behind enemy lines on the theory that the American parachutists might be mistaken for Germans and brought under fire. The U.S. Army Air Corps had also objected on the thesis that there would be no moonlight so the parachutists might be widely dispersed.

"Keeerist!" a Five-O-Four had exclaimed on hearing of the Air Corps protest. "The moon was bright enough in Sicily (six months previously) to read a newspaper, and the fly-boys scattered us over 60 miles of the island. So they couldn't do any worse at Anzio."

Now off Anzio in the early gray hours of the twenty-second, a loudspeaker from a control ship bellowed out an order to Colonel Tucker, the reluctant seaborne soldier: "Move your regiment onto Red Beach!"

As though the maneuver had been practiced for months instead of being one of largely improvisation, the LCIs carrying Tucker's parachutists headed for shore in precise formation. The only sound to be heard was the throbbing of the craft's powerful motors. The lead boats reached the shoreline and lowered ramps into the shallow water, and troopers began splashing toward dry land.

Moments later, the stillness at Anzio was shattered. Out of the blinding sun a flight of six Messerschmitt dive bombers pounced on the LCIs as they were debarking paratroopers. Several bombs hit on land and plunged harmlessly into the water. But one bomb struck directly on an LCI carrying G Company of the 3rd Battalion. An entire platoon was wiped out by the blast, and the craft was left a burning, blackened, twisted wreckage.

Having scored a bull's-eye, the six intruding Luftwaffe dive bombers pulled up and sped for their home base. Unloading of the 504th Regiment continued uneventfully and the troopers marched two miles inland to an assembly area in the Padiglione Woods.

That afternoon at Nettuno, Captain Carlos "Doc" Alden, the 33-year-old surgeon of the 509th Parachute Infantry Battalion, was growing restless. There had been total lack of enemy action—and action was what Alden sought. Since seeing his unarmed medics shot down in cold blood in ferocious fighting in North Africa, Doc Alden, a realist, made a realistic decision: he would arm himself and his medics, except for a few whose religious beliefs precluded their carrying weapons.

The surgeon from Buffalo, New York, always went into action armed to the teeth: Tommy gun, two pistols, trench knife and pockets full of grenades. And he was an expert at using all these weapons.

Alden approached one of his medics, Sergeant Pat Herr, who, like others in the parachute battalion in Nettuno, was sitting idly by awaiting orders. "Pat, let's go for a walk," Alden said.

Herr had been in action with his commanding officer for months and knew that "going for a little walk" with Doc Alden in a combat situation could lead to almost anything—probably a perilous trek through and behind enemy lines.

The two medical men, loaded down with their customary heavy arsenal of weapons, walked out of Nettuno and pushed on for about two miles until they reached outposts of the 3rd Infantry Division, the veteran outfit to which the 509th Parachute Battalion was attached.

"You'd better not go out there any farther," a young lieutenant told Alden. "There's nobody out there but Krauts."

Undaunted, Alden replied, "Well, thanks for the warning. But I don't see or hear anything that indicates the enemy is out there. So I think we'll just stroll on a little way."

The infantry lieutenant shrugged his shoulders as if to say, "Well, it's your funeral," and sat back to await developments.

Alden and Herr trekked onward for an hour, moving some four miles out in front of Allied lines. Obviously the Italian population had fled inland. The pair of parachutists did not see a single human being or any sign of Germans being in the vicinity.

"Guess we'd better be heading back, Pat," Alden observed. "It's going to get dark before too long."

Taking a different route back to American lines, the parachute captain and his medic arrived at the MLR (main line of resistance) of the 3rd Infantry Division just as shadows were starting to creep on D-Day. The surgeon was astonished to see infantrymen furiously digging in. There had not been a shot fired in the vicinity and Alden had been four miles forward without seeing a single German soldier.

"What're you fellows digging in here for?" the battle surgeon inquired.

"Orders," a dogface sergeant wielding a shovel replied. "Higher up's expecting a heavy counterattack at any time."

Offshore on the *Biscayne*, General John Lucas was looking over casualty figures for the seaborne assault which had just reached his desk. He still could not believe his eyes and his good fortune. A bloodbath had been anticipated, yet 36,034 Allied troops had been put ashore over the beaches with only 13 killed, 97 wounded and 44 missing.

Meanwhile in Rome on D-Day, many German officials were frantically packing for sudden departure from the Eternal City on hearing of the Allied landing at Anzio, virtually on the front porch of the Italian capital. American and British soldiers, possibly preceded by Allied paratroopers in a mass bailout, could be expected to bolt into Rome momentarily.

But the glittering jewel by the historic Tiber River, where centuries before Romulus and Remus cavorted, would not fall into Anglo-American hands like an overripe plum. *Obersturmbannführer* (SS lieutenant colonel) Herbert Kappler, the dreaded Gestapo chief in Rome, was almost gleefully confiding to aides on the afternoon of D-Day at Anzio plans to "blow up" the Eternal City as Allied tanks approached the gates.

Adolf Hitler, warlord of Greater Germany, had given orders to destroy certain powerplants, communications facilities, bridges and other structures in the event it became necessary to abandon Rome. But Kappler interpreted the order to an extreme degree.

Kappler disclosed to his confidants that his Gestapo agents, numbering some 100 in Rome, were already feverishly engaged in organizing enormous ammunition dumps at key locales in the Eternal City. After the Allies entered the city, sabotage teams left behind by the Germans would ignite the dumps, blowing up much of Rome.

That same night preliminaries for the destruction of Rome got underway.

Elsewhere in the electrified, tense Italian capital shortly after word had been received of the Anzio invasion, the American OSS spy, young Peter Tompkins, was huddled in a decrepit, second-level apartment with an assorted, seedy collection of Italian men who were members of various factions of the Rome underground. Each man was heavily bundled up against the bone-chilling cold of the apartment; and their reception of the American agent was equally frigid.

As the Italians stared coldly and with intense disinterest at the American, Tompkins began unfolding the reasons for his being in Rome—to establish an intelligence and sabotage network to assist the Allies in their drive for the capital from Anzio. The bearded intellectual urged the Italians to unfurl a campaign of destruction of German facilities and harassment of Wehrmacht troops.

Only silence resulted from Tompkins' impassioned plea. As the American had suspected, these underground faction leaders were dedicated to a single cause—establishing themselves in positions of political power when the Germans were driven out of Rome.

Tompkins, despairing and distressed, headed back through the streets to his lodging, his mission to generate a partisan uprising inundated by the underground power struggle. He concluded his worst fears would be realized: instead of assisting the Allies as they moved toward Rome, the warring factions would erupt in a bloody civil war.

While American and British fighting men were moving ashore at Anzio in almost parade-ground style on D-Day, some 60 miles to the southeast the Rapido River battle grounds had been ablaze for the second day. Texans of the 36th Infantry

Division were still clinging by their fingernails to a slender bridgehead on the German side of the river, but had been under the most intense artillery and incessant enemy ground attacks.

Combat engineers had repeatedly established foot bridges across the narrow and treacherous river through the day, suffering heavy casualties in the process from enemy fire. But almost as soon as the spans were erected, they were destroyed by German salvos.

Individually and in tiny groups, 36th Division men on the embattled far shore crawled and slithered through the mud back to the river bank and inched their way across. Many were blown to bits by shells just as they reached what they thought was the safety of the American side of the Rapido. Other desperate, mud- and blood-caked figures made it only halfway across the stream; weak and exhausted, they were hauled under by the powerful current, their pitiful screams drowned by the torrents of rushing water.

Night fell over the raging Rapido and the holocaust that had been flaming along its banks. The sound of American weapons on the far shore grew dimmer, then halted altogether. An hour before midnight, the echo of savage battle ceased. An eerie, grotesque hush blanketed the Rapido killing grounds. Here and there crickets chirped merrily along the river banks and in the marshland.

Sprawled out in front of German gunners were masses of bodies of American dead. Here and there the pitiful moans and pleadings of wounded 36th Division men wafted over the damp landscape. No medical help was immediately available. They suffered, and died.

The desperate struggle by General Fred Walker's fighting men from Texas to carve out a foothold on the German side of the swift-flowing Rapido had lasted for 48 hours—a lifetime to those caught in the hurricane of steel and explosives. Over 1,100 casualties were inflicted by the Germans.

But the sacrifices of the 36th Infantry Division were not in vain. The Anzio region had been virtually denuded of Wehrmacht troops.

5

"Fight the Battle Without Pity!"

For the next two days of the invasion, a hushed, almost eerie quietude hovered over the barren flatlands of Anzio. The VI Corps beachhead line remained roughly as it had been on the afternoon of D-Day, seven to eight miles deep at points and stretching for 16 miles from the Mussolini Canal on the south to the Moletta River on the north.

Most of the Allied "progress" took place at the shoreline where huge mounds of equipment and supplies were unloaded. General Lucas, the white-haired commander of VI Corps who was well-liked by all from privates to generals, recalled the parting words of General Mark Clark when the Fifth Army leaders visited the beachhead on D-Day:

"Don't stick your neck out, Johnny. I did at Salerno and nearly got it chopped off."

The methodical Lucas had no intention of placing his neck on the executioner's block. He would build up his supplies, await the arrival of additional troops, probe the front with small patrols and then launch limited objective attacks to expand his toe-hold around the peacetime resort of Anzio.

There had hardly been a shot fired on the bridgehead since the early hours of D-Day. Only the occasional gruff thump-thump-thump of Allied antiaircraft guns marred the silence when a flight of Luftwaffe warplanes would hurry over the harbor area, drop its bombs, strafe the docks, then high-tail it for home, the airfields around Rome.

American and British fighting men in the "front lines" remained astonished over the almost total lack of Wehrmacht opposition to their invasion. They had expected a bloody fight.

In the Padiglione woods in the British sector late in the afternoon of D-Day plus 1, the 24th Guards Brigade was in reserve and in the process of an ancient army ritual known as "brewing up"—heating their afternoon tea. Officers had spent most of the day playing bridge. None could understand why they were sitting in a woods instead of racing for Rome.

In particular, the Irish Guards had hoped to be in the vanguard of a dash for the Eternal City. Shortly after landing, a particularly enthusiastic Guardsman had called out to his comrades:

"We'll give the Holy Father a holiday and make Father Brookes (the unit chaplain) acting unpaid Pope!"

On the other end of the bridgehead, troopers of the 504th Parachute Infantry Regiment had grown restless from two days of almost total inactivity. When there was no enemy to fight, the parachutists often fought among themselves. Two fistfights erupted, and with the normal assortment of bloody noses and black eyes the impromptu bouts were called draws by wildly cheering comrades.

Two hours later the battered pugilists were drinking from the same bottle of Italian *vino* which had been "liberated" by an enterprising paratrooper from the cellars under Nettuno. He had gone there on a self-appointed mission to "assess the morale of the civilian population."

Despite the relative inactivity, men of the 504th Parachute Infantry were killed and wounded, and there were increasing indications of German movements into the area. Lieutenant Chester Garrison, personnel officer of the 2nd Battalion, recorded in his daily journal for Monday, January 24:

F Company suffered one killed (Rabb) and one wounded through the chest (Bishop) by snipers in house. Some of these snipers were Italians in German uniform, others were in civilian dress. F Company flushed the houses and found one Italian civilian hiding his gun, killed him on the spot much to the turmoil of other civilians.

Report at 1900 (7 P.M.) that 14 planeloads of German paratroopers had jumped east of Bridge Number 4 in Carrot Red area. Shortly afterward our password was changed.

Late that day, a shell exploded here and there on the beachhead. Enemy gunners displayed particular interest in the Anzio harbor area. There was no great cause for concern from this long-range shelling. But it did tell Allied commanders that the Germans were starting to build up forces out there in the unknown.

Shortly after dawn the following day, the twenty-fourth, a small task force of the Grenadier Guards, loaded in Bren-gun carriers, headed up the Albano-Anzio road toward the Alban Hills with the mission of probing the terrain to the front. The motorized patrol advanced for three miles to the village of Carroceto without being fired on. "Blimey, let's go all the way to Rome!" a Guardsman enthused to his comrades.

There had been no sign of the enemy, but the knowing eyes of the veteran Guardsmen soon observed a disquieting factor: farmhouses along either side of the road had been tightly shuttered. This had always been the normal procedure among civilians in a battle zone who had reason to fear violence was about to erupt around them.

Edging forward out of the cluster of houses known as Carroceto, the quietude was angrily shattered. Swissshhh-CRACK! A flat-trajectory shell, fired from Aprilia, Benito Mussolini's model town only a few hundred yards to the northeast, crashed into a wall next to the lead Bren-gun carrier.

Moments later the Guardsmen saw two huge self-propelled guns rumble out of Aprilia toward them and enemy infantry scrambling into position behind an embankment. Finally, the confrontation on Anzio beachhead had been joined.

Having achieved its mission of making contact with Germans, the Bren-gun carriers spun about and the patrol headed for the rear. Machine gun bullets and 88-millimeter shells chased the British vehicles for nearly a mile.

Word of the unexpected presence of a sizeable German force was passed along to higher levels, and at dawn the following

day, January 25, General Penney's Guards Brigade jumped off
to drive the enemy out of Aprilia (which had been dubbed The
Factory by the British). In Aprilia was the 29th Panzer
Grenadiers of the 3rd Panzer Division.

As the Guardsmen approached The Factory, they were met
by a torrent of fire, but fought their way into the large complex
of buildings. There a hand-to-hand fight among the houses
developed, with grenades, bayonets, rifles and automatic
weapons. Often Germans and Tommies found themselves in
adjoining rooms of the same house. Down in the dark, cold
cellars civilians huddled in fear, caught in the center of the
violence. Women sobbed. Children wailed and screamed. All
prayed.

It required 24 hours of bloody fighting but General Penney's
Guardsmen seized the battered town and captured 112 prison-
ers. Remnants of the 29th Panzer Grenadiers withdrew to
Campoleone, some four miles to the north.

When Penney's men dug in that evening, they had pushed
the Allied line forward for nearly four miles. But the Guardsmen had paid a heavy price for this elongated finger of real
estate sticking out toward the Alban Hills, a hazy land mass off
in the distance.

General Lucas was feeling more optimistic on January 25
when a regiment of the U.S. 45th Infantry Division came in
over the beaches and word was received that the remainder of
the 45th and elements of the U.S. 1st Armored Division, both
battle-tested formations, were en route to Anzio.

Reflecting his slightly buoyed spirits, Lucas penned in his
diary that evening:

"My days are filled with excitement and anxiety, although I
feel now that the beachhead is safe and I can plan for the future
with some assurance."

Other factors on the twenty-fifth contributed to General
Lucas' uplifted mood. General Alexander, the Briton commanding 15th Army Group, paid another visit to the bridgehead and remarked to Lucas, "What a splendid piece of work."

Although a high-level commander, Harold Alexander was
no stranger to the front lines. Within hours of the Anzio
landing, he had arrived by PT boat and gone ashore, along with
the hulking leader of British naval forces at the beachhead,
Rear Admiral Thomas H. Troubridge.

Wedged in a jeep and driving among troops moving along the coastal road, General Alexander halted to confer with Colonel Scott of the Irish Guards. "Good work," the ground commander in Italy declared.

Alexander's words were bitten off with the sudden nearby explosion of a salvo of enemy shells. "This is unfair!" Admiral Troubridge complained with a straight face. "On shore I'm a noncombatant."

General Mark Clark also arrived at Anzio that day and complimented Johnny Lucas on the way he was building up his supplies in preparation for the advance inland.

Most encouraging of all to General Lucas that day were reports received from General Penney at the British 1st Division which told of his men's seizure of The Factory.

But now a sobering thought penetrated the beings of top commanders at Anzio as well as those of many frontline fighting men. Field Marshal Albrecht Kesselring had rushed troops and guns to the beachhead far faster than Allied planners had anticipated. The Great Adventure of Anzio was a thing of the past. Now the bloody fighting would start.

Despite the British advance toward the Alban Hills—and Rome—General Lucas was not yet ready for a full-blooded offensive. "I must keep my feet on the ground and my forces in hand," he cautioned himself in his diary. "I must not do anything foolish. This is the most important thing I have ever tried to do and I will not be stampeded."

One who was all for a "stampede" to be launched toward Rome was the "father" of the Anzio landing, Winston Churchill. Anzio was the British Prime's "baby" and by D-Day plus 3 he was enraged at what appeared to him in far-off London to be a failure to exploit the surprise invasion behind German lines.

An impatient Churchill fired off a signal to his fellow Briton, General Jumbo Wilson, who had succeeded Eisenhower as supreme commander in the Mediterranean, demanding to know why the Allied troops on Anzio were not by now racing for Rome.

Wilson shifted the "blame" onto Foxy Grandpa Lucas, claiming in his response that "there has been no lack of urging from above," meaning General Alexander and General Clark,

as "both visited the beachhead during the first 48 hours to
hasten the offensive."

Churchill, wily, stubborn, egotistical, shot off another message to General Wilson: "Senior commanders should not 'urge'
but 'order.' "

It was a thinly disguised slap at Churchill's protege, General
Alexander, who The Prime had long believed was "too
gentlemanly" in his dealings with subordinate commanders.
The suave, astute, well-liked Harold Alexander had always
exercised command by "suggesting" courses of action to those
serving under him.

A subtle foundation was being laid for isolating an Anzio
scapegoat should the amphibious invasion flounder. The finger
seemed to be pointing at Johnny Lucas for that dubious role.

Pacing about in his London office like a caged tiger,
Churchill rasped to his confidants, "I thought we were throw-
ing a wildcat onto the beach to rip the bowels out of the Boche.
Instead we have a stranded whale."

Meanwhile, some 60 miles southeast of the Allied bridgehead at Anzio, German grenadiers on outpost duty along the
bloody Rapido River were maintaining an alert vigil, on guard
against further American attacks to secure crossings over the
swift-flowing stream. Many of the Germans wore handker-
chiefs or other material over noses—the putrified stench of
death and decaying flesh saturated the air.

Out in front of the German defenders of the Rapido, scores
of 36th Infantry Division bodies lay grotesquely sprawled in
death, men who had reached the far shore but were cut down
in ferocious fighting.

Hardly distinguishable from the cadavers of the Texas
division, Platoon Sergeant Charlie Rummel, who had been
seriously wounded in both legs on January 22 just before the
tenacious Germans crushed all opposition on the far shore, had
been crawling from foxhole to foxhole for three days and
nights. He had been passing out, then regaining consciousness
repeatedly, but had to drag himself about on his stomach in
search of food.

Rummel, ashen-faced, weak from loss of blood and in
intense pain, was constantly wet to the skin and shivering from
the cold. Each hole he crawled into was filled with icy water.
Nearby he could hear Germans chattering, but the American

remained undiscovered in the midst of German battle lines. It was now January 25, but the hazy-minded Rummel was unaware of that fact.

At one point, American artillery and mortars, firing mainly white phosphorous shells which inflicted hideous burns on victims, pounded the area around Sergeant Rummel as he took refuge in a water-filled hole. He thought that at any moment a shell would come right in after him.

In one of those periodic curious happenings in a savage war, the Germans observed a truce on the twenty-fifth to allow American medics to cross the Rapido River unmolested and remove their dead and wounded. But Rummel was in a confused state of mind and too weak to call out, even though medics moved about near him. He was overlooked and left behind as the truce ended.

An undetermined amount of time later the half-conscious Charlie Rummel was spotted by the Germans. He was removed to a field hospital where it was necessary to amputate both of his mangled and infected legs.

On the slender strip of Italian real estate around Anzio, frontline soldiers and commanders alike were growing increasingly aware that the Germans were rapidly building up around the entire length of the perimeter. An alarmed VI Corps intelligence was steadily identifying units which had moved to Anzio from France, Germany, the Balkans and northern Italy with far greater speed than the Allied planners had envisioned.

German artillery fire was now pounding American and British positions and installations with ever increasing intensity. The enemy had even moved in an enormous 280-millimeter railroad gun, later called the Anzio Express by Allied soldiers because shells from the huge weapon sounded like a train rushing through a tunnel as they raced toward the bridgehead. This frightening weapon pounded Anzio, the docks, Nettuno and other rear facilities.

Early in the morning of January 25, Sergeant Milton V. "Fuzzy" Knight of Colonel Rube Tucker's 504th Parachute Infantry Regiment, stuck his head out the window of a well-built, neat farmhouse along the *Canale Mussolini*. Knight briefly reflected that this was the way to fight a war. He and his intelligence section had been in the house for two days without being shelled or otherwise molested by the enemy.

Suddenly anger surged through Knight's being. Hanging on a wire fence in front of the structure were several GI drawers and undershirts—a sure tip to the ever-present German eye that Americans were occupying the house.

"Who the hell do these goddamned long handles on the fence belong to?" Sergeant Knight shouted.

Young Private Danny Karsch sheepishly admitted that they were his, that he had put the underwear out to dry in the darkness and had forgotten to bring in his apparel.

"Well, get your ass out there and bring them in!" Knight ordered.

Karsch was going out the door when the sound of incoming shells reached the ears of the men in the house and they all ducked for cover. Possibly zeroing in on the long-handle underwear, the German aim was accurate.

There were loud explosions and a wrenching of timber and stone. When the thick clouds of smoke cleared, Danny Karsch's underwear was no more—a shell had scored a direct hit on them. And the house received several hits and pieces of the roof fell in on the paratroopers below. The occupants, including Knight and Karsch, escaped serious injury. But for days Karsch had to endure the frigid glares of his comrades.

Elsewhere along the canal that night of the twenty-fifth, Private First Class Leon F. Mims of the 509th Parachute Infantry Battalion, a machine gunner, and two comrades had been sent forward to establish an outpost. One of them was a teenager who had not been in action before.

Mims recalled an episode on the troop transport as it sailed toward Anzio four days before. A prayer service was held and well attended. Going into battle, many soldiers were struck suddenly by acute attacks of religious fervor.

Leaving for the prayer service, Mims noticed that the youthful machine gunner was not going to attend and asked why.

"Aw, I don't go for all that religion stuff," was the reply.

"Maybe not," the Georgia-born Mims observed. "But if we're living 10 days from now, and we probably won't be, you'll come to me and tell me you've been praying."

"I will like hell," the youth responded. "Someone else can do the prayin'."

Now as the three paratroopers were digging in their machine

gun in the darkness of the moonless night, Mims moved forward to see if he could view or hear any ominous action. Suddenly the sky broke out in iridescence. The Germans to his front had fired a flare. Mims flopped to the ground. His heart beat faster. He peered forward and the thumping in his chest grew more intense. He didn't know if the Germans could see him, but he certainly saw them—an entire platoon of heavily-armed grenadiers.

As Mims lay motionless and held his breath, the flare flickered out and the blackness returned. He slithered along the ground back to his two comrades.

Manning the machine gun and silently, tensely awaiting developments, Mims and the others saw the shadowy silhouettes of the German force slipping across the canal, their coal bucket-shaped helmets outlined against the murky sky.

Now the silence was shattered. Mims squeezed the trigger and his machine gun spit streams of tracers at the advancing enemy, cutting down several and causing the other feldgrau (field gray, the average German soldier) to leap for cover. Moments later the German force opened up a withering burst of smallarms fire against the American machine gun crew. The echoes of the intense fire fight rolled for miles across the damp, frigid flatlands of Anzio.

Soon three German machine guns began pouring fire into Mims and his comrades. One paratrooper was killed. Mims was lying behind a low mound of dirt from the hole that had just been dug. Two bullets zipped through the canteen on his web belt and three other slugs passed through his jump jacket.

In the meantime, other members of the 509th Parachute Infantry Battalion had edged up to the scene of the firefight to lend assistance to the hard-pressed outpost. Mims slithered forward and tossed several grenades at two of the enemy machine guns, and both fell silent.

Now the American paratroopers pounced on the foe in the darkness. There was a thrashing of bodies, grunts, groans and an occasional scream as the intermingled feldgrau and American parachutists battled it out with grenades, bayonets and daggers. As the Germans fled the scene, they left 12 bodies behind. Several paratroopers lay dead.

Silence returned. Leon Mims had a curious thought: where

was the teenager who didn't believe in "all that religion stuff."
Had he been killed?"

The Georgian moved to the youth's foxhole, and the boy
called out, "Mims, is that you?"

"Yeah, it's me. Where were you while we were tangling
with the Krauts?"

After a short pause, the teenager replied softly:

"I was here in my hole—prayin'."

On the evening of the twenty-fifth, Field Marshal Kesselring
was discussing the battle picture in Italy with his chief of staff,
Major General Siegfried Westphal. Highly intelligent, energetic and decisive, Westphal had proven to be Kesselring's
strong right arm who took much of the burden off the shoulders
of the Wehrmacht commander in the Mediterranean.

Kesselring, always imperturbable, was now breathing easier. A master of parlor magic, a gifted piano player, affable and
courteous at all times, the field marshal inwardly had been
quite worried over the situation at Anzio since three days
before when the Allies landed and the Germans had virtually
nothing between the shoreline and Rome.

Now, on the Allies' D-Day plus 3, the Germans had
elements of eight divisions around the bridgehead with five
more divisions rushing to the new battlegrounds. The Anglo-
Americans had missed their golden opportunity, Kesselring
told General Westphal.

Rain, sleet and hail pounded the beachhead on January 26,
disrupting the Allied supply buildup which had been operating
smoothly until Mother Nature intervened. The deluge of
miserable weather sent General Lucas' spirits plummeting once
again.

Bundled up in his lined trench coat and wool scarf in the
gloomy, damp wine cellar in Nettuno that served as VI Corps
headquarters, Lucas wrote in his diary:

"I am doing my best, but it seems terribly slow. This waiting
is terrible."

The following day, General Harold Alexander, 15th Army
Group commander, walked into General Mark Clark's headquarters at Caserta. Alexander, cordial and suave as ever, was
deeply concerned about Anzio—particularly so with regard to
what he called "the command question," meaning Johnny
Lucas. Alexander had been stung by the sharp slap he had

received from his patron, Prime Minister Churchill, in the latter's signal to General Jumbo Wilson two days previously.

Alexander promptly launched into heavy criticism of Lucas, maintaining that the beachhead commander was not moving vigorously enough or rapidly enough. Clark bristled at Alexander's rebuke of a fellow American general whom he (Clark) had appointed to the post, and a sharp exchange bordering on a dispute resulted.

Clark found himself in an ambivalent position: he too had gnawing concern over General Lucas' handling of the Anzio operation, yet he felt compelled to defend Foxy Grandpa, who he recognized had been saddled with a difficult operation.

As the discussion became more heated, Mark Clark's blood pressure soared. He was particularly resentful of the fact that Alexander obviously was serving as a "mouthpiece" for Winston Churchill. The Prime, Clark felt, had again donned his Super Supreme Commander's hat and was endeavoring to direct the Battle of Anzio from the plush armchairs of far-off London. Churchill, it seemed to the Fifth Army commander, wanted a mad dash to Rome launched—and The Prime Minister was not concerned with tactical and logistical problems faced by General Lucas.

As a result of the intense discussion with his immediate superior over the command situation at Anzio, General Clark decided to visit the harassed Johnny Lucas on the beachhead. He came within a whisker of being killed in the process.

At dawn the following morning, the twenty-eighth, Clark went to the mouth of the Volturno River where he boarded a swift PT boat for Anzio. Another PT boat accompanied Clark's craft. With the Fifth Army commander were several aides and Frank Gervasi, an American war correspondent.

There was a thinly masked air of tension as the PT boats roared off. German air raids and shelling at and around the beachhead had become increasingly heavy, and reports were that enemy *Schnellboote* (small, fast craft similar to American PT boats) were roaming the coast to torpedo Allied shipping.

Slashing along through heavy waves in the early morning seven miles south of Anzio, the PT boats were challenged by an American minesweeper. The PT boat skipper ordered green and yellow flares to be fired and the designated signal to be flashed on the blinker to identify the craft as friendly.

Up until that time, the angular Mark Clark had been seated on a stool where the bridge of the boat afforded him some protection against the chilling bite of the wet wind blasts. When the minesweeper challenged the PT boats, Clark got up from the stool and moved a short distance to one side.

Moments later shells from the American minesweeper struck Clark's PT boat, one of which crashed into the stool he had abandoned only seconds previously. The skipper was wounded in both legs and writhed in agony on the deck. Another shell exploded below decks. Several men on the PT boat were knocked off their feet, and two of them were killed.

In the confusion which had erupted on deck, someone dropped a Very pistol. General Clark picked it up and fired the correct flare to again identify the PT boats as friendly. This brought another round of shelling. Clark fired the Very pistol once more—without result.

Now Clark cast a hurried glance around him. All three navy officers on the PT boat and two navy ratings were casualties, sprawled about, bleeding profusely, either dead or wounded. There was no one at the wheel to guide the craft, but a young ensign, though painfully wounded in both legs, dragged himself to the wheel and swung the boat around.

General Clark quickly kneeled down beside the ensign, who was too weak to get up from the deck, now awash with blood. "What do we do now?" the Fifth Army commander inquired evenly.

"I don't know," the navy officer replied through clenched teeth.

"Well, let's make a run for it," Clark suggested.

The army commander reached down and helped the ensign to his feet and held him in place so that he could direct the movement of the PT boat. With a noisy revving of motors, the two craft (the other PT boat escaped damage) sped off in the direction of Naples. The American gunners on the mine-sweeper continued to pepper shells at the fleeing PT boats, but scored no more hits.

While the battered PT boat and its companion craft sped southward for 30 minutes, examinations revealed that an ensign named Donald was in the most serious condition. One of his leg arteries had been severed and he was losing blood at an alarming rate. Other navy men on board received shell wounds, fractured bones, and one man had his kneecap shot off and was in intense pain.

Curiously, not one of the several army men, including General Clark, had been hit.

The wounded men were transferred to the approaching British minesweeper *Acute* which had a doctor aboard. Then Clark told the remaining naval crew, "Okay, head back for Anzio. "With a roar of motors, the pair of PT boats leaped northward.

Reaching the point seven miles south of Anzio from which the PT boats had been shelled, Clark and others on the two craft were concerned on seeing that the same minesweeper— with its nervous gunners presumably still fingering triggers— was still in place. Again the identification signals were flashed—and recognized. All on board the PT boats exhaled collective sighs of relief.

General Clark's new skipper, who had transferred from the other PT boat, edged his craft up to the minesweeper which went by the unromantic name *AM 120*. The young navy officer could barely contain the fury that had been surging through him for hours, ever since the "friendly" shelling that had killed and wounded several of his comrades.

Grabbing a megaphone, the skipper hailed the captain of the minesweeper and proceeded to launch a loud and profane lecture, beginning with, "You goddamned sons of bitches fired on General Mark Clark."

"Please accept our sincere apologies," the embarrassed captain of *AM 120* called back over his megaphone. "The rays of the early morning sun made it impossible for us to recognize your signals."

Ignoring the fact that he was addressing a naval officer superior in rank, the ensign responded loudly, "It's a wonder you ignorant bastards didn't shoot at the sun."

With the inauspicious beginning of January 28 now history, General Clark moved on toward embattled Anzio. He was held up in the harbor as Luftwaffe pilots, unaware that a prize target of an Allied army commander was bobbing around helplessly in a small PT boat just offshore, plastered the docks.

General Clark arrived at Johnny Lucas' deep, musty, dank wine cellar in Nettuno a short time later in an apprehensive mood. The episode of an American minesweeper ignoring recognition signals and raking his PT boat with fire seemed to reflect the gloomy atmosphere so evident in Lucas' subterranean headquarters and on the beachhead.

Clark alternately sought to lend encouragement to General Lucas and at the same time prod him on to greater progress. In view of the enemy's constantly expanding strength around the beachhead, Clark felt that bolder and more aggressive action was necessary. He urged Lucas to speed up his methodical attack by the U.S. 3rd Infantry Division toward Cisterna and the British 1st Division push in the direction of Campoleone, both key road centers Fifth Army wanted in the beachhead defensive line.

Although polite and soft-voiced as always, Lucas was inwardly deeply disturbed by General Clark's disclosure that the Fifth Army commander would set up a new advance command post in a pine grove on the grounds of the Prince Borghese palace outside Nettuno. This action made matters perfectly clear to Lucas: the Allied high command had totally lost confidence in him.

That night General Lucas, drawing thoughtfully on his corncob pipe, confided to his diary what he could reveal to no one else:

"Apparently the high levels think I have not advanced with maximum speed. I think more has been accomplished than anyone had a right to expect. This venture was always a desperate one and I could never see much chance for it to succeed, if success means driving the Germans north of Rome."

At the same time Generals Lucas and Clark were conferring in the deep wine cellar on the twenty-eighth, Albrecht Kesselring was perusing an exhortation just received from Adolf Hitler. There was a faint tone of creeping desperation to the German warlord's signal, as his *Armee Gruppe Sued* (Army Group South) had just suffered bloody reversals along the Dniepr River on the frozen Russian front.

Hitler declared:

The enemy's aim (in Italy) is to pin down and to wear out major German forces as far as possible from the English base in which the main body of the invasion force is being held . . . The significance of the battle (at Anzio) must be made clear to each soldier.

It will not be enough to give clear and correct tactical orders. The army, the air force, and the navy must be imbued with a fanatical determination to come out victorious and to hang on until the last enemy soldier has been exterminated.

The men will fight with a solemn hatred against an enemy who is waging a relentless war . . . against the German people. The battle must be hard and without pity.

Hitler indeed had taken a close and personal interest in Anzio, even to becoming involved in minor tactical details. The fuehrer contacted his rotund, flabby-jowled, high-living commander of the Luftwaffe, Reich Marshal Hermann Goering, and demanded that heavy air attacks be increased against Allied shipping.

Goering responded, and the Luftwaffe was constantly out in force, apparently not having read Allied communiques which spoke of Anglo-American air superiority over the beachhead. Every few hours, German fighter-bombers appeared over the bridgehead, bombed and strafed along the shoreline and at the front.

In addition to dropping conventional bombs, the Luftwaffe attacked Allied shipping with torpedoes and devious radio-controlled glide-bombs, which could be released from three miles away and sink a vessel without the ship's crew even realizing it was under attack.

These menacing glide-bombs were a serious threat to the Anzio invasion, and the American and British navies quickly took counteraction. The radio beam, by which the Luftwaffe pilot sent his explosives-laden robot to the target, was vulnerable to detection and jamming. Three Allied destroyers were hurriedly equipped with special jamming devices and monitors so sensitive that they could detect the German glide-bombers getting ready to take off from airfields around Rome.

Soon a cat-and-mouse game developed between Luftwaffe glide-bomb pilots trying to direct their radio-controlled missiles to an Allied vessel off Anzio and jamming teams on the

three American and British destroyers who struggled to bend
the beam and thereby cause the bomb to deflect from its course
and splash harmless into the sea.

The Allied beam-bending was not always successful. On
January 23 a glide-bomb broke through jamming efforts and
crashed into the British destroyer *Janus*. A series of tremendous explosions erupted on the ill-fated vessel, and in less than
a half-hour it plunged to the bottom with its skipper and 153 of
the crew.

A handful of survivors clung for their lives to pieces of
floating wreckage. Some sang "Roll Out the Barrel" while
other ships raced to their aid.

Two nights later the hospital ship *St. David*, brightly
illuminated and its red crosses fully exposed, was lying
offshore, crammed with wounded fighting men. A screeching
noise was heard and moments later an enormous explosion
rocked the ship. A glide-bomb had wiggled through Allied
jamming and found its mark.

The Luftwaffe continued to pound offshore shipping. Adolf
Hitler had always said that "the way to halt an invasion is to
drop bombs on their heads." In a five-day period, in addition
to the *Janus* and the *St. David,* German aircraft sank a British
antiaircraft vessel, sent a Liberty ship with vitally needed
supplies to the bottom, damaged another hospital ship, and
forced a cargo-carrying Liberty ship to run onto the beach in an
effort to escape cascading bombs.

These heavy Luftwaffe air attacks, along with the steadily
increasing shelling of all sectors by German artillery, although
they took a toll would not in themselves be decisive in the
death struggle at Anzio. That decision would be carved in
blood on the ground. Both adversaries were gearing up for that
looming showdown.

6

The "Lost Battalions" of Cisterna

Corporal Eric G. Gibson of General Lucian Truscott's 3rd Infantry Division was not content with the lot he had drawn in army life. A company cook on official records, Gibson should have remained far back from the fighting and prepared meals for his combat comrades. That he did—and he was an excellent cook, dedicated and talented in the culinary arts as practiced in the field.

But the company cook regularly insisted on volunteering for combat assignments, usually nasty ones which others did not relish.

In the heavy fighting in the rugged terrain of Sicily, he had volunteered to lead a pack-mule train across a mountain range fully exposed to enemy gunners to bring crucial ammunition, medicine and other supplies to an isolated unit of his 30th Infantry Regiment. Reaching the outpost, he volunteered as lead scout in a limited objective attack, killing a few Germans in the process.

On the Salerno beachhead and elsewhere in brutal mountain fighting in southern Italy Corporal Gibson was always in the forefront. After each fight, he would return briefly to his field kitchen in the rear, then when a hot action was in the offing he found some excuse for dashing up to the front to lead an attack as scout.

Now, at midnight on January 28, Gibson's company had

67

jumped off toward the enemy—and the cook was out in front as lead scout, an assignment not designed to promote one's longevity. Elements of the 30th Infantry had the mission of eliminating a German pocket prior to the impending major division attack to seize the key town of Cisterna, and Gibson's company had joined in the preliminary action.

Urging his comrades to remain 50 yards behind him, Corporal Gibson moved out in the eerie darkness toward enemy lines. He had gone 400 yards when the lead scout and his trailing comrades were raked with heavy enemy fire. The attacking dogfaces leaped into a huge ditch as bullets hissed past and into their ranks, but Gibson declined to take cover. He bolted forward for 30 yards to the point where he had detected the flashes from an enemy machine gun, poked the muzzle of his Tommy gun into some underbrush where the German weapon was concealed, and emptied an entire clip into the startled crew.

Now the Germans started shelling Gibson and his comrades. One projectile crashed near the cook, knocking him to the ground. He was stunned, but pulled himself to his feet and immediately was the target for withering bursts from another concealed machine gun. Gibson again charged ahead and raked a clump of bushes, killing the enemy crew.

"I wonder if we'll have to do any fighting at all with Gibby out in front," Private First Class John J. Slattery called to a comrade.

Once again the attackers moved forward down a ditch, with Corporal Gibson far out in front. A machine gun some 100 yards to one side sent bursts at the 3rd Division men. Gibson told his comrades to keep up a steady fire at the enemy automatic weapon from the cover of the ditch. The cook then slithered across an open field on his stomach with bullets zipping past him until he had reached a point 30 yards from the enemy machine gun.

Lying on his side, Corporal Gibson pulled the pins halfway from three grenades, raised up and tossed the missiles, one at a time, in the direction of the German crew. Then he leaped to his feet and charged the machine gun nest, killing two of the crew with his Tommy gun and capturing the third man.

Returning to the long irrigation ditch (which unknown to the Americans was named *Fossa Feminamorta*—Ditch of Dead

Women), Gibson took up the forward advance once again. He reached a sharp bend, and crawled back to the others to tell them to remain in place until he determined if any of the enemy were around the bend.

As his comrades tensely waited, the cook disappeared into the darkness around the curve in the deep ditch. Moments later Gibson's fellow soldiers heard the rip of a German machine pistol up ahead followed by the slower bark of a Tommy gun. They rushed forward and found two bodies—Gibson's and that of a Wehrmacht soldier.

Eric Gibson, who had shunned the safety of a rear area cook's assignment, lay dead with his gun in firing position.

At his command post in the underground wine cellar in Nettuno, General Lucas later that morning of January 29 concluded that there was sufficient strength ashore to launch a major offensive to methodically expand the beachhead. Lucas now had at his disposal 70,000 troops, 28,000 tons of supplies and in excess of 500 guns. The greater part of the veteran U.S. 1st Armored Division, commanded by the aggressive, flamboyant Major General Ernest N. "Gravel Voice" Harmon, had come over the beaches, bringing the Allied tank force to 238.

Lucas also had available a number of the United States Army's finest elite formations—Colonel Bill Darby's Ranger battalions, Lieutenant Colonel Bill Yarborough's 509th Parachute Infantry Battalion, and Colonel Rube Tucker's 504th Parachute Infantry Regiment. Also sailing toward the Anzio beachhead that day was another crack force of fighting men, the First Special Service Force, whose realistic motto was: "Killing Is Our Business." They were well versed in that enterprise.

The attack planned by Lucas for the thirtieth called for a two-pronged advance with the primary objectives to be the seizure of the key road centers of Campoleone and Cisterna. The heaviest blow would be struck on the left where the British 1st Division and U.S. 1st Armored Division would attack up the Albano road toward the Alban Hills. Prior to the jumpoff, aircraft, naval guns offshore and land-based artillery would pound German positions.

On the right Truscott's 3rd Infantry Division, with the Ranger battalions and the 504th Parachute Infantry Regiment attached, would capture the key road center of Cisterna and

maneuver into position to drive against the Alban Hills from
the east. Allied intelligence had told Lucas that enemy defenses
in front of Cisterna consisted only of scattered strongpoints.

Lucas, methodical and cautious, insisted on keeping a tight
rein on the attacking formations. Convinced that his beachhead
force was not strong enough for a precipitate dash for Rome in
the event of a sudden breakthrough at some point, the VI Corps
commander established phase lines beyond which his troops
could not advance without his specific approval.

General Mark Clark's cautionary words to him of a few days
before continued to echo and re-echo through Johnny Lucas'
being: "Don't stick your neck out. I did at Salerno and nearly
got it chopped off!"

On the evening of the thirtieth, American and British
fighting men had moved into position to jump off for the major
effort to push back the German defenders and deepen the
bridgehead. Colonel Darby's Rangers were to spearhead
the 3rd Infantry Division assault to seize Cisterna. The 1st and
3rd Ranger battalions were to infiltrate German lines, beginning at midnight, march six miles and assault Cisterna at dawn.
An hour after the first two Ranger battalions jumped off, the
4th battalion was to follow to clean up any resistance along the
road to Cisterna, after which the 3rd Division's 15th Infantry
Regiment would move forward to support the assault on the
town.

Stealth was the password in reaching the key German-held
town. Enemy forces were to be bypassed, sentries were to be
dealt with noiselessly by dagger or bayonet. It wa a daring plan
of attack for the Rangers. Much would depend upon reaching
Cisterna undetected—a large order.

While the Rangers were storming into Cisterna at daybreak,
Colonel Rube Tucker's 504th Parachute Infantry was to launch
a full-blooded assault on the right of the Rangers to protect the
flank of Darby's men.

As the three Ranger battalions were making final preparations to launch the infiltration, six miles away in Cisterna
Major Edwin Wentz, in command of defenses in the sector,
was nearing exhaustion. Since the Western Allies had stormed
ashore in their surprise landing on January 22, Wentz had
stolen only a few hours of sleep here and there.

The major was in charge of a hodge-podge collection of troops which had been hurriedly scraped together eight days previously and thrown into a semblance of a defensive position in front of Cisterna. In his provisional battalion was a large number of 18-year-old replacements who had never heard a shot fired in anger, service troops, assorted soldiers who had fled from Anzio, wounded convalescents, clerks, cooks and anyone else Wentz could find to throw into the line.

The veteran U.S. 3rd Infantry Division had chopped up his battalion in recent days, but Wentz was puzzled—the Americans had not made an all-out effort to push forward and capture Cisterna.

During the past 24 hours, Wentz's spirits had soared. Tough, experienced Wehrmacht units from the Gustav Line, 60 miles to the southeast, from the Balkans, from France and from the Third Reich had steadily arrived and were hurriedly sent to the front. Hour by hour, the German position improved. "Perhaps we can hold when the Allies hit us in strength," Wentz told himself.

Outside his command post at midnight of the thirtieth, the roar of powerful tank motors and grinding of treads echoed through the night air and shook the old buildings as iron monsters roared through the darkened streets of Cisterna on the way to the front lines. Wentz lit a cigarette and propped his feet upon the desk. Now, for the first time in over a week, the major could relax to a degree.

Some seven miles south of Major Wentz' command post, Colonel Bill Darby sent out several Ranger patrols across the Mussolini Canal in the direction of Cisterna. They reported the area as lightly held. The ground to be crossed was flat, cut by irrigation ditches, dotted by an occasional stone farmhouse and with virtually no cover.

The night was moonless and cold. Loaded down with personal weapons, pockets crammed with grenades, bayonets affixed to rifles, and extra bandoleers of ammunition draped over shoulders, the Ranger battalions moved out from their bivouac area behind the Mussolini Canal at 9 P.M. Voices were raised in a popular tune of the day, "Pistol Packing Mamma," as the Rangers swung along toward jumpoff positions across the canal. Nearing the front, the singing ceased.

As they reached the outposts of the 3rd Infantry Division, an eerie silence blanketed the pitch-black night. Not a rifle shot. Not an artillery shell. The quietude caused an uneasy feeling in some of the Rangers—could this be the calm before the storm?

Faces blackened and gear taped to prevent its rattling, the two lead Ranger battalions stole off silently into the ominous night. Approaching a perpendicular road, Major Alvah Miller's 3rd Battalion was preparing to cross when they heard a sudden roar of motors in the blackness. The Rangers flopped to the ground and lay motionless as a procession of German armored cars rolled past, close enough for the American infiltrators to reach out and touch them.

Hearts thumped furiously and perspiration dotted foreheads as the Rangers clung to the ground. Trailing the armored cars were trucks loaded with German infantry, and bringing up the rear were 10 or 12 tanks, their powerful diesel engines shooting off sparks and loud roars that echoed for great distances across the flatlands.

As the final German tanks clanked off into the darkness and silence again settled over the road, Major Miller got to his feet, a worried man. "Where in hell did all this heavy stuff come from?" he whispered to an officer. "I thought this sector was supposed to be lightly held."

The major waved his men onward, and they scrambled over the road and resumed the trek toward Cisterna, now only two miles away. Minutes later a whispered warning filtered down the column of Rangers: "Kraut bivouac just ahead. Many Krauts sleeping on ground."

Major Miller knew his orders were to avoid a fight until the Rangers reached Cisterna. As he mulled over his next course of action, a strident shout rang out through the darkness: *"Wer da?"* (Who is there?)

"Let the bastards have it!" a Ranger officer yelled, and a withering burst of Tommy gun and rifle fire was poured into the sleeping Germans in the field. Shouting at the top of their voices, the Rangers rushed forward and pounced on the now aroused Germans, knifing and bayoneting many before the enemy soldiers were fully awake. The entire field was now alive with thrashing figures as Ranger daggers and bayonets slashed and were plunged into German bodies. In minutes it was all over; nearly an entire company of the Wehrmacht had been butchered.

But a few of the enemy got away and fled into the darkness.

A short time later, the field telephone jangled urgently in Major Wentz' command post in Cisterna. A colonel commanding an adjoining sector was on the line. In a voice tinged with anxiety, he told Wentz: "We've been getting reports men in our listening posts have been killed. Throats slashed. Better be on the alert. I think we've been infiltrated!"

Again Wentz' phone rang. This time it was a captain commanding an infantry company in front of Cisterna. *"Herr Major,"* the deep voice said calmly, "the *Amis* (Americans) are in the fields only a few hundred yards from town. An entire German company has had their throats cut."

As the pair of Ranger battalions deployed outside Cisterna to attack the city, the follow-up 4th Battalion was fighting for its life. Under Lieutenant Colonel Roy A. Murray, the 4th Battalion had jumped off precisely one hour after the others had moved out. Only a half-mile down the road leading to Cisterna, the same one the 1st and 3rd Battalions had negotiated 60 minutes previously without incident, Murray's men were suddenly raked with machine guns from out of the darkness.

As Rangers dived pell-mell for ditches, the black night was illuminated with enemy tracer bullets hissing past the prostrate column. The automatic weapons were on three sides. Colonel Murray's men, although in a supporting role, had stumbled into an ambush.

Near the front of the long battalion column, several Rangers edged forward, and with bayonets and grenades wiped out the crews of two machine guns. But others kept spitting away, and the remaining Rangers were pinned to the ground. Captain George Nunnelly, commander of the lead company, was killed, as were many others. Wounded, some screaming as bullets tore into vulnerable flesh, lay where they fell, unable to receive medical attention.

Colonel Murray contacted two company commanders and ordered them to assault the German defensive line. Each rose from the ground, waved his men forward and charged toward the chattering, lethal enemy automatic weapons. Both captains were killed in the futile assault, as were many others in the charge. Ranger wounded were strewn about the terrain in front of the enemy guns.

Bill Darby, the Rangers' founder and leader, had his
command group up forward with the trailing 4th Battalion.
Lying almost face down in a ditch as mortar rounds exploded
around him and tracers hissed and sang just overhead, Darby
contacted the 1st and 3rd Battalions outside Cisterna. He was
alarmed by what he heard: these two outfits had also been
ambushed and nearly surrounded and were fighting for their
lives.

Instead of going up against the widely dispersed strongpoints
expected to be confronted, Darby's leading battalions had
bumped into an assembly area of a tough, experienced *fallschirmjaeger* (paratrooper) division supported by heavy panzers. The enemy parachutists and tanks poured torrents of
artillery, mortar and machine gun fire into the ranks of the
Rangers, who were strung out for nearly three-quarters of a
mile along an irrigation ditch half-filled with icy water.

A desperate Bill Darby ordered Colonel Murray's 4th
Battalion to attack in an effort to break through to the two
trapped battalions outside Cisterna. It was now daylight, the
terrain was flat and without cover, and the Germans were
entrenched in thick-walled stone farmhouses that served as
miniature forts and deeply-dug field fortifications. German
tanks kept up a steady stream of fire from places of concealment behind and in haystacks and farm buildings.

Roy Murray's men charged forward but were met with a
solid steel wall of bullets and flat-trajectory tank fire. A single
platoon charged an enemy machine gun emplacement and the
lieutenant in the lead, four sergeants and 10 others were cut
down in their tracks. The attack to join the two Ranger
battalions trapped outside Cisterna bogged down.

Just outside the key town, the 1st and 3rd battalions
now realized they had been ambushed. They formed into
skirmish lines and charged toward Cisterna. Now the area was
alive with German paratroopers, grenadiers of the experienced
Hermann Goering Division and swarms of Mark VI tanks,
huge, lumbering monsters with hides so thick American
bazooka rockets bounced off, much as a flea would bounce off
a rhinoceros.

Major Alvah Miller, leader of the 3rd Battalion, led his men
in a charge across open ground. Armed only with a carbine and
a few grenades, Miller rushed toward a menacing Mark VI,

apparently with the intention of climbing up onto it and dropping a grenade through the turret. The panzer's 88-millimeter gun barked and belched flame and a shell exploded at Major Miller's feet. He died instantly—facing the enemy.

A Ranger company took cover in a water-filled irrigation ditch. Minutes later they heard the rumble of approaching tracked vehicles and looked on in horror as three German self-propelled guns took up positions astride the trench, depressed their long, ominous barrels and began firing rounds into the huddled and helpless Rangers.

Firing upward against the vulnerable underside of the SP guns, the trapped men in the ditch set all three German vehicles ablaze. The crews quickly scrambled out of the burning vehicles and under a hailstorm of Ranger bullets fled to the rear.

Now a fourth self-propelled gun rumbled up and straddled the ditch. A Ranger hurried up to it, slapped a "sticky" grenade to its underside, then splashed away through the water-logged trench as the SP gun blew up.

The German fire on all sides appeared to be increasing in intensity. Out in the center of a field, Major John Dobson, the 1st Battalion commander, stood up, waved an arm forward, and shouted to his men, "Let's go! Let's go!" He had taken only a few steps when a shell exploded nearby, a white-hot fragment tearing a huge chunk of flesh out of his thigh.

"Take over, Shun," he called out weakly to his second in command, Captain Charles Shunstrom. "Keep 'em moving!"

But Shunstrom, who long before had gained a reputation as a fearless leader in combat, could not move forward. Every effort to do so was greeted by withering machine gun fire and direct fire from tanks. The two Ranger battalions attacking Cisterna were now compressed into an area only some 300 yards square.

German commanders, scenting the total destruction of an elite American fighting formation, urged their men to move in for the kill.

Now the fighting, already intense and bloody, became dirty and vicious. No mercy was asked for or given by either side. German tankers deliberately ran their tracks over wounded and helpless Rangers. Bill Darby's men rushed up to Mark VIs and flung sticky grenades against the iron monsters. When the tanks caught fire and the surviving crew members scrambled out, Rangers cut down the fleeing tankers with Tommy gun blasts. The Rangers took no prisoners, for there was no place to keep them. The Germans, in turn, accepted surrenders only when it was beneficial to them.

German tanks, trapping an individual Ranger, blew him apart instead of taking him prisoner. A makeshift Ranger aid station was set up outside a stone farmhouse, and German marksmen poured a steady stream of fire into the medics and the wounded.

A Ranger battalion surgeon, tending to some seriously wounded men, did not see a squad of Germans approaching. The enemy soldiers took him prisoner and insisted that he accompany them, but the medical doctor refused to leave his injured comrades. Grabbing a German's gun, the surgeon killed the enemy soldier. But the German's comrades riddled the Ranger doctor, and he fell dead in a pool of blood.

Taking 10 wounded but mobile Rangers with them, the Germans marched the captives toward a position held by Lieutenant Warren Evans and several Rangers of the 3rd Battalion. One German called out in English: "Surrender or die! Surrender or die!"

In response, Evans and his tiny group of Rangers opened fire, killing several of the Germans. In retaliation, the enemy grenadiers thrust bayonets through two of the captive Rangers, then opened fire against Evans' little contingent as the life-blood of the two pierced Americans flowed out of them and they died.

Lieutenant Evans was in a quandry. He and his men were nearly out of ammunition and to continue to resist would result in the deaths of other wounded Rangers being held by the opposing Germans. An anguishing Evans surrendered, along with his men.

The new Ranger prisoners were joined by others just made captive and the Americans were formed up into a column and ordered to march ahead of the German contingent toward a Ranger defensive position. Lieutenant Evans was out in front. Nearing the Rangers, who were huddled in an irrigation ditch, prisoners and captors halted and a German officer shouted in fluent English:

"Come out with your hands up or we will shoot these prisoners!"

Captain Frederick Saam told his Rangers in the ditch, "Hold your fire until they get closer. Then pick off the Krauts."

The German force and its captives were 150 yards away, but a nervous Ranger fired his rifle, and a full-fledged smallarms duel erupted. A score or more of Germans were cut down, but their comrades opened fire against Saam and his men while others raked the helpless Ranger prisoners with bursts of Schmeisser machine-pistol fire at point-blank range.

Several miles to the rear of the beleaguered 1st and 3rd Battalions, Colonel Bill Darby agonized over the disaster being inflicted upon his fighting men outside Cisterna. Only a short time before he had escaped death by a whisker at his command post in the front lines of Colonel Roy Murray's 4th Battalion which also was fighting for its life.

A heavy German mortar barrage had pounded Darby's CP and while the Ranger commander continued to lead a charmed life, his close friend and valued assistant through many months of fierce combat, Major Bill Martin, was killed beside Darby by shell fragments.

Darby's despair was increased minutes later when another mortar pounding of his CP killed his loyal runner Corporal Presly Stroud and three medics who were working over those wounded around Darby in the previous barrage.

Colonel Darby, his eyes red-rimmed and his strong heart grieving for his trapped men, was wallowing in the pits of frustration. His beloved "boys" were being cut to pieces a few miles up the road at Cisterna and he was helpless to do anything about it.

He had spoken with an aide of trying to "slip through by foot and join my boys" but was dissuaded by the other who knew it would be suicide for Darby to go forward against a strongly-entrenched foe blocking the road ahead.

As Colonel Darby hovered by his radio at noon, hoping for the best but expecting the worst, up ahead outside Cisterna the melodrama in blood was nearing its foregone conclusion. Rangers, now out of ammunition and armed only with daggers, bayonets and a few grenades, continued to battle the larger enemy force and its supporting swarms of tanks. The Ranger pocket grew smaller, now only about 100 yards square.

A glimmer of hope surged cautiously through Bill Darby's being at 12:15 P.M. when the radio at his CP crackled. The reception was spotty, but the colonel recognized the voice, and another lump formed in Darby's throat. It was Sergeant Major Robert E. Ehalt of the 1st Battalion, one of the Old Sergeants who had been with Darby through thick and thin in battles on two continents.

"Colonel, it's me . . . Ehalt," the weak but firm voice on the transmitter stated. A tear formed in Bill Darby's eye as he recognized his trusted Old Sergeant.

"They're closing in on us, colonel . . ."—an explosion was heard near the transmitter and there was a pause—"but the bastards won't get us cheap."

"Issue some orders," Darby pleaded in a choked voice. "Don't let the boys give up! Get the officers to tell them to shoot! Don't give up!"

The radio cracked loudly, then calmed as the colonel called into the transmitter in an anguished tone:

"Get the old men (those long in unit) together . . . Lam for it . . . We're coming through . . . Hang on to your radio until the last minute . . . How many men are still with you? Stick together."

Again the field radio began buzzing, roaring and crackling. Darby beat on the instrument with his fist. The instrument began to function once more.

"Hello . . . hello . . . Ehalt . . . Ehalt . . . Use your head and do what is best . . . You're there, I'm here, unfortunately . . . and I can't help you . . ."

Darby's voice trailed off as he fought back the tears.

"But whatever happens, God bless you, sergeant! God bless all my boys!"

The radio outside Cisterna went dead. Darby never knew if Ehalt heard his final words.

Bill Darby let the transmitter slip from his hand. He sat motionless and stared at the ground. He couldn't believe it—his invincible Rangers destroyed, cut to pieces. Darby had not cried since childhood. Now he struggled desperately to hold back a deluge of tears. Those were his Rangers, his boys, lying dead and mangled in the fields before Cisterna while comrades marched away to captivity.

In less than 12 hours, two of his battalions had been wiped

out, and his 4th Battalion was still fighting for its life after suffering 50 percent casualties, including three company commanders killed, in less than a half-day.

Without a word, Bill Darby rose from a stool and headed the few yards to a farmhouse. Several of his command group looked on in anguish as their steel-willed, resolute commander disappeared through the doorway. There, in solitary loneliness, he sobbed out the agony and the frustration which racked his being.

Minutes later Darby emerged from the farmhouse, shoulders square, eyes clear, a determined chin thrust out in customary fashion. He was a West Pointer, a professional soldier, a resolute man. Two of his battalions had been destroyed and a third mauled. But the war must go on. The Germans would pay for what they had done—and pay dearly.

"Get General Truscott on the phone," he snapped to an aide in a confident, crisp tone. "I want to get our orders to continue the attack."

7

"The Situation Is Clouded With Doubt"

At the precise time three Ranger battalions had jumped off for Cisterna, at 1 A.M. on the thirtieth, two battalions of Colonel Rube Tucker's 504th Parachute Infantry Regiment crossed the *Canale Mussolini* and moved forward into the night. Their mission was to attack and protect the right flank of Bill Darby's force.

Hardly had the last paratrooper crossed over the murky waters of the stream than the two battalions were raked by murderous fire from several German flak wagons mounted with 20-millimeter automatic guns. The flak wagons were guarding a bridge which was one of the objectives of the 1st Battalion.

Caught in the open, the parachutists flopped to the ground. They felt naked and defenseless. Shells from the enemy's multi-barreled antiaircraft guns hissed and sang just over their heads.

Flat on his face, Lieutenant Colonel Warren R. WIlliams, a 28-year-old North Carolinian who commanded the 1st Battalion, heard the roar of a powerful motor as a Sherman tank edged out of the darkness and halted about 25 yards from him. The tank was buttoned up as a protection against the withering bursts of enemy fire.

Williams sprang to his feet, ran to the Sherman and leaped onto the iron monster. With streams of bullets zipping past him, he banged on the turret with the butt of his rifle and shouted above the din, "Open up, goddamn it!" There was a wrenching of metal, the hatch flew open and a helmeted head popped out.

The parachute colonel pointed toward the flak-gun muzzle flashes and shouted, "Those 20-millimeters are giving us hell! Lay a few rounds into the bastards!"

Nodding his head in agreement, the tank commander began rolling the Sherman into firing position as the infantry officer leaped to the ground. Moments later the tank's 75-millimeter gun barked and a brilliant orange muzzle flash erupted. Peering from under the rims of helmets, the prostrate paratroopers felt like cheering—the first round had hit right in the center of the concentration of enemy guns. The lone Sherman continued to pour shells into the German position, and within minutes the flak wagons fell silent.

Rising to their feet, the parachutists moved on toward the bridge. As they neared it, there was a mighty roar and flash of light—the Germans had blown the span in the paratroopers' faces. But the enemy fled the scene, and Colonel Williams' men took over the crossing site. As the paratroopers continued to advance through the inky blackness, they halted periodically to clean out an enemy strongpoint in an old stone farmhouse, or in an irrigation ditch, or in freshly-dug earthworks, but no organized line of resistance was encountered.

At noon Williams' battalion was ordered to hold in place. Darby's men on the parachutists' left flank had run into fierce opposition. In contrast, all was quiet around the 504th Parachute Infantry, and most of the men did not even bother to scrape slit trenches out of the frozen soil.

Meanwhile that day, the 15th and 30th regiments of the 3rd Infantry Division had jumped off to protect the left flank of the Rangers in the attack to seize Cisterna. At mid-afternoon, the 30th Infantry Regiment company in which Private First Class Lloyd C. Hawks was a medical aid man, was engaged in a ferocious firefight with an entrenched enemy force near the town of Carano. In charging the German positions, two infantrymen had been seriously wounded and were lying in an exposed position some 30 yards from the enemy line.

Two riflemen volunteered to try to rescue the pair of wounded comrades. They slowly crawled forward, but before they could reach the injured men were driven back by heavy smallarms fire. In the savagery of Anzio, the Germans had no intention of bringing the wounded Americans the 30 yards into their lines nor allowing 3rd Division men to reach them.

A medic next inched forward on the mercy mission, but he was shot and lay semiconscious in No-Man's-Land.

Undaunted by the fate of the other would-be rescuers, Private Hawks volunteered for the job. Leaving American positions, he crawled 50 yards ahead under intense German rifle and machine gun fire and reached his fellow medic. Administering first aid to the wounded man, Hawks continued edging toward the pair of injured riflemen.

An enemy machine gun bullet zipped through Hawks' helmet, knocked it off his head and stunned him. Now the Germans began a cat-and-mouse game with Hawks before finishing him off. They peppered his helmet with 13 bullets, kicking it along the ground beside him like a young boy would bounce a tin can by tossing one rock after the other at it.

Ignoring his taunting adversaries, the medic once more slithered forward on his stomach and reached the pair of wounded comrades. He gave each of the suffering dogfaces a shot of morphine, then bandaged the more seriously injured man and arduously dragged him some 25 yards to cover in a small depression in the ground.

Crawling back toward the other wounded man, Hawks now became the target of mortar fire. Explosions rocked the ground around him. Reaching the soldier, the medic raised up to remove bandages from his kit when his hip was shattered by a burst of machine gun fire, leaving a gaping, bloody wound. A second burst splintered his forearm. The arm hung limply at his side, shredded and bleeding profusely.

Hawks, using his remaining good arm, managed to finish bandaging the injured rifleman and drag him to the same depression in the ground where he had taken the first victim. There was not enough room for three men to take cover there, so Hawks, with enemy bullets thudding into the ground around him and whistling just over his head, crawled and slithered along on his stomach 75 yards back to his company positions.

Moments later, ashen-faced and weak from shock and loss of blood, Private Hawks passed out in the arms of a comrade.

Major Oliver G. Kinney, commanding the 1st Battalion of

the 30th Infantry Regiment, was a frustrated man late in the afternoon of the thirtieth. He and his men had jumped off the night before just to the left of the ill-fated Rangers and had suffered heavy losses in fighting their way forward against a wall of German mortar, artillery and automatic weapons fire.

Kinney's battalion had reached a point only 1500 yards from Cisterna and possible rescue of the trapped Ranger battalions. But in so doing the major's men had advanced far out in front of other attacking 3rd Division units and was in danger of being cut off.

A call came in from regimental headquarters: "You'd better pull back from your exposed position."

"Hell, no!" Major Kinney shouted back. "We fought our way here and had a hell of a lot of casualties. We're staying! We can hold!"

"General Truscott has personally ordered that you pull back," the voice on the other end of the line stated. "He can't take a chance that you'll get cut off. You've got to withdraw to protect your exposed flanks and get within range of our artillery. That's an order!"

Reluctantly, Major Kinney sent word to pull back. His grimy bearded men, near physical and emotional exhaustion, turned the air blue with their curses. They knew that they would have to purchase the same real estate a second time at the customary high price—in blood.

Fighting along the 3rd Infantry Division sector raged on into the night as the Germans kept throwing in reinforcements as they arrived at the beachhead. Most of the assault battalions had suffered heavily during the day and on into the evening. The 1st Battalion of the 7th Infantry Regiment was ordered to dig in behind the crest of a small knoll, in a horseshoe pattern.

Sergeant Truman C. Olson of Company B and his six-man crew hurriedly dug in their machine gun about 25 yards in front of the riflemen, who were holding the central portion of the battalion front. The automatic weapon was sited to cover a flat, clear area stretching out for 600 yards to enemy positions on a slight terrain rise.

Sergeant Olson's gun was of particular significance in the defensive line. All other machine guns in the company had been destroyed in the day's heavy fighting.

All during the night the Germans attacked the 1st Battalion

positions, and Olson and his men, out in front of the riflemen, kept their weapon blazing. When dawn broke over the rugged Apennines, five of Olson's six men had become casualties. The sergeant, left alone with his gun, refused to budge.

The tense men of the 1st Battalion peered out across the flatland shortly after daybreak and saw long skirmish lines of German feldgrau advancing steadily toward American positions. When the attackers were in range, Sergeant Olson, operating his gun single-handedly, opened fire. As the enemy infantry moved closer Olson traversed his automatic weapon up and down the ranks of the oncoming Germans. Many went down before his chattering gun; the attackers halted, floundered around for several minutes, then beat a hasty retreat.

Soon the Germans reorganized and advanced once more toward the 1st Battalion. This time, aware of the carnage wrought in the earlier attack by the American machine gunner, the Germans concentrated their fire on Sergeant Olson. A mortar shell exploded near Olson, sending white-hot jagged pieces of metal into his back and legs.

Although in intense pain, the sergeant, still operating his weapon alone, continued to rake the advancing enemy with withering bursts of fire. Weak from loss of blood, Olson remained at his exposed post for an hour and a half, until the German assault was halted.

Platoon Sergeant John H. Earl and two medics rushed to the machine gun position and found Sergeant Olson near death, his blood saturating his uniform and covering the ground around the weapon. The medics tenderly eased the grievously wounded man onto a stretcher and hurried him to an aid station. Olson died on the way.

While Lucian Truscott's 3rd Infantry Division and attached Rangers were suffering horrendous casualties in their effort to reach Cisterna, on the left flank of the bridgehead General Penney's British 1st Division and General Harmon's U.S. 1st Armored Division, had run into a buzz saw in their joint drive on Campoleone.

The attack plan to seize the key town of Campoleone called for elements of the British 1st Division to push directly up the Albano-Anzio road, the only hard-surfaced road in the area, while the tanks of Combat Command A, commanded by Colonel Kent Lambert, of the U.S. 1st Armored Division, would sweep around to the left across open fields toward Campoleone—and possibly beyond toward the Alban Hills (known to the Italians as the *Colli Laziali*).

In the inky blackness of midnight, at the same time Bill Darby's American Rangers were jumping off for Cisterna on the right flank, General Penney's Scotch and Irish Guards moved out of The Factory and up the main road toward Campoleone. Advancing abreast, the two Guards formations were to secure a start line about two miles up the road after which the trailing 3rd Brigade would pass through and launch the final attack against Campoleone, nearly two miles farther along.

Colonel Lambert's American tankers quickly ran into trouble after moving out into the flat fields to the left of the Albano-Anzio road. The terrain was rough and criss-crossed by narrow streams, irrigation ditches and ravines, which provided natural tank obstacles. German mines blew up several of Lambert's tracked vehicles, and other tanks became bogged down in the muddy, sponge-like fields.

The attack by the 1st Armored Division in support of the British infantry ground to a halt not far from the jumping off point.

Advancing cautiously in the stillness of the night, anxious Irish and Scotch Guardsmen suddenly froze in place. The blackness was turned into the light of day as Germans to the front fired Very pistol flares. Starkly outlined against the dark background, the attacking force was raked by dug-in Germans with machine guns, flak guns, rifles and 88-millimeter fire from concealed panzers.

A fierce firefight broke out, but the Scots and Irish fought their way on to their objective, the start line two miles south of Campoleone. Sprawled in the wake of the advance were scores of dead and wounded Guardsmen.

Dawn was approaching. As the exhausted and depleted Irish and Scots dug in to brace for the certain German counterattack, their commanders radioed urgent pleas to Brigadier Murray, commander of the Guards Brigade! "Send up our heavy friends immediately!" The heavy friends were tanks.

Murray was in a dilemma. He had few "heavy friends" available, not enough to support both the Scots and the Irish. Feeling that the Scots on the right were the most vulnerable,

Brigadier Murray sent his only five tanks there. By now both Guard units were under heavy German attack.

Sensing that the Irish Guards were on the verge of being overrun, Murray radioed repeated orders for the unit to withdraw. There was no reply. All radios in the Irish Guards had been put out of commission. So the men remained in their shallow slit trenches and fought the oncoming German grenadiers and panzers.

Lance Corporal Holwell of Number 2 Company moved to a shallow hole far to one side of his comrades as he knew the muted glow of the flashlight he would use in trying to repair his balky radio would draw enemy fire. As the hours of darkness slipped by, Holwell took his radio apart, pausing periodically as mortar shells attracted by his dim light crashed about him. After each salvo, Holwell would switch on the flashlight and continue his tedious work.

Corporal Holwell, as with his Irish comrades, had no way of knowing that repeated orders to withdraw were being beamed by Brigade headquarters. All the time the Germans edged closer.

It was nearly 6:30 A.M. when an excited radioman at Brigadier Murray's CP called out: "Number 2 Company's on the air! It's Corporal Holwell."

Murray grabbed the transmitter and told the beseiged Irish Guards, "Come back—as quickly as you can!"

Holwell acknowledged receipt of the order.

Moments later the lone radio contact with the battered Irish Guards again fell silent. Lying beside the instrument, his battle dress saturated with blood, was Corporal Holwell—dead. He had saved his comrades, but paid for it with his young life.

As daylight broke on January 30, Brigadier Murray of the 24th Guards Brigade had mixed feelings. He felt good about the fact that the Scots Guards on the right of the Albano-Anzio road, with the help of the five "heavy friends," was holding firm though under fierce attack. But the Irish were back to their jumpoff point, and another attack would have to be mounted to secure the start line.

General Penney, as was his custom, wasted no time in launching that attack. A thunderous artillery barrage pounded German positions in front of Campoleone as a company of the Irish Guards and one from the King's Shropshire Light

Infantry, jumped off early that morning, supported by the 46th Royal Tank Regiment and the U.S. 894th Tank Destroyer Battalion.

Leading the advance, the American tank destroyers sent shells into every farmhouse along the route. General Penney's infantry hurriedly mopped up each house in the wake of the iron vehicles' belching guns, and by early afternoon the task force seized the start line.

The short winter day was rapidly running out of light, but the aggressive General Penney ordered the attack on Campoleone to continue. Shortly after 3 P.M. a battalion of the King's Shropshire Light Infantry on the right advanced against spotty resistance, captured over 100 Germans, and by nightfall reached a low ridge a short distance from Campoleone.

On the left, a battalion of the 1st Duke of Wellington's Regiment ran into fierce resistance. Efforts by the Dukes to reach a point abreast of the KSLIs were thwarted by heavy German fire.

As his men dug in for the night, General Penney reviewed the situation of his 1st Division. He didn't like what he saw on the battle maps. Elements of his command were reaching out "like a sore thumb" in the direction of Campoleone. The thumb almost beckoned to German commanders to chop it off at the base.

As darkness blanketed the Italian killing grounds the night of January 30, General Lucas' VI Corps attack to seize Cisterna and Campoleone had bogged down short of the objectives. A combination of miserable weather which had grounded Allied aircraft and limited the vision of artillery observers, mud and unexpected tenacious resistance from the Germans had combined to thwart the limited objective assaults.

Reviewing gloomy field reports in his damp, musty subterranean wine cellar in Nettuno near midnight, General Lucas found little to cheer him. He penned in his diary:

"There is never a big breakthrough except in story books. The situation, from where I sit, is clouded with doubt and uncertainty. I expect to be counterattacked in some force, maybe considerable force, tomorrow morning."

While Lucas was wallowing in gloom in his wine cellar, General Mark Clark was at his new advance headquarters on Prince Borghese's palace grounds north of Nettuno. Clark remained a worried man. All that day he had been trekking through the mud near the leading attack forces and was disturbed by what he had viewed—primarily the surprise strength of the Germans. He wrote in his diary:

"I have been disappointed by the lack of aggressiveness on the part of VI Corps, although it would have been wrong, in my opinion, to attack and capture (the Alban Hills). I have told Lucas to push vigorously to get (Cisterna and Campoleone). He has not insisted upon this with his division commanders . . . I have been harsh with Lucas today, much to my regret, but in an effort to energize him to greater effort."

At his command post near Conca that night, General Truscott was limping about on a leg that had been paining him since he had been struck by a bomb fragment six nights previously. He was thankful that he had had on his ever-present cavalry boots at the time he was hit, as the thick leather absorbed part of the fragment's impact.

Truscott, his face a mask of solemnity, was going over reports by the flickering light of a kerosene lantern. Those reports were revealing. The 3rd Division had suffered heavily in that day's assaults to capture Cisterna. The full impact of the disaster that befell the two lightly-armed Ranger battalions outside the town exploded across the pages of Truscott's casualty reports. Of the 767 Rangers who had jumped off to spearhead the drive, only six returned.

As daylight began to streak the murky winter sky the following day, January 31, a thunderous artillery fire began to plaster German defensive positions along the entire VI Corps front. The assault to expand the narrow confines of the bridgehead by seizing Cisterna and Campoleone erupted anew.

One battalion of the 3rd Infantry Division, its ranks dwindled from the ferocious fighting of the previous 24 hours, jumped off to lead the attack against Cisterna. Leading elements immediately came under heavy German artillery fire, but the 3rd Division men advanced nearly a mile and burst into enemy positions in an orchard. The Germans, confronted at grenade range, fled, but many of them were picked off by American riflemen as they ran.

The battalion's advance continued to a railroad embankment, but there it ground to a halt. Nearly out of ammunition, fatigued from 54 hours of incessant fighting and exposed to enemy fire from three sides, the dogfaces dug in for the night. Not many remained to dig. Some 800 men had jumped off in the assault—150 survived.

Early that morning, remnants of Colonel Darby's 4th Battalion, which had bumped into a solid wall of tough, tenacious German paratroopers the night before when it followed an hour later in the wake of the doomed 1st and 3rd Ranger battalions, launched an attack. Sixty 4th Battalion men had been killed and 120 wounded the previous day, chopping the unit down to half-strength.

Led by Lieutenant Colonel Roy Murray, the remaining Rangers had blood in their eyes. The disaster that befell their comrades up ahead near Cisterna would be avenged, of that they were certain. Murray's men dashed forward into entrenched German paratroopers blocking the road to Cisterna and in vicious head-to-head fighting forced the enemy to fall back. At the end of the day, the decimated Ranger battalion had fought its way forward for a mile, killing 300 German paratroopers and capturing the rest—reluctantly.

At mid-afternoon on the west flank of the bridgehead, General Ernie Harmon, the scrappy commander of the U.S. 1st Armored Division, was standing in the turret of a Sherman tank far up in the salient thrusting out toward Campoleone which by now had become known to the Allies and Germans alike as "The Thumb." That morning Harmon had sent his tankers up the Albano road in an effort to help out the hard-pressed British, and now he was looking for a higher elevation from which he could observe his tanks swapping fire with German panzers.

Harmon was in a tank for one reason—in a jeep he would never have arrived at this forward position, so intense was the German fire.

Harmon ordered his driver to push on up a relatively steep slope he had spotted, and as the Sherman neared the top the general got out and walked the rest of the way forward. A savage hand-to-hand battle had obviously just taken place on the slope. Dead bodies lay sprawled on all sides. They were so close together Harmon had to watch his step. A veteran of numerous combat actions in two wars, the armored commander reflected that he had never seen so many dead soldiers in one place.

Just before reaching the top, General Harmon saw a row of foxholes and several soldiers. He shouted for the commanding officer.

A few moments later a mud-caked, blood-stained corporal of the Sherwood Foresters edged out of his hole. The Britisher was the highest-ranking leader in the group still alive. He stood stiffly at attention before Harmon.

"How are things going?" the general inquired. He knew it was a silly question. All around him lay the answer.

The Foresters had fought their way through to the ridge where they were overlooking German positions outside Campoleone. There they had bogged down due to heavy enemy fire. All day they lay there, pounded relentlessly by mortar fire.

"Well, sir," the corporal with a handle-bar mustache replied calmly, "there were 116 of us when we first came up here. Now there are 16. We've been ordered to hold until sundown. I think with a little good fortune we can manage it."

At nightfall the remaining 12 British Tommies pulled back as ordered.

For three bloody days and nights American dogfaces and British Tommies had slugged it out in front of Campoleone and Cisterna with larger numbers of feldgrau strongly supported by artillery, mortars and panzers. The Allied attack to gain beachhead elbow room ground to a halt.

Allied intelligence reports had been that the Germans held only screening positions before the two key towns, and that their main line of resistance was back on the heights of the Alban Hills and Lepini Mountains. Instead the Wehrmacht had rushed in forces in front of Cisterna and Campoleone to strengthen Field Marshal Kesselring's iron noose.

Every house and village before the two towns had been converted into a strongpoint, connected by well-camouflaged rifle pits and machine gun nests. Roving panzers and self-propelled guns, massed artillery and nebelwerfers (multi-barreled mortars) fire supported these positions. Each thick-walled stone farmhouse required a separate tank, mortar, artillery and infantry assault to reduce.

If the Road to Rome ever were "open" to the Anglo-American invaders, a detour sign had been erected in the form of a maze of German strongpoints and massed artillery.

At his headquarters at Monte Soratte north of Rome, Kesselring was breathing deep sighs of relief on learning from field commanders that General Lucas' major attack had ground to a halt and that the Americans and British were digging in. Confidence was running high at Monte Soratte—and well it should have.

"I wonder if they'll ever know how close they came to breaking through," Kesselring mused to his aides. "We were thin—paper thin. If only the Allies had made a greater effort with more troops . . ."

The implication was clear: Smiling Al Kesselring had shuddered inwardly at the specter of Allied tanks dashing for the prized plum of Rome.

But Kesselring had grossly overestimated Allied capabilities and resources. He had no way of knowing that Mark Clark had no more troops to bring in to exploit a breakthrough to the Eternal City, that the Allied perimeter had already been stretched to the breaking point, nor that the Anglo-Americans had limited shipping with which to land ammunition and supplies.

German staff officers with Kesselring, though keeping their thoughts to themselves, believed they knew the cause for the German "Miracle of Anzio"—thousands of mutilated feldgrau corpses sprawled about the muddy fields outside Cisterna and Campoleone.

One fact was evident to Field Marshal Kesselring at Monte Soratte and General Mark Clark at his CP outside Nettuno some 40 miles to the south: the initiative at Anzio had now passed over to the Wehrmacht.

Meanwhile at his chalet at Berchtesgaden high in the Bavarian Alps, Adolf Hitler, Chancellor of Nazi Germany and Commander in Chief of the German Wehrmacht, was carefully scrutinizing plans designed to throw the Allies back into the sea at Anzio. Hitler was in a jubilant mood; he had just been advised by his trusted aide, Colonel General Alfred Jodl, that the Anglo-Americans were digging in all around the beachhead perimeter. The anticipated Allied "lightning bolt" to Rome had failed to materialize.

The plans to inflict another "Dunkirk" on the Anglo-Americans had been drawn up by the staff of Colonel General Eberhard von Mackensen, a monocled Prussian aristocrat, experienced and capable. Kesselring had ordered von Mackensen to rush south from Verona in northern Italy on January 24 and take charge of German operations at Anzio. Von Mackensen's command would be known as the Fourteenth Army.

Kesselring's instructions to the general with the monocle had been simple and to the point: (1) halt the Allies, and (2) launch a decisive counterattack at the earliest possible time to drive the invaders back into the Tyrrhenian Sea.

Von Mackensen's plan to inflict disaster upon the Allies, approved by Kesselring and Hitler, was to cut the beachhead in half by attacking along the Albano-Anzio road to the white sands of the shoreline. Then he would assault each half of the Anglo-American force and destroy it, one after the other.

As von Mackensen was shuffling assault troops into position for the all-out drive to the sea, American General Lucas was growing ever more despondent. He wrote in his diary:

"The strain of a thing like this is a terrible burden. Who the hell wants to be a general?"

PART TWO
Death Struggle

1

Escape From a Steel Trap

As January turned into February, Fifth Army commander Mark Clark had ample reason for ordering VI Corps to dig in. Reading a continuing flow of alarming secret German signals intercepted by Ultra, Clark knew that his foe at Anzio, General Eberhard von Mackensen, had ringed the beachhead with 90,000 troops and was preparing to launch a massive counterattack to drive the Anglo-Americans into the Tyrrhenian Sea.

In the first few days of the Allied landing, Field Marshal Kesselring had thrown a hodge-podge collection of units into the path of the invaders. But now some of the Third Reich's finest formations were maneuvering into position for the impending assault.

These first-rate German outfits, which had reached Anzio far more rapidly than the Allies had anticipated, included the Hermann Goering Division, the SS Reichsfuehrer Division, the 735th Grenadier Regiment, the 16th SS Division, the 35th Panzer Grenadier Division, the 26th and 29th Panzer Grenadier Divisions.

Several hundred miles away in Berlin, Adolf Hitler, supreme warlord of the Third Reich, hourly was demanding that Kesselring destroy the Anglo-American force at Anzio.

"It must be driven home to the enemy that the fighting power of Germany is unbroken," the fuehrer declared, "and that the invasion is an undertaking that will be crushed in the blood of British and American soldiers."

Hitler had a grudging respect for the fighting capabilities of the British, but held the Americans in contempt. "The Americans are ribbon clerks, effeminate and cowardly," he had often told his generals.

On the beachhead, General Lucas was dismayed over Clark's decision to cease attacking and dig in. "We must continue to attack to keep the enemy off balance," he declared. But Lucas did not have available to him the all-knowing device that the Fifth Army commander had at his disposal—Ultra.

General Lucas, as with other Allied commanders at the division level, had no knowledge of the existence of Ultra. He knew the Germans were rapidly building up to his front, but not that von Mackensen was nearly ready to strike.

At his unit's CP along the Mussolini Canal on February 1, Lieutenant Louis A. Hauptfleisch of Illinois, intelligence officer of the 2nd Battalion, 504th Parachute Infantry, was conferring by telephone with frontline companies, warning them to be on the lookout for a German reconnaissance car loaded with heavily-armed soldiers. Hauptfleisch had received reports that the recon vehicle had apparently slipped through a 500-yard gap between the paratroopers and elements of the 3rd Infantry Division on the left and for nearly an hour had been dashing about behind American lines. By now dusk was gathering.

A short time later Lieutenant Hauptfleisch received a call from his F Company: "Scratch the Krauts in the recon car!"

In the gloaming, F Company troopers along the canal had heard a vehicle racing toward them from behind. There was a loud splashing noise and the roaring motor fell silent. Several paratroopers rushed to the site and pulled two seriously injured Germans from the wreckage of their recon car in the canal. The vehicle had been bolting for home when it plunged off a blown bridge. Three other enemy soldiers fled to the German side of the canal under a hail of American bullets.

Under a murky, forboding sky on February 2, the First Special Service Force, a mixture of 2,300 tough and resourceful American and Canadian troops, took up positions along the southwest sector of the *Canale Mussolini*. Led by Brigadier General Robert T. Frederick, a slight, soft-spoken, mustachioed officer who had become a legend among his elite fighting men in the savage mountain warfare in southern Italy, the men of the Force took an immediate deep-rooted dislike for the defensive role to which they had been assigned.

During the first few hours after burrowing in along the canal, the Forcemen suffered casualties from artillery and mortar fire, as well as from snipers.

"Hell, this ain't our kind of fighting!" a Canadian called out to his comrades, who echoed the sentiment. "Let's go after the bastards."

There was an informal, loosely-knit relationship between officers and men in Bob Frederick's outfit. As long as the Forcemen were killing Germans, no one bothered too much about the chain of command or rank.

As night fell, Frederick's men blackened their faces, replaced helmets with knit caps, taped loose gear to prevent rattling, and slipped across the canal. Five different patrols stealthily edged nearly 1000 yards through German positions, slashed the throats of a number of sleeping Germans, performed similar emergency surgery on enemy sentinels and outposts, and returned to the canal at dawn with a bag of prisoners.

Since the Rangers and the 504th Parachute Infantry Regiment had pushed ahead on January 29-30, the Germans dropped back from outposts along *Canale Mussolini* and set up defensive positions about one-half mile from the stream. The stone farmhouses, each a miniature fortress due to its thick walls, that dotted the flat terrain in No-Man's-Land became nightly sources of contention.

Frederick's Forcemen roamed about the area at night, dueling with enemy patrols, driving Germans out of the houses, ambushing isolated outposts. One Force patrol returned with a diary taken from the body of a German lieutenant who had been dispatched by the American-Canadian group. A recent entry stated: "The Black Devils (Forcemen) are all around us at night. They are upon us before we hear them coming."

General Frederick, who believed in inspiring his men by example and not through dramatic gestures, in the tense situation along the Mussolini Canal allowed himself a brief departure from his normal low-key approach to violent combat.

He ordered stickers printed which displayed the insignia of the First Special Service Force and the wording: DAS DICKE ENDE KOMMT NOCH! (The Worst Is Yet to Come!)

Going on night patrol, each Forceman would pocket a batch of these stickers and after killing a German would paste a sticker on the corpse's face or helmet. The psychological impact on the Germans from these nefarious antics was devastating.

At his Fourteenth Army headquarters, General von Mackensen, despite relentless exhortations from the fuehrer to get moving, felt he was not yet ready to launch his massive counterblow to drive the Allies into the sea. The additional troops, guns and tanks he wanted were rushing toward Anzio, but had not arrived.

As with his foe at Nettuno, General Lucas, von Mackensen had grown extremely cautious. His intelligence had far over-estimated Allied strength and he even feared another Anglo-American landing north of Anzio. But to keep the Allies off balance, the German commander planned to strike the British Thumb sticking out for more than three miles at Campoleone and perform surgery to amputate it.

It was clear to General Lucas on the beachhead that the looming German offensive would strike down the Albano-Anzio road, so he ordered the 3rd Battalion of the U.S. 504th Parachute Infantry Regiment to move out of the unit's defensive positions along the *Canale Mussolini* and attached the battle-tested battalion to General Penney's 1st Division in the Campoleone sector.

Whatever the bickering based on Nationalistic jealousies may have been in the upper strata of Allied command, on the front lines the fighting men of America and Great Britain operated in close harmony.

On reporting to Colonel Andrew Scott, the aggressive commander of the Irish Guards, Lieutenant Colonel Leslie Freeman, leader of the paratrooper battalion, with his opening words charmed his new battlefield comrades.

"Those goddamned Krauts, I sure hate their guts!" Freeman spit out.

There were smiles all around the battered Irish Guards CP. "Now here is an American who speaks our language!" was the common thought.

From the tall Colonel Freeman, a first-rate fighting man from Virginia with a slow drawl and a winning manner, and his rugged paratroopers the Irish Guards took to the word "Kraut." Never again would they describe the hated foe in such terms as Boche, Jerries or Heinies—always it would be "Kraut."

Each morning shortly after dawn, Colonel Freeman would breeze into the Irish Guards CP to exchange notes on the previous night's action and plans for the day. Each morning the dapper Irishman commanding the Guards would call out cheerily in "Americanese": "Hiya, Colonel Freeman, what d'ya know?"

Always the American parachute officer would smile and respond: "Not a goddamned thing!"

Freeman and his veteran 82nd Airborne paratroop battalion were put in a back-up position across the Albano-Anzio road in front of the village of Carroceto. General Penney felt that a back-up force might soon be needed, for he was disturbed about the disposition of his troops in the three-mile-long Thumb sticking out toward Campoleone. There were broad holes in British lines in The Thumb with wide sweeps of ground between units uncovered by rifle or machine gun fire. Under cover of darkness, the Germans had proven themselves masters of infiltration. Penney's positions were ideal for this type of penetration.

Von Mackensen's initial target in his limited attack down the Albano-Anzio road was Aprilia, known to the Allied fighting men as The Factory. This collection of stone buildings had been constructed by Benito Mussolini in 1936 as a model farm community, and the thick-walled structures were ideal as miniature forts. The Factory controlled the road network leading to Anzio and Nettuno, and the Germans had to seize this area in order to launch their do-or-die offensive to destroy the Allied invaders.

It was cold and wet on the night of February 3 when von Mackensen struck. At 11 P.M. the barren flatlands of Anzio erupted with a tremendous roar as scores of German guns began to pound Colonel Andy Scott's Irish Guards huddled miserably in water-filled slit trenches in the nail of The Thumb.

West of the Albano-Anzio road a regiment of the German 65th Division had massed in deep, brush-covered ravines. Even before the barrage ceased, elements of the 65th charged the Irish Guards shouting *Seig Heil! Gott mit Uns!* (All hail! God is with us!) A shell had set several hay stacks on fire and as the German grenadiers charged out of the darkness their forms were starkly silhouetted by the flaming background.

Machine gunners of the Guards opened up and mowed down the charging masses by the score.

Front line Guards commanders reported Germans had infiltrated their positions, and in the blackness, a hectic hand-to-hand fight broke out. Streams of tracers ripped through the sky, orange bursts flashed into the air where grenades exploded. Artillery and mortars of both sides pounded the same area, killing friend and foe indiscriminately. Throughout the night the Irish Guards and the grenadiers of the 65th Division battled each other.

At dawn the 6th Gordons on the right of the Albano-Anzio road were struck a vicious blow by elements of the German 715th and 3rd Panzer Grenadier Divisions and in a short period of time the Gordons were driven from their positions. Panzers were now rushed forward into the gap and began raking the road with 88-millimeter gun fire. As General Penney had feared, the 3rd Brigade, which included the Irish Guards and the Gordons, had been cut off in the tip of the Campoleone Thumb.

As the icy rain beat down in sheets and the wind howled, the isolated Tommies fought for their lives. The Germans kept pouring in reinforcements and closing in from four sides to wipe out the 3rd Brigade. The overcast sky prevented Allied air forces from supporting the beleaguered British fighting men.

General Penney knew if he was to save his 3rd Brigade from extinction he would have to counterattack—and soon. But he had nothing to counterattack with. At this crisis point, the Gods of War intervened—on the side of the British.

In a happenstance General Penney told his aides was "providential," at that very moment the veteran 168th Infantry Brigade under Brigadier Kenneth Davidson had just finished unloading on the docks at Anzio. "I've got to have that brigade—now!" Penney told General Lucas.

The VI Corps commander hesitated. He wanted the just-arrived British brigade as part of his reserve for the even more massive counterattack he was sure would strike him. Penney was adamant. Either he gets the new brigade or his trapped 3rd

Brigade in the tip of the Campoleone Thumb will be wiped out. Reluctantly, General Lucas agreed.

General Penney rushed the 168th Brigade, an element of Major General Gerald Templer's 56th Division, to the base of the crumbling Campoleone Thumb and hurriedly formed up the three battalions for the counterattack. There was no time for planning. Supported by the 46th Royal Tank Brigade, the rain-soaked, shivering and weary Tommies jumped off northward from The Factory at 4 P.M.

Penney rushed to the farmhouse CP of Brigadier James just north of The Factory. James had been put in a difficult situation due to the German attacks from both flanks into The Thumb— he was cut off from his troops.

"You'll have to get them out in daylight," Penney told the brigadier.

James hurriedly formed a sketchy withdrawal plan, then radioed his units trapped in The Thumb: "On getting the code-word 'Tally Ho,' start the pullback."

Now the tables were turned on the Germans in The Thumb. Just as the Wehrmacht had caught the Gordons by surprise and overran them that morning, a spirited attack into the unprepared Germans in the salient by the 168th Regiment resulted in a corridor of sorts being opened.

It was time for the Great Escape. Brigadier James, in his battered farmhouse CP, flashed the code-word: "Tally Ho."

The withdrawal got underway. But it was not an easy one. The 3rd Brigade Tommies had to fight their way out and were pounded relentlessly by accurate German artillery. As the battered columns started back along the Albano-Anzio road, the icy rain turned to sleet. The temperature dropped. The sky turned from gray to black.

All through the night bone-tired Tommies, many supporting wounded comrades wearing blood-stained and mud-caked bandages, stumbled toward the rear. The darkness was broken regularly as Germans shot Very lights into the air, outlining the long columns of British troops, tanks and trucks for their gunners. Everywhere there were the dead—those killed in the savage fight that morning, others who died fighting their way out of The Thumb.

At midnight the last man had returned. The 3rd Brigade had of necessity left behind many dead and wounded comrades, and much equipment had been destroyed or abandoned. Despite their losses and near-brush with total destruction, Brigadier James' men emerged intact as a fighting formation.

The two-day Battle of the Anzio Thumb had been a costly one for the British. They suffered 1400 casualties, some 900 of whom were captured after the Germans had sprung their iron trap around the salient.

On the other side, the 800 German casualties had largely been in vain. The key objective, The Factory, which von Mackensen considered vital to launch his massive counteroffensive, remained in British hands.

Kesselring and von Mackensen, feeling the hot breath of Adolf Hitler gusting down their necks, were not about to give up efforts to seize The Factory. They would be back soon—in even greater numbers.

As Tommies in The Thumb braced for the certain resumption of German efforts to seize The Factory, a company of the U.S. 509th Parachute Infantry Battalion on the British flank was jumping off on February 5 to drive the enemy from its entrenched positions in several farmhouses. The paratroopers of the 509th were a cocky lot—fierce and seasoned fighting men.

The 509th was intensely proud of its battle accomplishments. It had been the first American parachute outfit to go overseas (in July 1942), the first to make a combat jump in the invasion of North Africa (in November 1942), and had fought the Germans tooth and nail in the jagged, freezing mountains south of Naples. The Gingerbread Men, as they were called due to their distinctive insignia of a stylized paratrooper standing in the door of a C-47 which some said resembled that figure, had helped to save the Salerno beachhead the previous September when the 509th Battalion jumped 20 to 40 miles behind German lines.

Now on the flaming Anzio bridgehead, parachutists of the 509th had hardly advanced from their water-filled slit trenches when they were raked with intense automatic weapons fire from the stone farmhouses out in No-Man's-Land. Several Gingerbread Men went down and the cry of "Medic! Medic!" rang out over the din of battle.

Captain Carlos "Doc" Alden, the battalion surgeon who had made it a habit to go into the attack with leading elements, dashed about from one wounded man to the other despite the heavy machine gun fire which whipped past his head. Alden, the brilliant red beret he habitually wore into battle shining like a beacon, injected morphine shots, applied splints and bandages, and supervised the removal of wounded men from the line of enemy fire.

As Alden's patrol steadily worked its way closer to the spitting German machine guns behind their thick-walled enclosures, the surgeon would halt his battlefield medical chores periodically to raise up and fire bursts from his Tommy gun at enemy grenadiers.

The parachute rifleman, having driven the Germans from several houses, began to dig in as nightfall arrived. Alden felt an intense weariness overtake him from his labors on the savagely-contested flatlands of Anzio. He had been treating patients all the previous night and had been without sleep for nearly 36 hours. Now all he wanted to do was to lie down on the ground and sleep.

A shadowy form edged up to the surgeon, a trooper who told Alden that there were two seriously wounded Gingerbread Men somewhere in the darkness out in front of company positions, toward the German lines. Despite his near exhaustion, the doctor leaped to his feet, rounded up several volunteers to join him in the search for their wounded comrades.

With Captain Alden in the lead, the little search party stealthily edged out into the eerie, ominous No-Man's-Land along a ditch which, unknown to the parachutists, was covered by an enemy machine gun. On hearing movements to their front in the pitch black darkness, the German gunners opened fire along the trench. The Americans flopped face downward in the water-filled ditch as angry bullets hissed and whined over their heads, like a swarm of angry bees.

Presently the enemy machine gunners lifted their fire and the parachute surgeon and his comrades resumed their crawl forward. They paused periodically to listen for some sound which would indicate that the pair of wounded Gingerbread Men were nearby.

"It's me, Doc Alden, where are you?" the doctor would call out in a stage whisper. It was a hazardous venture. A whisper on the night air might carry to the enemy machine gunners only a short distance away. But he had to call out. Otherwise he would never locate the wounded men out there somewhere in the blackness.

This procedure was carried out several times as the parachutist patrol edged onward. Each time the only response was silence. Finally, convinced that his mission was an impossible one, the battalion surgeon made a final effort before heading back to friendly lines. "It's me, Doc Alden, where are you?" he whispered gently.

Alden's heart skipped a beat in elation as he heard a soft nearby voice in the darkness: "Here."

As noiselessly as possible, for they were now virtually under the muzzles of the German machine guns, Doc Alden and his three volunteers slithered on their stomachs toward the sound of the faint voice. There they found the seriously wounded pair of Gingerbread Men.

Suddenly the area was illuminated in a brilliant light. Nervous Germans, hearing movements to their front, had fired flares which hovered ghost-like over the huddled group of paratroopers. All froze in place, not daring to move a muscle. They feared the furious thumping of their hearts would give them away, and braced for the expected bursts of enemy fire into their midst.

But the flares flickered out and total silence and blackness covered the area.

Alden administered first aid to the wounded men as best he could in the darkness. Now the real test would begin—getting the helpless pair back to American lines. The rescue party would have to take turns dragging the two Gingerbread Men back along the ditch covered by German machine guns.

In short order the heavy huffing and puffing of the able-bodied troopers engaged in the physically taxing effort seemed to float across the barren landscape. Progress was painfully slow. But at no time did the wounded and half-conscious troopers moan or utter a word of complaint.

The faint rippling of water in the trench, the muted snap of a stick under the dead weight of the bodies being dragged along or a rustling of gear resulted in the alerted enemy periodically sending bursts of fire in the direction of the parachutists.

After a period that seemed an eternity, the rescue party heard a low voice call out to their front in the depth of the darkness: "Halt! Who the goddamned hell are you?"

Alden and his volunteers breathed a collective sigh of relief. They were back to the relative safety of the front lines.

It was a typical moonless, cold but dry night on February 6 as three American paratroopers manning a machine gun post along the Mussolini Canal turned up their coat collars against the raw, biting wind. Behind them comrades of the 504th Parachute Infantry Regiment were burrowed into the frigid, wet mud in the banks of the canal. Nearby were elements of General Bob Frederick's First Special Service Force.

The three parachutists at the outpost perked up their ears as they thought they detected the faint grinding of treads out in the darkness to their front in No-Man's-Land. They cupped hands to ears in order to hear better against the howling of the wind.

There, they heard it again. The sound of clanking treads and powerful motors grew louder out on the barren flatlands. No doubt about it, the enemy was moving armor right in front of 504th positions.

The parachutists along the canal were alerted for an imminent attack, but the rest of the night passed with no further activity in the dark to the front—at least none that could be heard by the tense Five-O-Fours.

As dawn broke over the battlefield, several haystacks were spotted to the front of the 1st Battalion. These haystacks had not been there when darkness had settled the previous day.

Lieutenant Colonel Warren Williams, the battalion commander, turned to a forward observer for a 4.2-inch mortar platoon supporting the paratroopers: "Dump some WP on those haystacks and let's see what happens."

Minutes later a drumfire of explosives erupted around and on the haystacks as the mortar platoon fired volley after volley of white phosphorous (WP) shells. The WP caught several of the haystacks on fire, and the Americans looked on in astonishment as Germans scrambled out of halftracks hidden in the stacks and started beating at the flames.

Now Five-O-Four machine gunners opened up on the stacks and the German grenadiers, caught in the open on the flatlands, hopped back into the halftracks to escape the withering bursts. More mortar fire was called for, and cascading white phosphorous particles again ignited the haystacks. Out jumped the Germans and once more they beat at the flames.

German drivers began furiously spinning treads in an effort to get the iron-plated vehicles out of the mud, but their frantic efforts were in vain. Several 4.2 mortar shells scored direct hits and the halftracks blew up.

Enemy crews and grenadiers who had not been killed or wounded fled for the relative safety of a nearby house, with paratrooper bullets licking at their heels every step of the way.

As the halftracks burned fiercely, the mortars were turned on the house. "HE (high explosives)!" the forward observer shouted gleefully into the radio. "Fire for effect!"

Soon the ground rocked as repeated salvos of 25-pound shells hit on and around the house. When the smoke cleared, the American parachutists could see that the house had been flattened by several direct hits. Off in the distance a handful of Germans who had escaped the destruction of the building were seen high-tailing it at full speed for their lines.

At Caserta, some 70 miles southeast of Anzio near the German Gustav Line, British General Harold Alexander and American General Mark Clark, were having a heated debate over reinforcing Anzio. Alexander indicated he wanted to withdraw the battered British 1st Division from the bridgehead. Clark, anxious to have every man possible on the imperiled strip of real estate, strongly protested.

Alexander declared the 1st Division was tired. "So is the (U.S.) 3rd Division," Clark responded. The Fifth Army commander added that "if the situation gets any more critical everyone will have to fight, tired or not."

That same day in far-off London, an impatient and exasperated Prime Minister Churchill fired off a telegram to Field Marshal John Dill, British representative on the Combined Chiefs of Staff in Washington: "All this (Anzio) has been a great disappointment."

On the morning of February 7, the crisp cool winter day was cheered by the bright sun which only a short time before had peeked timidly over the majestic Apennines of central Italy. The front lines were unusually quiet—an occasional shell explosion, the periodic crack of a rifle. Soldiers on both sides took advantage of the lull to cautiously edge out of foxholes to stretch aching muscles or to relieve themselves.

At 8:15 A.M. Americans and Britons along the shoreline far to the rear heard the ominous thump-thump-thump of scores of antiaircraft guns which told them the Luftwaffe was paying an early morning visit. All eyes were instinctively cast skyward to see 21 Messerschmitt 109s and Focke-Wulf 190s dive out of the sun, one after the other, and loose their bombs over Anzio and Nettuno.

Bombs demolished several buildings in Nettuno, blew up four ammunition trucks and killed or wounded 13 soldiers.

Three hours later Luftwaffe dive bombers again knifed over the shoreline and dropped explosives and strafed the docks at Anzio, damaging two large landing craft and killing or wounding 72 Allied servicemen.

As German bombers and dive bombers ranged up and down the shoreline areas on a regular basis that day, doctors, nurses and orderlies at the tented 95th Evacuation Hospital on the beachhead largely ignored the crescendo of explosions all around them and continued to administer to the needs of the wounded.

The unsung heroes of Anzio were the men and women of the army medical corps who staffed the several evacuation hospitals. The nurses were tremendous boosters of morale at a time it badly needed building. So inspiring was the battlefield work of the nearly 200 nurses on the beachhead that an attitude evolved among combat troops: "If-they-can-do-it-so-can-I."

The nurses went about their work wearing helmets and facing danger as great as anyone else on the bridgehead. They labored with the doctors in the canvas-covered operating theaters and among the patient cots in the tents—often under shelling and air bombardment and sometimes on an around-the-clock basis.

It was mid-afternoon that day, February 7, when 20-year-old Corporal Charles H. Doyle, a member of the 509th Parachute Infantry, was reclining on his cot as a patient at the 95th Evac. Doyle had mixed feelings. In the tent, he was warm and dry, fed hot food and had a reasonable comfortable cot on which to sleep. But like other combat men who were patients in the four tented hospitals southeast of Anzio, Doyle had been infected by a creeping suspicion that it might be "safer" in frontline foxholes than it was in the rear areas—at least during periods of static warfare.

As Corporal Doyle lay on his cot, he could hear shells screaming to earth all around the hospital. Periodically there was the frightening rustle of a huge shell from the Anzio Express, the enormous German 280-millimeter railroad gun, just before it rocked the terrain with a terrific explosion. And there were the regular visits from the Luftwaffe. The tented hospitals were plainly marked with huge red crosses on fields of white, but the beachhead was so jammed with troops, supply dumps and installations that errant artillery shells and bombs from the air on occasion struck hospitals and aide stations.

In the Devil's Inferno of Anzio, there was no such thing as a "rear area."

Now Charlie Doyle's sensitive ears perked up as he heard a familiar roar in the sky. He could not see it from under the canvas, but a Luftwaffe bomber swept over Anzio, chased by British Spitfire fighter planes. Seeking to escape his tormentors by gaining altitude and speed, the German pilot jettisoned his bomb load. The bombs fell in the center of the 95th Evacuation Hospital, killing 23 persons, including three nurses, a Red Cross lady, a number of Medical Corps men and patients. One of those killed was Lieutenant Blanche F. Sigman, Chief Nurse.

Sixty-eight were wounded, including Colonel George Sauer, who commanded the hospital. Much valuable equipment was also lost in the bombing.

Minutes after the hospital was struck, the Luftwaffe pilot who had jettisoned the bombs was shot down. Parachuting to earth, the German airman was found to be wounded and was taken to the hospital for treatment—the 95th Evac which had just been leveled by bombs from his aircraft.

During this period, when the Anglo-Americans were awaiting the all-out German offensive on Anzio (which top commanders knew was coming through Ultra), Fifth Army commander General Mark Clark had inaugurated a virtual shuttle service between the beachhead and his headquarters at Presenzano, facing the German Gustav Line. The trips back and forth were made in Clark's Cub plane, piloted by Lieutenant Colonel Jack Walker.

In order to escape detection by enemy planes, the trip was normally made only 20 feet or so above the water. Colonel Walker had equipped the aircraft with pontoons as the landing strip on Anzio was often under intense enemy artillery fire and the landing had to be made on the water.

When touchdown was on the water, Walker would land near

the beach, jump out and use ropes to pull the Cub up on the sand.

On leaving the beachhead one afternoon, the Tyrrhenian Sea was thoroughly angry, and it was necessary for Walker to bounce the light craft from wave to wave in order to get it airborne. One wave struck the pontoons with terrific impact, but seconds later the Cub was airborne. General and pilot breathed sighs of relief.

A few minutes later, Colonel Walker asked in a calm voice: "Did'ja see what happened, general?"

Clark looked over the side of the plane and saw that both pontoons had been broken off and were dangling by a single wire.

Trying to keep his voice calm, the general replied, "I see." It was all he could think of to say.

"What do you want me to do now?" the pilot inquired.

Clark thought that was a curious question, and with a tinge of anger in his tone responded:

"Hell, you're the pilot. Don't ask me!"

"The only reason I asked the question, sir," Walker stated evenly, "is that it is merely a matter of where the hell you prefer to crash."

"Well, in that event, make it Sorrento. It's a pretty place."

"Yes, it is. Sorrento it will be."

The Cub flew down the coast for about two hours, and near the Albergo Vittoria, a luxury hotel serving as a rest center for Fifth Army officers, Walker came in low near the beach and put the craft down hard in four feet of water. Neither man was injured.

As Clark climbed out of the plane and waded ashore with his long strides, he looked back at the Cub that had long served him so well. "It's fit now only for the salvage heap!" he thought.

As the bloody battle of attrition raged on the flatlands of the beachhead, with no quarter asked and very little given, General Ernie Harmon, leader of the 1st Armored Division, had become known as The Fireman of Anzio. He had been given command of the beachhead reserve by General Lucas.

American and British units relieved from front-line duty for brief periods of "rest" came under Harmon's control. The "resting" dogfaces and Tommies were pounded incessantly by long-range German artillery. As General Harmon was in command of mobile, fast-moving units, he rapidly became the unofficial trouble-shooter on the embattled beachhead.

At any hour of the day or night Harmon was called by General Lucas or his chief of staff and ordered to dash to this hot spot or that one with his tanks and mobile guns. Almost every night 1st Armored tankers, standing by in the Padiglione Woods on half-hour alert, clanked off to back up the infantry at points where the Germans were on the verge of breaking through.

"All we need to be real firemen," a Harmon tank commander observed as he jumped into his Sherman turret, "are red hats and sirens on these goddamned iron crates!"

On the sector held by the 509th Parachute Infantry Battalion, Lieutenant Kenneth Shaker's platoon had been in an exposed position for nearly a week. It had been pounded night and day by the heaviest shelling Shaker had been under during the war. And the 27-year-old Californian had fought in bitter battles in North Africa and Italy for 17 months. One by one, Shaker's men were being killed and wounded by the relentless bombardment.

It was nearing twilight when Lieutenant Shaker sent a runner back to his company headquarters to find out when his steadily dwindling platoon was going to be relieved. It was dark when the messenger returned.

"Well, what did Captain Winsko say?" the platoon leader asked.

"Nothing," was the reply.

"Then what did the XO (executive officer) say?"

"Nothing."

"You mean neither one of them said anything?"

"They couldn't. They were both killed in the same foxhole. A shell came right in after them."

Meanwhile, another battle-hardened warrior of the 509th Parachute Infantry Battalion was stealthily peering out of the window of a sturdy farmhouse located but a short distance from German lines. Sergeant Nicholas R. DeGaeta of Brooklyn, New York, had volunteered to sneak into the farmhouse, far in front of his unit's positions, and direct naval gunfire into a locale where enemy troops thought to be assembling to launch an attack.

The 25-year-old DeGaeta spotted the German force only 75 yards to his front and radioed its position. Minutes later came the reply from warships offshore: "On the way!" DeGaeta heard the eerie sound of many huge shells rushing through the air, and then the ground shook violently as salvo after salvo exploded around the farmhouse and the German force.

Moments later a shell crashed into the house and the paratrooper was knocked unconscious by falling ceiling timbers. When DeGaeta regained his senses the battalion surgeon, Captain Carlos Alden, was ministering to his wounds.

"Too bad, Nick," the irrepressible combat doctor remarked drily. "You were only knocked goofy. You aren't hurt seriously enough to be sent back to the States."

Two days later Sergeant DeGaeta was back in action.

2

"After the Bastards!"

Aprilia, the village so insignificant that Field Marshal Kesselring could not locate it on his maps the night of the Anglo-American invasion at Anzio, now loomed large in the councils of the Allied and German high commands. Von Mackensen considered seizing Aprilia, a cluster of sturdy stone buildings located on a slight rise in the ground, as crucial. He wanted to use it as a springboard for his massive offensive.

On the Allied side, Generals Lucas and Clark sought to hold on to Aprilia, called The Factory by the Anglo-American fighting men, to deny von Mackensen this springboard.

British Tommies defending The Factory heard the familiar rustling sound of shells cutting through the air at 9 P.M. on the seventh. Moments later a series of heavy explosions erupted on and around the buildings. The Germans continued the bombardment for 15 minutes. Then enemy infantrymen crossed over the Moletta River and attacked The Factory from the British left flank, reaching almost to the Tommies' line before being halted and driven back.

Less than one hour later, elements of the 3rd Panzer Grenadier Division, heavily armed with machine pistols and machine guns, struck the British defenders from the right flank and succeeded in establishing small pockets behind the lines of General Penney's men. At midnight, von Mackensen threw units of the 715th Division into the battle to exploit the gains of the 3rd Panzer. Although sustaining heavy casualties, the British halted the 715th just short of the hotly-contested Factory.

With the arrival of dawn, the Germans again lashed out toward Aprilia, and came within an eye-lash of seizing the town even though an American and two British cruisers had been rushed in during the night and heavily pounded the attackers.

At his underground headquarters in Nettuno that night, VI Corps commander John Lucas was especially concerned with the touch-and-go situation around The Factory. He penned in his diary:

"I wish I had an American division in there. It is probably my fault that I don't understand them (the British) better. They are certainly brave men but ours are better trained, in my opinion, and I am sure that our officers are better educated in a military way."

General von Mackensen that night had no time for evaluating the relative merits of officer corps. He issued specific orders for Aprilia to be seized the following day. Von Mackensen knew that the Allies for several days had been stringing barbed wire, planting thousands of mines and establishing automatic-weapons strong-points along the front in anticipation of the Wehrmacht's looming all-out offensive. With each passing day, the Anglo-American defenses grew stronger, the German Fourteenth Army commander knew. Aprilia had to be seized—immediately.

Shortly after dawn on the ninth, German artillery bombarded British defenses around The Factory. As the fire lifted, grenadiers surged forward and fought their way into the prized objective.

Both sides suffered heavy casualties in the savage fighting for the cluster of stone buildings. But now von Mackensen had the springboard he needed. He would strike hard—and soon— to drive the Allies into the Tyrrhenian Sea.

Meanwhile on February 8, the Germans were launching probing attacks at various points along the entire beachhead perimeter, seeking soft spots for their impending offensive. One of the sectors hit that day was held by Lieutenant Colonel Yarborough's 509th Parachute Infantry Battalion. The American paratroopers were defending a stretch of terrain between the 45th and 3rd Infantry Divisions, near the town of Carano.

Yarborough's men were spread out thinly and in an exposed position some distance to the front of 45th and 36th Division units on either flank. The German fire hit particularly hard at A Company of the 509th Parachute Infantry. Corporal Paul B. Huff volunteered to lead a patrol out ahead of company lines to determine the enemy's strength and location.

As a youth growing up in Cleveland, Tennessee, Corporal Huff had been a staunch admirer of Sergeant Alvin C. York, the famed World War I hero who lived only a few miles from Huff, at Pell Mell. Huff had always hoped that if the occasion arose, he would conduct himself on the battlefield in much the same manner as did his fellow Tennessee mountaineer of the previous war. Unknown to the parachute corporal, that moment was at hand.

At 7:30 A.M. Huff and his six-man patrol slipped out of American lines and began cautiously advancing up a draw toward the enemy. With Corporal Huff in the lead, the patrol had moved forward about 100 yards when it was raked by withering bursts of machine gun and rifle fire. The parachutists flopped to the ground as swarms of enemy bullets hissed and sang over their heads.

Flat on his stomach and peering forward from under his helmet, Huff quickly surveyed the situation. He told his men to remain under cover while he advanced up the draw toward the chattering German machine gun and its supporting riflemen. He had moved out about 100 yards in front of his patrol when two other machine guns and a .20-millimeter flak gun began pouring fire at the young corporal.

His predicament was serious enough as it was, but matters got worse. Huff discovered that he was in the middle of a minefield. Slithering forward along the edge of the draw, the corporal reached a point 75 yards from the spitting German machine guns which continued to pepper Huff with bursts of fire. Bullets thudded into the ground around him and hissed just over his head.

Grasping his Tommy gun tightly, the parachutist crawled forward until he reached the enemy automatic weapon. He leaped to his feet and poked the muzzle of his Tommy gun into the machine gun position, squeezed off a long burst of fire, and killed the five-man German crew.

Having located the enemy positions, some 400 yards from American lines, Huff began working his way back to his waiting patrol as the enemy continued to rake him with machine gun and mortar fire.

Huff reported to his company commander, giving detailed information on Germans to the front. A larger patrol, led by Sergeant Kelly C. Bath, was quickly formed, and at 1 P.M. moved out toward enemy lines. Corporal Huff, without resting from his arduous mission that morning, accompanied Bath and his men.

Nearing the German positions identified earlier by Huff, the paratrooper patrol opened fire on a company of 125 men, and after an intense firefight lasting over an hour, drove the enemy from the site. Huff, Bath and the others captured 21 grenadiers and 21 Germans lay sprawled in death around the defensive position. Three of Colonel Bill Yarborough's paratroopers were killed in the afternoon action.

As General von Mackensen continued to probe Allied lines in search of vulnerable points, some of the more enterprising American and British units were reacting in kind—often in a bizarre, but effective, manner. Sergeant William Karnap, a member of the 504th Parachute Infantry Regiment, almost daily harassed the Germans across the Mussolini Canal.

Karnap was an expert marksman, and his soft-spoken manner and mild appearance belied his ferocity on the battlefield. His favorite pastime during this period was to slip out into No-Man's-Land just before dawn and hide until he spotted a German climb out of a foxhole or emerge from a house to relieve himself. Karnap then would kill the unlucky soldier while he was in the act of heeding the call of nature.

Sergeant Karnap's excursions soon created mild panic among German troops opposite the 504th Parachute Infantry. Word got around in enemy ranks that it was "not safe to take a leak" without risking sudden death at the hands of the skulking "black-hearted devils in baggy pants."

One night during this period, a Special Service Force patrol slipped out into No-Man's-Land and into the back of a farmhouse. The black-faced Forcemen froze. From the front of the house they heard voices—German voices. The Americans waited and listened. A German-speaking Forceman whispered that the enemy was using this house as an assembly point for a raid on the Mussolini Canal and that they apparently were waiting for more comrades to arrive.

Suddenly the Forcemen dashed into the front part of the house, brandished Tommy guns at the startled Germans, and shouted, "*Hande hoch!* (hands up), you Kraut bastards." Some 20 enemy soldiers were disarmed and marched back over the canal under guard of a lone Forceman.

Lieutenant George "The Mustache" Krasevac, who led the Force patrol, knew he had a good thing going. He decided to remain with his men and milk the situation for all it was worth. As small groups of Germans walked nonchalantly into the house assembly point during the night, they were greeted by Tommy gun muzzles in the hands of a group of black-faced, sinister looking Americans.

German faces turned ashen as they realized they had fallen into the evil clutches of The Black Devils of Anzio. Since the Forcemen arrived on the beachhead 10 days previously, word had quickly spread through German ranks that the members of Bob Frederick's outfit were ex-convicts—murderers and rapists—who took no prisoners and showed no mercy.

Each new group of Germans was sent back across the canal.

It had been the procedure of the Forcemen to melt back to friendly lines at dawn after having committed assorted mayhem inside and behind German positions during the night. But now Lieutenant Krasevac believed that business was thriving and it would be poor policy to shut down the shop just because daylight had arrived.

A total of 108 Germans had been seized at the house by 8 A.M., so Krasevac, believing no more of the enemy were on the way, decided to return with his men across the Mussolini Canal. Just as the Forcemen were ready to depart their place of business after a productive night and early morning, three more Germans were spotted approaching the house.

The trio of Germans ground to a halt, stared in astonishment at the Americans leaving the structure they were to assemble in, spun on their heels and fled for the safety of their own lines. Krasevac was dismayed. His mission had been perfect so far—a prisoner bag of 100 percent. He didn't want the last three to elude him.

"After the bastards!" the lieutenant shouted, Krasevac and two of his men sped off in pursuit of the three fleeing Germans.

The Forcemen could have shot them at any time they chose—but somehow that wouldn't be "sporting."

Krasevac and his two men chased the quarry for nearly a mile before nailing the enemy soldiers with flying tackles.

A short time later, Force intelligence officers found a written message from higher German headquarters on one of the prisoners:

> You are fighting an elite Canadian-American force. They are treacherous, unmerciful and clever. You cannot afford to relax. The first soldier or group of soldiers capturing one of these men will be given a 10-day furlough.

On the flatlands of Anzio, cooped up on a narrow strip of real estate only 16 miles long, hemmed in by strong enemy forces with heavy artillery support, and with German observers looking down the throats of the invaders—literally—from the heights on the Alban Hills, American and British troops were developing a curious malady which would infect their beings for months. They felt naked and defenseless.

"With those goddamned Krauts up in the hills, they not only can see what they're shooting at, but shoot at what they see!" a frustrated American dogface sputtered to comrades after being forced to flop face downward in the mud when a German 88-millimeter gun started firing at him as he emerged from his slit trench to heed the call of nature.

"Only goddamned place I ever heard of where the Krauts use 88s as sniper weapons," another chipped in.

Indeed the Wehrmacht had plenty of artillery ammunition at Anzio. And they didn't spare it, even though they were building up for a massive offensive.

Lieutenant Colonel Warren Williams, commander of the 1st Battalion of the 504th Parachute Infantry, defending a stretch of terrain along the *Canale Mussolini*, left his CP shortly after dawn during this period and headed for his forward elements to check on any sign of German activity. As he was striding along the flat ground, he heard the rustle of shells cutting through the air and heading his way. He flopped on the ground as the projectiles exploded around him.

Unhurt, he got to his feet to continue his trek forward. Again the rustle of shells, the explosions, the face-down plunge. Now Colonel Williams knew that the German gunners were firing battery salvos at him—one man.

"Totally inspired," as he explained later, Williams once more scrambled to his feet and took off across the fields toward the front lines at a dead run. Shells continued to fall around him as he reached an outpost foxhole manned by one of his men and jumped into it without waiting to be invited.

The parachute colonel instinctively ducked as another shell approached. The German gunners refused to let their quarry escape. There was a terrific explosion near the foxhole and Williams could hear the ominous whirring of shrapnel hissing by just over his head.

"Damn, that was close!" Williams exclaimed as he raised up in the hole.

There was no answer. His companion's head had been blown off by the blast.

Lieutenant Leo L. Rodrigues was a platoon leader in the veteran 509th Parachute Infantry Battalion and one of the shortest men in the outfit. The 26-year-old officer in C Company had always said that lacking physical height had its advantages and disadvantages in combat. "I make a smaller target for the Krauts," he would say with tongue in cheek.

One of the disadvantages had occurred when Lieutenant Rodrigues was leading his platoon ashore on D-Day. The landing craft let down the ramp and Rodrigues and the others jumped out. They had been so intent on feeling the reassuring crunch of dry sand under their feet that no thought had been given to the depth of the water, nor how far from shore they would be forced to leave the landing craft.

Taking a long step off the ramp, Lieutenant Rodrigues, heavily burdened with combat gear, like the proverbial rock sank out of sight. Like any good cork, he bobbed up again, and with the help of a taller trooper found his footing. He scrambled up on the shore, a little heavier (with sea water) but thankful that his guardian angel was nearby in the form of a taller comrade.

Now, more than two weeks after he nearly drowned, Rodrigues was leading his platoon across the flat terrain in a probing mission. From their balcony seats on the Alban Hills, German observers spotted the patrol and began bombarding it with heavy artillery salvos. The paratroopers flopped to the ground.

The platoon leader heard a dull thud to his immediate front. He peered forward under the rim of his helmet, and what he saw made his heart beat faster—and skip a beat. An enormous shell was sticking halfway into the ground not more than 20 feet from him.

It was a cold day, but perspiration broke out on Rodrigues' face. He could do nothing but hope and pray. He lay motionless for what seemed like an eternity, awaiting the expected explosion that would blow him and several of his platoon members to smithereens.

The lieutenant looked up again and murmured a prayer to the Almighty. The shell apparently was a dud. Rodrigues scrambled to his feet, gave one last glance at the ominous shell, and shouted, "Let's haul ass!"

His obedient platoon needed no further encouragement. With a clop-clop-clop of jump boots and the rattling of gear, Lieutenant Rodrigues and his men dashed off at a gallop.

Meanwhile, heavy fighting raged around The Factory on the left flank of the Allied perimeter. Now that von Mackensen had the cluster of buildings which controlled the road network to Anzio town, he wanted terrain to protect it. The German 65th Division seized the ground the enemy commander wanted, but lost it again when the British 1st Division launched a counterattack.

That evening the Germans lashed out in a counter-counterattack and drove the British from the contested territory around The Factory. Both sides were now exhausted from the three day, bloody, see-saw struggle for Aprilia. General Penney's Tommies were particularly hard hit, down to 50 percent of fighting effectives.

General Lucas, VI Corps commander, knew that the 1st Division was in no condition to hold its ground. So two regiments of the U.S. 45th Infantry Division were rushed into the line to relieve Penney's decimated formation. Known as the Thunderbirds, the 45th had performed well in Sicily and on the Salerno beachhead. A National Guard outfit with most of its original men from Oklahoma and New Mexico, the Thunderbirds were commanded by Major General William W. Eagles, a tall, graying, bespectacled officer who was soft-spoken but highly regarded by the Allied upper councils.

Lucas promptly issued orders to the Thunderbirds' Eagles: attack, recapture The Factory, hold it.

General Eagles assigned the mission to one of his regiments, which selected a battalion which, in turn, gave the task to a rifle company. Supported by 8 or 10 tanks, the assaulting company was taken under heavy fire shortly after jumping off. Going under an overpass, the leading tank was struck by a flat-trajectory round, careened crazily and came to a halt, its crew killed or wounded.

A second tank pulled around the knocked-out Sherman and advanced for 200 more yards. There was an enormous explosion and the tank seemed to lift off the ground in a cloud of acrid black smoke. It had struck a mine.

Suffering heavy losses on the flatlands leading to Aprilia, the assault company fought its way into the town. Only a handful had reached the objective, advancing the last few hundred yards under a thick smoke screen. Inside Aprilia, the Thunderbirds ran into a buzzsaw. An entire battalion of seasoned German grenadiers had taken refuge in deep wine cellars as Allied artillery plastered the sturdy stone buildings. But when the fire lifted the enemy troops scrambled out of the subterranean chambers and loosed withering machine gun bursts against the few Americans who had knifed into Aprilia.

The assaulting rifle company remnants were driven out of town. The following morning the same company tried to capture the heavily-defended objective once more, but again was forced to pull back. In two days of fighting, eight American tanks had been knocked out, several more damaged, and the 45th Division company chopped down to three officers and 40 men, including the walking wounded.

Aprilia remained in German hands.

At his headquarters at *Wolfsschanze* (Wolf's Lair) behind the Russian front in East Prussia, Adolf Hitler was taking a deep personal interest in wiping out the Anglo-American bridgehead at Anzio. If the Allies could be smashed, a disaster inflicted upon them, they would have to postpone—perhaps abandon— plans for a cross-Channel assault against Northwest France in the spring, the fuehrer was convinced.

Speed and daring were vital.

After intensely reviewing even the most minute details in the counterattack plan drawn up by the able General von Mackensen and his skilled staff of professionals, Hitler sent a flood of "suggestions" to the Fourteenth Army commander. Coming as they did from the fuehrer, commander in chief of the Wehrmacht and absolute master of much of Europe, "suggestions" were interpreted by field commanders as direct orders.

Field Marshal Kesselring at Monte Soratte north of Rome and von Mackensen at the bridgehead were appalled by the "suggestions" from on high.

Hitler "suggested" assaulting the Anglo-Americans on "a very narrow front." Massed formations on the flatlands of Anzio, devoid of cover or concealment, would subject the attackers to powerful shelling from Allied warships and heavy bombing from the air, Kesselring and von Mackensen knew.

The fuehrer wanted a "creeping barrage," such as was used by both sides in World War I and with which Hitler, who as a lowly lance corporal had won a high decoration for valor, was thoroughly knowledgeable.

And finally, the commander in chief of the Wehrmacht designated the assault unit to make the main effort—the elite Berlin-Spandau Infantry Lehr Regiment, which Hitler considered "politically reliable"—meaning staunch Nazis.

The latter "suggestion" seriously disturbed Kesselring and von Mackensen. Although picked troops and fine physical specimens, the Lehr Regiment had been engaged solely in putting on demonstrations for other German units on how attacks should be conducted. But the regiment had never been under fire. How would this green German unit hold up when suddenly immersed in the crucible of savage combat?

For four days and nights, beginning on February 12, an eerie silence descended upon the beachhead, a silence broken only by an occasional shell and nighttime clashes in No-Man's-Land between patrols of each adversary.

Patrolling out in front of the lines was a vital, and extremely hazardous function. Commanders on each side had to know if the other side was building up for an attack. On a cold, dark and damp night near the little town of Carano on February 14, Lieutenant Jack M. Darden of the 509th Parachute Infantry Battalion was assigned a patrol mission to probe enemy lines. He selected to accompany him Sergeant Joseph Anslow,

Private First Class James Buzzard and several other members of his platoon.

Darden and his men replaced steel helmets, which could give away the patrol's presence if the metal headgear were to scrape against branches or rocks, with wool knit caps. They removed gear which might rattle and blackened faces, then moved out into ominous No-Man's-Land and were swallowed up by the inky blackness.

Edging cautiously ahead, eyes straining to part the darkness and ears cocked for any ominous sound, Darden and his men had advanced about 300 yards when the patrol leader suddenly signaled his men to halt. Unable to see, most bumped into the man to his front in domino fashion. There was no place to hide on the barren terrain, so the parachutists flopped face downward.

The men lay still for several moments, reluctant to breath for fear the noise would give away their presence. Then the sounds were heard again to their front. Sounds like shovels hacking into the hard terrain. Two minutes passed. There, again the digging noises.

Lieutenant Darden and his men, seasoned troopers, knew that they had bumped into the enemy. Probably Germans at an outpost in front of the main body. The patrol's mission was to determine enemy positions and strength out to the front of the 509th Parachute Infantry Battalion. There was only one way to achieve that goal: open fire and see how much lead was received in turn.

Darden and his men opened up with Tommy guns and rifles in the direction of the digging sounds, and in seconds a wide stretch of black-shrouded terrain to their front erupted with chattering machine guns and rifles sending converging fire against the American paratroopers.

After a firefight lasting several minutes, the paratrooper patrol withdrew under a hail of bullets. The needed intelligence had been gained. A large German force had moved into No-Man's-Land, presumably for the purpose of launching an assault.

In line with Lieutenant Darden's report to intelligence officers that he had run into a heavy concentration of enemy troops, captured Germans along the central portion of the Allied defensive perimeter had been saying for days that the

Wehrmacht was planning to unleash a powerful attack on February 16. Even the precise time was pinpointed by POWs— 6:30 A.M.

Word went out to all American and British units: brace yourselves, the long-awaited major effort to drive the Allies into the Tyrrhenian Sea is at hand.

3

Evil Eye on the Hill

Sixty miles southeast of tense Anzio beachhead, in the barren valley below towering Monte Cassino, a bearded, mud-caked, red-eyed American artillery commander peered upward into the wintry gray sky toward the massive Benedictine monastery perched on its peak. "I don't give a goddamn about the monastery," he snapped at an inspecting officer from Fifth Army on this February 14. "I have Catholic gunners in this battery and they've begged me for permission to fire on it."

The captain added in a mixture of bitterness and resignation: "But I haven't been permitted to give them that permission. They're mad as hell. They don't like it."

Founded by Saint Benedict in 529 A.D., the monastery was as famous and revered as any in the Christian world. It was destroyed by the Lombards in 581, by the Saracens in 883 and by an earthquake in 1349. Each time it was rebuilt by dogged Benedictine monks.

Working tediously over the centuries, monks in the abbey had laboriously copied an irreplaceable wealth of Latin literature that might otherwise have been lost to civilization.

But down in the valley and in shallow foxholes scraped into the rocky soil of the slopes of 1,702-foot tall Monte Cassino, embittered American infantrymen had no concern with the preservation of ancient literature nor the art treasures said to be stored within the 10-foot-thick walls of the abbey. Rising 150 feet, 660 feet long and made of stone, the monastery represented one thing to the young, weary fighting men huddled miserably in the cold and dampness under its brooding, omnipresent gaze—it was a German observation post from which death and destruction were rained on the mortals down below.

Under the evil eye of the awesome edifice, American assault troops, principally the 34th Infantry Division under Major General Charles W. Ryder, had been attacking relentlessly toward Monte Cassino and its abbey, which commanded a panoramic view of the entire Liri Valley through which the Allies would have to advance to link up with the forces on Anzio and push on to Rome.

Colliers magazine correspondent Frank Gervasi told his alarmed readers back home: "I saw 800 (Americans) go out and 24 come back, because the Germans could see every move they made and turn their fire on them."

The terrain approaching Monte Cassino was so treacherous that attacks could be made only in small groups of determined American dogfaces picking their way up flinty slopes, through jagged, deep ravines and over ridges made slippery by ice and snow—always under the gaze of the Evil Eye on the Hill. In many places the ground was frozen so hard and laced by stone that it was impossible to claw out even slit trenches. Then the heavy German artillery screamed in—lethal, deadly accurate.

Exposed constantly to the brutal rawness of the Italian winter, many of the assaulting American infantrymen were stricken with dysentery, pneumonia and trench foot. Casualties among the 34th Division on the approaches to Monte Cassino were horrendous. German infantrymen, protected by concrete bunkers carved out long in advance on the upper slopes, poured withering machine gun and rifle fire into the ranks of the Americans as they sought to scramble forward.

Some rifle companies had 80 percent of their combat effectives chopped down, and in three weeks of savage fighting the division suffered 2,250 killed or wounded. Through it all, the Evil Eye on the Hill looked down mockingly on the slaughter.

The massive presence of the Abbey of Monte Cassino now became an ominous, frightening and pitiless ogre to those who shouldered the ultimate burden—the Allied fighting men

whose job it was to storm the edifice. Some combat commanders on the slopes and in the valley, acutely aware of the
hundreds of bodies strewn about the enormous mountain, were
convinced that the Germans were using the ancient building for
military purposes.

"That goddamned old fort's gotta go!" a bitter American
foot soldier barked, summing up the sentiment of most of his
comrades.

A regimental commander in the 34th Infantry Division
reported he saw the flash of field glasses in the monastery.

An Italian Civilian who moved into American lines, said he
had left the abbey two days previously, and that he had seen 30
machine guns and 80 German soldiers inside the building. The
ominous report swept through the ranks of the front-line
fighting men, adding to their embitterment over the order not
to fire artillery at the monastery.

Another report was sent to higher headquarters from an
American artillery battery in the valley: "Our observers have
noted a great deal of enemy activity in the vicinity of the
monastery, and it is clear that they are using the abbey as an
observation post . . ."

The report added that a member of the battalion had been
seriously wounded the day before "by a sniper hiding in the
monastery."

As a steady flood of reports of this type continued to flow
from the front, two American generals sought to determine
first-hand if the Wehrmacht had occupied the 1400-year-old
Abbey of Monte Cassino. On February 13, Lieutenant General
Jacob L. Devers, deputy to the Supreme Allied Commander in
the Mediterranean, and Lieutenant General Ira C. Eaker, leader
of the Mediterranean Allied Air Forces, climbed into a Piper
Cub and flew off toward the abbey on top of Monte Cassino.

The generals were aware that it had been the custom of the
Germans to ignore small Allied aircraft to avoid drawing heavy
attacks by fighter-bombers. Counting on the enemy to continue
this practice, the Cub, with General Eaker at the controls,
knifed in low over the walls of the abbey—at less than 200
feet.

Banking sharply, Eaker flew the light plane back to the
landing strip. Hopping to the ground, the high-ranking observers were in agreement: they had viewed a military radio aerial

inside the monastery and German soldiers moving in and out of the structure.

Earlier, Fifth Army commander Mark Clark, realizing the U.S. 34th and 36th Infantry Divisions had been badly chewed up in three weeks of brutal fighting on the approaches to Monte Cassino, assigned the task of seizing the monastery and breaking out into the Liri Valley toward Anzio to the newly arrived 2nd New Zealand and 4th Indian Divisions, later to be joined by the British 78th Division.

Called the New Zealand Corps, it was commanded by General Bernard Freyberg, a heavy set, rugged and aggressive leader who had won the Victoria Cross for gallantry in World War I and had distinguished himself in fighting on Crete earlier in World War II.

Freyberg, studying previous American attacks and military maps, developed a daring plan. He concluded he would have the 4th Indian Division assault and capture the monastery on the peak of Monte Cassino and push on beyond it into the valley. Meanwhile the 2nd New Zealand Division would assault and seize the town of Cassino, in the valley down below.

It was a tall order, as two American divisions had been butchered in attempting to advance toward and up Monte Cassino. But General Freyberg would employ more assault troops than the Americans had thrown into the bloody struggle.

On learning that his 4th Indian Division had been assigned the monumental task of seizing the monastery, Major General F.I.S. Tuker, the commander, sought information from Allied intelligence on the massive building. Intelligence could provide none.

Undaunted, General Tuker hopped into a jeep and drove to Naples. There he prowled through the dusty shelves of book stores and was elated to find what he was seeking—an 1879 volume which detailed the monastery's construction, dimensions, wall thickness, and entrances. There was only one entry, a huge door guarded by an enormous wooden gate.

Returning to the battlefront along the Gustav Line, Tuker went immediately to confer with General Freyberg. The Indian Division commander declared that it would be foolhardy and fraught with looming disaster if his men were to assault Monte Cassino with the "fortress at the top intact." He added that it made no difference if Germans were in the enormous building at the outset of the attack, that the enemy most certainly would move in once the battle was underway.

General Tuker hauled out the diagrams and descriptions of the abbey's construction in the 65-year-old book he had found in Naples. The structure was so strong and immense, Tuker pointed out, that there was only one way to wipe it out—by blockbuster bombs from the air.

And Tuker made one point clear: he wanted the 1,400-year-old abbey destroyed.

Freyberg concurred in General Tuker's request and relayed it on to General Harold Alexander, commander of Fifteenth Army Group. Alexander, in turn, put in a call for U.S. Major General John Cannon, commander of the Twelfth Air Force: "Can bombs destroy the Abbey of Monte Cassino?"

General Cannon could hardly control his enthusiasm. He and other Air Corps commanders had long pined for the opportunity to dramatically demonstrate the awesome power of the heavy bombers when utilized in support of ground troops to obliterate a target to the front. The technique had never been tried before.

"If you let me use the whole of our bomber force against (the Abbey of) Cassino," Cannon enthused, "we'll whip it out like a dead tooth!"

Freyberg's proposal to heavily bomb the ancient abbey triggered a flood of calls among concerned Allied commanders. General Mark Clark, Fifth Army commander, was on the Anzio beachhead at the time but was reached by his able chief of staff, General Alfred Gruenther.

"I do not consider the destruction of the monastery necessary," Clark declared.

He added that, in view of General Freyberg's emphatic demand that the abbey be destroyed, this was a matter that placed the Fifth Army commander in a difficult position. In the event the attack on Monte Cassino failed, Clark would find himself the commander who refused to give full support to his fighting men.

Gruenther next called Major General Geoffrey Keyes, leader of the U.S. II Corps which had been battering its bloody head against the Gustav Wall and Monte Cassino for three weeks.

Asked if bombing the monastery would be a military necessity, Keyes replied:

"Bombing it would probably enhance its value as a military obstacle, because the Germans would then feel free to use it as a barricade."

Keyes observed that General Charles Ryder, leader of the U.S. 34th Infantry Division which had suffered frightful casualties advancing by inches toward Monte Cassino, also thought wiping out the abbey was unwarranted.

Minutes later Gruenther received a call from Lieutenant General John Harding, chief of staff to the commander of Fifteenth Army Group:

"General Alexander has decided that the monastery should be bombed if General Freyberg considers its destruction a military necessity."

Suave and diplomatic, General Gruenther stressed that Mark Clark believed that no military necessity existed, that a heavy bombing would probably kill refugees and monks, and that a pounding from the air would probably not demolish the ponderous, thick-walled abbey, but rather enhance its value as a fortification.

Harding bristled at Gruenther's recitation of General Clark's views. He replied coldly, "General Alexander has made his position quite clear. He regrets very much that the monastery should be destroyed, but he sees no other choice."

The delicate question of destroying the ancient monastery, which would undoubtedly result in a world-wide flurry of indignant protests and furnish the Nazi government with an enormous propaganda tool, was bucked on up the ladder of command to General Jumbo Wilson, a Briton and supreme commander in the Mediterranean.

Before rendering his decision, Wilson presumably went clear to the top—the British Bulldog, Winston Churchill in London. Later in the day General Alexander received word on the abbey bombing from Jumbo Wilson—Go!

During the day of February 14, a flight of Allied aircraft winged over the abbey and the town of Cassino, nestled in the valley at the foot of the towering mountain. This time bombs were not dropped, but leaflets:

Italian Friends:

Until this day we have done everything to avoid bombing the abbey. But the Germans have taken advantage. Now that the battle has come close to your sacred walls we shall, despite our wish, have to direct our arms against the monastery. Abandon it at once. Put yourselves in a safe place. Our warning is urgent.

—Fifth Army

A leaflet was brought to the 80-year-old abbot in the monastery who promptly sent his secretary to confer with a German officer. It was agreed that all civilian refugees and monks would depart the building at 5 A.M. on February 16, climbing down from the peak by way of a mule path.

At 9:30 on the sunlit morning of February 15, General Fridolin von Senger und Etterlin was peering through binoculars at the wide sweep of terrain he could view from his position in a concrete bunker on the upper slopes of a lofty mountain adjacent to Monte Cassino. Von Senger, a devout Catholic and Benedictine lay brother, commanded the German XIV Corps responsible for blocking Allied efforts to force a passage through the narrow Liri Valley toward Anzio.

The bunker was the forward command post of Major General Ernst-Gunther Baade, the eccentric but capable leader of the crack 90th Panzer Grenadier Division. Baade had been known to wear Scottish kilts as part of his battle uniform, and in the North African desert fighting had sent his British foe a New Year's greeting.

Von Senger turned his binoculars toward majestic Monte Cassino across the valley and its abbey sitting on the sunlit crown in early morning splendor. The German aristocrat had taken Christmas dinner in the historic old building to make sure his troops were obeying his off-limits edict. At that time he had been so scrupulous that he insisted on eating with his back to the window so he could not glance out at the Allied positions in the valley far below.

It was 9:38 A.M. when the two German generals in the forward bunker heard the faint throbbing of powerful airplane motors in the distance. The noise grew louder and over the snow-capped peaks a flight of lordly American B-17s—Flying

Fortresses—winged steadily toward Monte Cassino. Probably on their way to bomb targets in northern Italy, von Senger and Baade agreed.

In the valley below Monte Cassino, thousands of American soldiers, whose buddies had died on the slopes, often in agony, gazed upward through squinted eyes at the Flying Fortresses. The dogfaces felt like cheering, but instead remained nearly mute, transfixed by the awesome spectacle about to unfold.

Inside the thick walls of the old abbey, 10 monks and lay brothers were reciting their beads. Strung out through the enormous structure were some 800 civilian refugees, many elderly and ill. Few could hear the approaching bomber flight, so broad were the walls.

Bomb-bay doors opened. From the mountain peak, came great orange bursts of flame, billowing thick clouds of black smoke. Gushers of masonry and earth shot upward. The muffled crunch of explosives drifted over the barren, frigid valleys. The combined detonations of the blockbusters sounded like the roll of thunder.

Three minutes later the humming of powerful motors in the sky foretold the arrival of the second wave of Fortresses. The third wave roared over at 9:45.

Gazing upward from the valley, an Allied division commander cried out: "Beautiful! Beautiful!" He was doing his best to "direct" the bombing formations: "That's the way, keep them over a little to the left. Oh, oh, that one's off target. Now, that's it! Beautiful! Beautiful!"

Onward came the bombers, 226 of them—Fortresses, Mitchells, Liberators and Marauders, roaming the cloudless sky undisturbed, dropping bombs with precise accuracy. Between bomber waves, 155-millimeter Long Toms and huge 240-millimeter howitzers pumped shells into the hill and the monastery. To the fighting men down below, Monte Cassino seemed to quake and quiver.

Watching American foot soldiers of the 34th Infantry Division, whose comrades had been cut down by the score on the approaches to Monte Cassino, wept with joy. They had one regret: that the massive structure they considered a German fortress had not been pulverized sooner.

Inside the abbey, the monks and refugees prayed, wailed—

and died. Some 300 of them were buried under tons of masonry.

As the motor of the last American bomber faded into the distance, it could be seen that while the monastery took a terrific battering, the lower part of the building remained intact. There were no breaches blown in the thick walls through which attacking Allied infantrymen could enter.

Now, as Mark Clark had feared, tough, tenacious German paratroopers were rushed into the tangle of pulverized stone and masonry that was the Abbey of Monte Cassino and set up machine gun and mortar positions in the rubble. The ruins of the monastery now became an almost impregnable bastion.

When night fell, eight hours after the abbey had been pulverized, elements of the 4th Indian Division attacked the slopes leading to the monastery but were bloodily repulsed by German gunners dug in above in concrete bunkers. At daybreak, 102 American P-40s darted out of the sun and pounded the abbey and surrounding peaks with bombs. Again the Indians tried to move forward but were driven back.

At the base of Monte Cassino, Maori elements of the New Zealand Division moved forward under heavy fire and seized the railroad station at the southern edge of Cassino town, now a battered, smoking pile of masonry. German counterattacks drove the Maoris back out of town. The Allies had been stopped—cold.

The utter failure of the air bombardment of the Abbey of Monte Cassino added to the pall of doom and gloom that hovered over General John Lucas' headquarters in the underground dark cellar at Nettuno on the Anzio beachhead. Now Lucas knew that Allied forces along the Gustav Line were not going to plunge into the Liri Valley and make a dash northward for a linkup with beachhead formations.

Fifth Army commander Mark Clark was also tormented by deep inner concerns. Secret German messages intercepted and deciphered by Ultra told him that General Eberhard von Mackensen was ready to strike with a maximum effort to drive the Anglo-Americans at Anzio into the Tyrrhenian Sea.

4

Thunder Over the Flatlands

An eerie hush had fallen over the cold, wet and dark Anzio beachhead on the night of February 15. A few German shells exploded in rear areas. Here and there a rifle shot punctured the silence.

At an outpost in front of the 45th Infantry Division two gunners were peering intently into the inky blackness. "I don't like all this one goddamned bit," one whispered. "It's too goddamned quiet. Those Heinies are up to something."

Lying in a water-logged shallow trench along the sector held by the 509th Parachute Infantry Battalion Lieutenant Justin T. McCarthy also was filled with mild apprehension. "Listen to those sounds out there," he murmured to a comrade. "The Krauts are moving some tanks around."

Along the Mussolini Canal, Sergeant Sam DeCrenzo of the 504th Parachute Infantry Regiment remarked to a cronie, "The calm before the hurricane." Across the canal, a German flare briefly illuminated the dark sky, flickered and expired.

Suddenly, Allied and German troops alike heard a terrific roar from the direction of Anzio and a brilliant flash of light gushered into the air. The Liberty ship *Elihu Root,* loaded with artillery shells and anchored in the harbor, had blown up when struck by a radio-guided bomb from a Luftwaffe aircraft more than three miles away. The *Elihu Root* burned fiercely for hours, creating ghost-like shadows from its flames around the harbor area.

To add to the nervous pall that hovered over the beachhead on this day, several news correspondents suddenly remembered that they had important stories to write and could do so only in the tranquil environment of the Sin Capital of Italy—cosmopolitan Naples. Lugging portable typewriters, the reporters boarded a PT boat that afternoon, adding to the sense of desperation which saturated the beachhead with sinister forecasts of "another Dunkirk."

At his wine-cellar headquarters at Nettuno, General Lucas waited nervously for the massive German blow to strike. In addition to his worries over the bleak battle picture on Anzio, Lucas had a deep personal concern—an intuitive gnawing which told him his "head was about to fall into the basket," as he had predicted to his diary previously.

In the dim light of the subterranean chamber, cold, damp and musty, he wrote that night:

"I am afraid that top side is not completely satisfied with my work. They are naturally disappointed that I failed to chase the Hun out of Italy but there was no military reason why I should have been able to do so."

Lucas added thoughtfully:

"In fact, there is no military reason for Shingle."

Johnny Lucas, the methodical general who looked far older than his 54 years, could have taken heart that night of the fifteenth had he known what was transpiring in the German high command directing the Anzio struggle. General von Mackensen, the monocled Prussian aristocrat in a highly unusual action on the eve of the crucial offensive, asked his superior, Field Marshal Kesselring, to be transferred to another command, presumably anywhere other than the Anzio beachhead.

Outwardly unruffled as always, Kesselring was deeply concerned by the request. His answer to von Mackensen was concise and to the point—"No."

Twice previously, since arriving on January 25 to take command of German forces on the beachhead, von Mackensen had requested an immediate transfer. Each time Kesselring had turned thumbs down to the appeal from the commander of Fourteenth Army.

Von Mackensen's repeated efforts to extricate himself from the hot seat at Anzio resulted from the inner concerns he had felt since arriving on the beachhead. He was convinced the German forces ringing Anzio were not powerful enough to push the Anglo-Americans into the sea, a mission demanded by the fuehrer from the isolated atmosphere of *Wolfsschanze* in East Prussia.

Kesselring, always the optimist, was convinced the Wehrmacht could break through Allied lines and race all the way to Anzio once the impending full-blooded assault was unleashed. He brushed aside von Mackensen's recitation of shortcomings—iron will and valor could carry the day.

Adolf Hitler, detached from the realities of the death struggle at Anzio, sent a signal that he not only expected von Mackensen to break through to the Tyrrhenian Sea, but gave him three days to succeed in the task.

At 7:35 P.M. that evening of the fifteenth, alarmed prisoner of war interrogators at VI Corps headquarters flashed a signal to American and British units on the bridgehead:

"Captured German said his officer had told him to 'take a good look at the terrain' as something big is coming off on February 16. PW said there was a rumor of a big attack, the object being to reduce the bridgehead and split it down the center."

At five minutes past midnight on the sixteenth, a radar report read by General Truscott at his 3rd Infantry Division headquarters told of a large concentration of armor to the front of his lines, in the direction of bomb-battered Cisterna.

Thirty minutes later Truscott received another report from the commander of his 30th Regiment: "Patrol just returned. Said enemy might be forming for an attack."

Along the *Canale Mussolini*, Colonel Rube Tucker, the scrappy commander of the 504th Parachute Infantry Regiment, called higher headquarters at 12:40 A.M.:

"Outpost reports sounds of Kraut activity to the front. Sector quiet."

The flood of ominous reports was well founded. Out to the Allied front in the hushed darkness, thousands of grim-faced German troops and vehicles were moving into position to smash into the Anglo-American lines and wipe out the beachhead. Von Mackensen had issued specific orders for the night before the massive onslaught: there would be no unusual activity on the part of his troops, and tanks were not to move into position until between the hours of midnight and 4 A.M.

General von Mackensen hoped to gain total surprise. He would need it to achieve Hitler's demand to wipe out the bridgehead in 72 hours.

With all indications pointing to the massing of German infantry and tanks, artillery commanders at VI Corps hurriedly organized a "Bingo" to disrupt the enemy preparations. At 4:30 A.M. every gun and many mortars on the bridgehead opened fire at selected targets.

The black sky was constantly aglow with lightning-like flashes, and the roar of powerful guns sent rolls of thunder streaming across the barren flatlands. For 30 minutes Allied artillery pounded German frontline positions, road junctions, gun emplacements, likely assembly areas, suspected headquarters and routes of supply. Along 16 miles of beachhead the ground shook and quivered under the most thunderous barrage the Anglo-Americans had yet fired in the Anzio fighting.

Hardly had the echo of the final Allied shell explosion drifted off into infinity than the procedure was reversed. From the German side the big guns belched and moments later hundreds of projectiles came screaming into American and British frontline positions. Lieutenant Ralph L. Niffenegger, commander of a platoon of 30 riflemen and eight machine gunners in the 157th Regiment of the 45th Infantry Division, clung to the bottom of his shallow trench as shells rocked the ground around him and sent white-hot fragments hissing by just over his head.

Niffenegger soon became aware of an obvious fact: this was the heaviest barrage he had been under during the war.

Niffenegger and his comrades had no way of knowing it, but their sector had been selected by General von Mackensen as the point where his assault troops would break through to the sea. Adolf Hitler's personal favorite, the Berlin-Spandau Infantry Lehr Regiment, would spearhead that main effort, along with the 3rd Panzer Grenadier Division and the 114th and 715th Divisions.

Once the first wave had penetrated the 45th Infantry Division, defending a six-mile-long sector, von Mackensen would hurl a second wave of two divisions into the breach. Assaulting

German grenadiers were told that they could expect minimal resistance from the 45th Infantry Division, as it was a National Guard outfit from Oklahoma composed mainly of Red Indians who were far from anxious to fight.

Up and down the entire front a thunderous barrage of shells was rained on American and British fighting men. The pounding continued for 30 minutes. Then eerie silence.

Tense Allied infantrymen peering out of shallow slit trenches and bracing for the certain charge of German foot soldiers and tanks, were awed by the ghost-like setting that draped the barren, pock-marked terrain. Early morning ground fog and haze, mixed with the thick black smoke of thousands of exploding shells, clung fiercely to the ground and sifted into deep, jagged ravines. Visibility was only a few yards.

Without waiting for orders, many American and British infantrymen fixed bayonets to be ready for the German charge out of the fog. Machine gunners tested mechanisms. Riflemen laid out extra clips along the lip of slit trenches. It was cold, but foreheads perspired. Stomachs churned and knotted. Hearts thumped furiously. All knew this was the Wehrmacht's all-out, do-or-die effort to destroy Allied forces on Anzio.

Suddenly, in the ominous fog and smoke blanketing No-Man's-Land, infantrymen of the 45th Division spotted ghost-like silhouettes, dim figures wearing coal bucket-shaped helmets advancing in long skirmish lines.

All along the 45th Infantry Division sector riflemen and machine gunners opened a withering fire toward the oncoming feldgrau. The entire front now was alive with the rattle of automatic weapons and rifles, the din echoing as far as the Alban Hills and for great distances up and down the Tyrrhenian shoreline.

Lieutenant Niffenegger and his Thunderbird platoon were rushed by about 45 Germans who charged out of the concealment of a fog-filled ravine some 50 yards to the front. An angry chatter of American machine guns erupted and cut down about half of the charging grenadiers. Those who could fled back to the safety of the ravine. Left behind, dead or wounded, was half of the attacking force.

Niffenegger and his men could hear the moans and cries of the German wounded, hidden by the fog just outside the young lieutenant's positions.

Niffenegger took advantage of the brief lull to crawl along his line of foxholes. Four of his men were slumped in death, six wounded. One man's hand was bloody and mangled. He refused an order to be evacuated, stubbornly remaining in his hole.

Sneaking out of Aprilia (The Factory) under cover of the early morning fog, groups of four to eight panzers rumbled toward elements of the 179th Infantry, south and southeast of the cluster of buildings, and the 157th Infantry, astride the Albano-Anzio road. Grinding to a halt to assure better aim, the panzers poured fire into the line of American foxholes at point-blank range. When out of ammunition, the tanks withdrew to The Factory, loaded up with shells, and clanked back toward 45th Infantry Division lines.

In the wake of the tanks, German grenadiers, weird-looking figures in their long overcoats which flapped about as they trotted, rushed the 179th Regiment lines and were beaten off with heavy losses. Hurriedly reforming, the Germans struck again.

Huddled in a stone oven next to a frontline farmhouse, Lieutenant Donald E. Knowlton was adjusting fire for the 160th Field Artillery Battalion. When panzers and grenadiers attacking out of The Factory forced back outposts, Knowlton refused to budge from the oven. Now there was no one between his observation post and the oncoming Germans.

Knowlton continued to radio fire adjustments as German troops swarmed about the stone oven. The lieutenant halted periodically to raise his carbine to shoot at the enemy soldiers, killing two of them and wounding a third.

Soon bullets were whistling into and around the stone oven. One of the slugs caught Lieutenant Knowlton in the head. When the handful of men with him had to pull back in considerable haste, Knowlton was left behind for dead.

Minutes later, probing the oven, Germans discovered the artillery observer, noticed that he was still breathing and gave him first aid.

The Germans heard the incoming hiss of American shells—salvos brought down by Knowlton before he was hit—and withdrew from the vicinity. Thunderbird infantrymen moved back into the hotly-contested site and "recaptured" the seriously wounded lieutenant.

As fierce fighting raged along the entire 45th Infantry Division sector, American artillery observers peering through binoculars could not believe the sight that greeted their eyes several hundred yards to the front. What appeared to be miniature tanks, no more than five feet long and three feet high, were edging toward them.

Unknown to the perplexed observers, these were Hitler's latest "secret weapon," known as Goliaths. The Goliath was loaded with explosives and remotely controlled by electrical impulses transmitted through a long cable connected to the unmanned pygmy tank.

Thirteen Goliaths were dispatched toward American lines that morning, their function being to blow up strong points, explode minefields, rip up barbed wire, and in general clear a path for the infantry.

Minutes after crawling out into No-Man's-Land, all 13 Goliaths bogged down. Wide-eyed Thunderbirds along the front line had no way of knowing that German engineers considered Hitler's Goliaths as "troublesome and dangerous toys" nor that the tiny tanks were employed only because they were creatures of the fuehrer.

Directly across from the sector defended by the 179th Infantry early that morning of the sixteenth, the Berlin-Spandau Infantry Lehr Regiment, Hitler's own, was confidently jumping off behind the massive German artillery bombardment. Even though the picked troops of the regiment had never been under fire, spirits were high. After all, the grenadiers were aware that they were considered by the fuehrer himself as the elite.

None knew that they had been chosen to spearhead the assault to break through to the sea despite the intense misgivings of the Wehrmacht's seasoned field commanders, Field Marshal Kesselring and General von Mackensen. They were in the forefront for one reason: that was where Adolf Hitler had ordered that they be.

As he moved forward with his comrades over the barren flatlands, Sergeant Hans-Rudolf Grunther couldn't understand why he was perspiring so profusely. Must be the damned heavy overcoat, he thought. Or maybe the intense excitement from knowing that his elite Infantry Lehr Regiment had been given

the high honor of being rushed all the way from the Third
Reich to punch a hole in Allied lines and race for Anzio.

Now Sergeant Grunther tensed as American artillery shells
exploded far off to his right. Nothing to worry about. His
leaders had already told him that the Allies on Anzio were
already reeling from incessant Wehrmacht assaults, had been
cut down to far inferior numbers, and that the morale of the
American and British foot soldier had reached rock bottom.

Churchill, the "war criminal" and "the Jew" Roosevelt had
abandoned their fighting men on Anzio and left them to wither
on the vine and die, the regiment had been told. And Grunther
and his comrades had heard from their leaders many times that
the American foot soldier was "nothing but an effeminate
ribbon clerk" who would be only too anxious to surrender.

Even if the Infantry Lehr had to fight, so what? After all, its
members were the elite, so gifted in warfare that they had been
chosen to demonstrate to other outfits the correct manner for
executing an attack.

As Grunther and his comrades advanced across the flatlands and neared the lines of the 45th Infantry Division,
artillery began to pound the area around them. Suddenly:
CRRRAAACCCKKK! CRRRAAACCCKKK! Two frighten-
ing airbursts exploded above Grunther. The Germans around
him were showered with jagged shell fragments and several fell
dead. Others flopped to the ground and refused to budge.
Cursing officers shouted at the men, "Move forward! Move
forward!"

Continuing the advance, Sergeant Grunther felt his ankle-
length overcoat getting even warmer. He was perspiring
heavier than ever. Breathing was labored. His ears picked up
the ominous sing-song of approaching shells, then the roaring
noise as the projectiles raced earthward. The gray-green
skirmish line plunged face downward. A crescendo of explosions rocked the ground around the grenadiers, causing ears to
ring and hearts to pound even faster. Mouths went dry. Some
defecated in their pants and urinated down legs.

On all sides cries and screams pierced the din as jagged
pieces of hot steel ripped into fragile flesh, hacked off arms,
legs and heads.

Now American artillery had the range. Shells continued to
rush toward the Infantry Lehr grenadiers as they tensely

hugged the ground or leaped for ravines or irrigation ditches. Officers stood up in the midst of the holocaust: "On your feet, goddamn it! On your feet! Move forward!" Exploding shells cut down most of the leaders.

A few of the Infantry Lehr, now totally unnerved by the thunderous bombardment and the gruesome sight of scores of mangled comrades, started inching to the rear. Others joined them, slithering over the cold, wet ground on their stomachs.

As the shelling became more intense, a few scrambled to their feet and raced for the rear. Comrades followed suit. Now the vaunted Infantry Lehr Regiment, Hitler's own, was in full retreat, fleeing in disarray. A few officers seeking to halt the wild stampede with drawn pistols, curses and threats, were nearly trampled.

The mass flight of the elite demonstration regiment in its first action under fire did not halt until the huffing and puffing grenadiers slumped to the ground exhausted, far behind their original jumping off line.

The rout of the Infantry Lehr Regiment, the spearhead of the German assault, eased the pressure on the 179th Infantry Regiment and robbed the offensive of its momentum. Blackened, knocked-out panzers, some still smoking, dotted the flatlands. Hundreds of feldgrau, lay grotesquely sprawled in death in No-Man's-Land.

Still the Germans came on. Sergeant Charles W. Keyser of the 191st Tank Battalion was in the turret of his Sherman, concealed behind a farmhouse only 600 yards from The Factory. Two other tanks were with him. One of the iron monsters was knocked out by enemy fire and the other was disabled.

Keyser's tank, in support of a group of Thunderbird riflemen, beat off two attempts by German infantry to seize the house. Two Mark VI panzers rumbled out of The Factory and down the road directly at Sergeant Keyser's tank. With three rounds from his 75-millimeter gun, Keyser knocked out a Mark VI, and four more rounds set the other panzer afire. As the black-uniformed German tankers scrambled out of the flaming vehicle, they were cut down by Keyser's machine gun.

Nearly out of ammunition and his radio knocked out, the sergeant heard the grinding of steel treads and the roaring of powerful motors. He looked up to see six more panzers bearing down on him, much like monstrous angry beasts set on avenging the deaths of comrades. Recognizing that a dead American tanker would be of little use to anyone, Sergeant Keyser whipped his Sherman around and set off cross-country at full throttle.

Three hundred yards from the house, Sergeant Keyser felt a terrific jolt. His head was sent spinning and intense pain shot through his body. An 88-millimeter shell had crashed into his tank, setting it aflame.

He glanced at his driver who was slumped over—dead. Keyser was in excruciating pain with serious burns over much of his body.

The sergeant pulled himself out of the turret, leaped to the ground and staggered to a nearby ditch. There he lay all afternoon as the battle swirled around him, hardly moving for fear of death or capture.

As darkness cloaked the killing grounds, Keyser began crawling, painfully, toward his own lines. He arrived an indeterminate length of time later, near collapse from shock and severe burns.

Given a shot of morphine, Sergeant Keyser lapsed into a semiconscious state of mild euphoria. He reflected that it had been a productive day at the office. All three of his Shermans had been destroyed, some of his men killed and he was badly injured. But he and his fellow tankers had repeatedly thwarted all-out efforts by larger numbers of German panzers to break through his position.

At the same time the main German assault struck the dogged 45th Infantry Division, in General Lucian Truscott's 3rd Division sector the enemy launched diversionary attacks at six points with forces ranging from single platoons to two companies. One of the feints was made by the tough, cocky but inexperienced *Fallschirmjaeger Lehr Battalion* (paratrooper demonstration battalion) from the vicinity of Cisterna.

Seeing the German parachutists in their bowl-type helmets and camouflaged smocks advancing across the barren plain in perfect skirmish line formation, 3rd Infantry Division artillery observers called down fire. Soon heavy explosions blanketed the advancing airborne men.

Within a few minutes nearly half the attacking German force had been wiped out, either killed or captured.

Sullen prisoners from the *Fallschirmjaeger Lehr Battalion* explained to 3rd Infantry Division dogfaces the reason for the utter failure of their attack. Many members of the crack unit had come down with dysentery. The battle-tested Americans recognized the symptoms. The malady often occurred to combat men under fire for the first time.

Another German feint was launched against the sector held by the veteran 509th Parachute Infantry Battalion on the left flank of the 3rd Division. Waves of feldgrau charged out of the fog against the American paratroopers, but were mowed down by rifle and automatic-weapons fire.

The Germans nearly broke into 509th lines, and here and there hand-to-hand fighting broke out. An enemy grenadier with fixed bayonet charged Private First Class Leon Mims. As the German was preparing to thrust his steel-pointed weapon through the American, in the last split second Mims quickly raised his .45 Colt and shot the enemy soldier through the chest.

The German's forward momentum continued to carry him toward Mims and in his dying throes he lunged at the American. With a thud, the bayonet plunged into the hard ground between Mims' feet.

After the German force was driven back, Lieutenant Ernest T. "Bud" Siegel removed the bayonet which had nearly speared Leon Mims and edged up to the intended victim.

"Here's the Kraut's pig-sticker, Leon," Siegel said to Mims. "Thought you might want it for a souvenir."

"What in the hell would I want that for?" the 25-year-old machine gunner asked, staring intently at the nasty looking bayonet.

"Well, you might not want it now, but you will in the years ahead," Lieutenant Siegel replied.

Mims shrugged his shoulders, took the bayonet and stashed it in his bedroll.

Fleetingly he conjectured what would happen if he were captured with a German bayonet in his possession. He knew that American paratroopers, including himself, did not take kindly to enemy soldiers taken prisoner with American items on their person.

Mims dismissed such thoughts. He returned to his machine

gun and waited for the next attack. It was sure to come, he knew.

During the all-out German assault that morning, Lieutenant Carl J. Kasper, a forward observer with the 30th Infantry, 3rd Division, was feverishly engaged in adjusting fire onto the waves of German grenadiers and tanks assaulting his lines. Despite the intense artillery fire from Kasper's battery, the enemy swarmed over the open fields toward the house serving as an OP (observation post).

Corporal Jack H. McDurman, one of Kasper's men, looked out the window to see a salvo of shells explode among gray-clad Germans only 50 yards to his front. When the smoke cleared, McDurman saw many bodies sprawled about the artillery impact area, but other Germans scrambled to their feet and continued toward the observation post.

In a calm voice, Lieutenant Kasper radioed an adjustment to the fire direction center: "Five zero, over." (Shorten the range of the previous salvo by 50 yards.)

There was a brief pause. Corporal McDurman presumed that the officer at the fire direction center pointed out that the salvo would land on Kasper's house.

"I know," the lieutenant responded. "That's it. Fire on me."

Kasper hurriedly set fire to his map and told McDurman to destroy the radio, after which the lieutenant told the corporal and a few others to "take out."

As McDurman and his comrades slipped out a rear door to dash for a drainage ditch about 50 yards behind the house, the corporal took a quick look over his shoulder as he ran and saw Lieutenant Kasper firing his pistol out the front door at a force of Germans who had worked their way up to the structure.

McDurman reached and dived into the ditch, looked back once more just in time to see American shells exploding around and on the house. He estimated that at least eight projectiles struck the building, engulfing it in a mushrooming cloud of smoke and dust. When the thick pall cleared, the corporal saw that only one wall was left standing. Buried beneath the rubble, McDurman feared, was Lieutenant Kasper.

Unknown to the corporal, Kasper survived the artillery barrage he had called on his own head. Out of ammunition but still defiant, Lieutenant Kasper was taken prisoner.

Meanwhile that morning on the left flank of the Allied

bridgehead, elements of the German 4th Parachute Division charged out of the fog and smashed into the lines of the British 56th Division. It was a diversionary attack to pin down the British, and the *fallschirmjaeger* were not expected to advance.

But the tough young Germans broke through 56th Division lines and pushed on for two miles, nearly reaching General John Lucas' previously designated Allied "no-retreat" line.

In the chaos of heavy fighting, German commanders on the beachhead were unaware of the wide and deep hole that unexpectedly had been ripped in British lines so failed to send in troops to exploit the penetration. Had they done so, the momentum of the breakthrough might have carried the Germans to the sea.

Alarmed Allied commanders rushed in reserves to block the onrushing German paratroopers, and as the morning wore on the enemy airborne men were driven back a mile, with the aid of a mammoth artillery pounding.

Guarding the right flank of VI Corps along the *Canale Mussolini*, the 504th Parachute Infantry and the First Special Service Force came in for their share of attention to help mask the German main effort down the Albano-Anzio road. Supported by several panzers and SPs (self-propelled guns) enemy grenadiers drove back a number of paratrooper and Forcemen outposts on the far side of the canal. But withering bursts of fire from American machine guns and rifles, together with heavy artillery fire and the guns of a company of the 894th Tank Destroyer Battalion, sent the enemy force reeling back.

Scores of German dead and wounded were sprawled about on the far bank of the canal. Three panzers and an SP sat motionless and mute, victims of accurate American gunnery.

At mid-afternoon a German advanced toward the canal with a large white flag on a pole. An American officer and two men went out to meet him. He was a medical officer and requested a one-hour truce to remove the large number of German dead and wounded. Permission was granted.

While the battle raged along much of the front, silence descended for an hour in front of the 504th Parachute Infantry and the Special Service Force. About 15 German medics, large red crosses on arm bands, scurried about the battleground as the Americans looked on with disinterest from the canal bank.

One American medic who 'spoke fluent German took

advantage of the lull to go out to the enemy medics and discuss the battle. He also had the foresight to make a reasonably accurate count of German dead. Information he obtained was hurried back to Allied intelligence officers.

As night pulled its black veil over the bloody battlegrounds, each side took a short respite to lick its wounds. In the first day of the do-or-die offensive, the Germans had made dents in the lines of the U.S. 45th and British 56th Divisions at a frightful cost in men and panzers. But the Americans had suffered heavy losses also.

General von Mackensen felt confident at the end of the first day. He had considerably weakened the Anglo-American force, and on the morrow would launch his Sunday punch—a second wave of fresh divisions.

In his wine cellar at Nettuno, General John Lucas scratched in his diary: "It gets worse and worse."

5

A Crisis Looms

"Disgraceful! Absolutely disgraceful!"

Field Marshal Albrecht Kesselring, customarily unruffled, was furious over the conduct of the elite Berlin-Spandau Infantry Lehr Regiment which fled the scene of battle in near-panic after it had been chosen by Adolf Hitler to spearhead the all-out German offensive.

But Kesselring's normal optimism soon returned that night of February 16 at his headquarters at Monte Soratte north of Rome. Both he and von Mackensen felt certain that the commitment of two fresh and battle-tested formations, the 26th Panzer Division and the 29th Panzer Grenadier Division, on the following day would score a decisive breakthrough.

One nagging concern dampened the German outlook: despite the heavy assaults of the day all along the flaming line the Allied command had not found it necessary to hurl General Gravel Voice Harmon's powerful 1st Armored Division into the fray. The 1st Armored was General John Lucas' ace in the hole.

Hardly had the last gray streaks of daylight disappeared across the Tyrrhenian Sea than Eberhard von Mackensen was on the telephone to his subordinate commanders: give the Allies no rest, attack through the night with strong assault units, pound the enemy lines with artillery, give the Americans and British no sleep, push, push, push!

147

At 10:15 P.M., concealed by darkness, two companies of the German 715th Division made a frontal assault against Company E of the 157th Infantry Regiment down the Albano-Anzio road, the axis over which von Mackensen was making his main effort. As the exhausted American dogfaces engaged the attackers in a firefight, two other German companies hit Company E on the left and on the right flank.

As the fighting raged in the blackness of night, Company E was squeezed into a tight perimeter, shooting in all directions, much like a circled wagon train in the Old West which was surrounded by Red Indians. Aided by three tanks of the 191st Tank Battalion under Lieutenant Tommy L. Cobb, Jr., which had been trapped in the tight pocket with the foot soldiers, the Americans held their ground.

By daybreak, only 14 riflemen remained. The little force was nearly out of ammunition and its supply route had been cut. A few hundred yards across the flatland, five panzers were rumbling toward the tiny isolated group, set on administering the *coup de grace*.

At 5 A.M. Captain Felix L. Sparks, beleaguered commander of Company E, was radioed permission to withdraw his remnants. Paced by Lieutenant Cobb's three Shermans, the little group had to fight its way to the rear. The virtual decimation of Sparks' company left a yawning gap in 45th Infantry Division lines, a fact quickly recognized by German commanders who began hurried planning to exploit the situation.

It had been a long, exhausting day for General Lucian Truscott, and the clock was nearing midnight when the 3rd Infantry Division commander retired to steal a few hours sleep at his headquarters at Conca. Minutes later Truscott felt a tug on his shoulder and through sleep-filled eyes saw his chief of staff, Colonel Don E. Carleton, standing beside him.

"I hate like hell to wake you up, general, but you'd shoot me if I waited 'til morning to give this to you," Carleton said in an apologetic tone.

Truscott sat up on his cot and read a field message from General Mark Clark:

Orders issued this date as follows. Major General Truscott relieved from command of Third Division and assigned as deputy commander Sixth Corps. Brigadier General O'Daniel to command Third Division. Colonel Darby transferred from Ranger force to Third Division. All assignments to take effect seventeen February.

Lucian Truscott was stunned. He had no previous inkling of his new role, although well aware of top-level dissatisfaction with General Lucas' handling of VI Corps on Anzio, particularly by the British.

Truscott was also furious. He had trained and led his beloved 3rd Infantry Division through heavy fighting in North Africa, Sicily and now in the crucible of Anzio. No American division had performed more courageously and effectively. Yet he was being separated from the authority and responsibility of his division command for a hollow figurehead post as a deputy corps commander.

But Lucian Truscott was a soldier. He would carry out his new duties, if any, loyally, energetically and to the best of his ability.

Brigadier General John W. "Iron Mike" O'Daniel, who would take over the reins of the Third Division, was a soldier's soldier. He looked, acted and was tough. But his men admired him, and to Truscott he was a "natural" to succeed to 3rd Division command.

Colonel Bill Darby's transfer from Ranger force was a bookkeeping transaction. For all practical purposes, a Ranger force no longer existed. Two of Darby's battalions had been wiped out when the lightly armed Rangers were ambushed by panzers, artillery and grenadiers in the attack on Cisterna. The remaining battalion had been chopped down to less than half of its combat effectives.

On learning of his new assignment, General Truscott promptly called a commanders' conference with Iron Mike O'Daniel, Colonel Darby (affectionately known to his Rangers as *El Darbo*) and regimental leaders. As details of the new assignments were being worked out at Conca shortly after daybreak on February 17, Truscott received a call from Lieutenant Colonel William Yarborough, leader of the 509th Parachute Infantry Battalion on the left flank of the 3rd Division sector. The battle-tested paratroopers were thinly spread out in a sector between the 3rd and hard-pressed 45th Infantry Division.

Yarborough said he was on the farmhouse roof of his command post. "I can see thousands of Krauts streaming across the flatlands toward the 45th," the parachute leader related. "I've directed several artillery fire missions on them, but they keep coming."

Later that morning, the VI Corps chief of staff at Nettuno called and talked to Colonel Carleton, Truscott's top aide.

"When's Lucian coming?" the corps officer inquired.

"He's on the way now."

"Well, he'd better hurry, because I don't know whether there'll be any corps headquarters by tomorrow morning. We'll probably all be driven into the sea!"

Arriving at the VI Corps' gloomy, musty underground headquarters, General Truscott was immediately struck by the suffocating pall of despair and desperation. He soon learned there was some cause for the wine celler atmosphere as field reports and urgent pleas for reinforcements poured in:

• The 180th Infantry Regiment of the 45th Division was under heavy pressure from infantry and swarms of panzers and was falling back.

• An estimated 35 Messerschmitt 109s and Focke-Wulf 190s had zipped up and down 45th Division lines, bombing and strafing with telling effect.

• Elements of four German divisions, supported by an estimated 60 panzers, had struck the beleaguered 179th Infantry Regiment, and two battalions were forced to pull back 1000 yards.

At 8:55 A.M. German assault formations had ripped open a wedge two miles wide and a mile deep in the center of 45th Infantry Division lines.

General John Lucas conferred with his new deputy, Truscott, on the looming crisis on the beachhead. As a result, Lucas ordered General Bill Eagles of the 45th Division to commit his reserves to restore his badly dented middle sector, and he directed General Ernest Harmon to rapidly dispatch a battalion to come to the aid of the hard-pressed 179th Infantry Regiment.

Now Dame Fate took a hand in battlefield proceedings—on the side of the Germans. Communications to VI Corps were disrupted and General Lucas received no report from Generals Harmon, Eagles and Templer, the British commander.

Lucian Truscott, seeking to lift at least one corner of the heavy veil of gloom hovering over the VI Corps wine cellar, smiled and said cheerily to two staff officers:

"Cheer up! Nothing ever looks so bad on the ground as it does on a map at headquarters!"

General Truscott's effort to practice psychology availed him nothing. Gloom and doom continued to saturate the wine cellar. The periodic crash of long-range German shells around the subterranean headquarters served to thicken the morose climate inside.

Despite Lucian Truscott's outward optimism, one factor was inescapable: the Allied force on Anzio was facing a crisis. General von Mackensen was making an all-out attempt to crash through the 45th Infantry Division and reach the sea.

Now the full arsenal of resources of VI Corps was brought to bear in a desperate effort to halt the advancing gray-green human tidal wave. German bodies were piling up by the hundreds, yet on came the feldgrau.

All 432 guns on the beachhead, scores of mortars, tank and tank-destroyer fire, four batteries of depressed antiaircraft 90-millimeter guns, and the powerful guns of two offshore cruisers pounded the oncoming German grenadiers and panzers with a thunderous barrage that shook the ground and echoed for miles around the countryside and all over the seascape.

So enormous was the Allied bombardment that Romans outdoors in the southern outskirts of the Eternal City, nearly 30 miles distant, could detect the faint sound of the masses of explosions on the bridgehead.

Big four-engined Flying Fortresses and Liberators dropped tons of bombs on German-held Campoleone and other targets up the Albano-Anzio road. Closer to the front swarms of fighter-bombers blasted the battered Factory, Carroceto and adjacent Wehrmacht assembly points, command posts, artillery positions and supply routes.

Altogether, 731 American and British warplanes pounded

the advancing Germans. The total weight of bombs dropped and the number of heavy bombers employed (288) in direct support of ground forces was the most in history to that point.

Weary, mud-caked, battered American and British fighting men, looking into the gray wintry sky, received a tremendous boost in morale on viewing wave after wave of Allied warplanes sweeping majestically past and loosing their lethal cargoes on the enemy.

Even when a flight of Flying Fortresses missed its target of Campoleone, several miles to the German rear, and rained bombs instead on The Factory, only a few hundred yards ahead of 45th Infantry Division lines, the dogfaces and the tankers failed to explode with the chorus of oaths normally reserved for such circumstances.

"Give the bastards hell!" was the common refrain up and down the Thunderbird lines.

About noon of that day, the seventeenth, General Truscott, now the deputy corps commander, set out from the headquarters wine cellar to determine for himself if it was true what he had told the VI Corps staff a few hours earlier, that a battle situation always looked worse on headquarters' maps than it did at the front.

Truscott was greatly encouraged by his findings. He called on General Ernie Harmon, the scrappy, salty leader of the 1st Armored Division. Harmon, as usual, was in fine fettle. His armored task force had not regained any lost ground, he told Truscott in an optimistic tone. "But we beat hell out of a lot of goddamned Kraut tanks and halted the bastards cold!" he roared.

General Eagles, the studious, professional commander of the hard-pressed 45th Infantry Division, told Truscott that the battle situation was serious and that he was out of communication with his frontline battalions. But he said he had great confidence in his battalion commanders and their men and thought they would hold or slow down the onrushing Germans.

With communications reestablished, General Eagles ordered elements of his weary 179th and 157th Infantry Regiments to launch a counterattack to regain some of the lost ground along the Albano-Anzio road. It was a tall order. Eagles' battalions had been hacked down to some 275–300 men each.

Two depleted Thunderbird battalions jumped off at 11 P.M.

into the pitch-black night. The 3rd Battalion of the 157th Infantry was delayed when its commander, Captain Merle M. Mitchell, received stomach and shoulder wounds from enemy tank fire. Despite the pleas of other officers, Captain Mitchell refused to be evacuated.

Instead, he climbed into a jeep and personally reconnoitered the route of advance, then returned to lead his men forward past the line of departure.

The attacking Thunderbirds immediately ran into a buzzsaw. The Germans were dug in and waiting. They raked the exposed Americans with machine gun fire and enemy tanks fired broadside into the ranks of the Thunderbirds. Enemy panzers and grenadiers riding in half-tracks rushed down the Albano-Anzio road and were promptly hurled against the 45th Division men.

General Eagles' counterattack by two depleted battalions ground to a halt.

Again a brief hushed lull settled over the killing grounds. Despite the savage German onslaught for two days, Allied lines were relatively intact, although dented in several places. But the Anglo-Americans, particularly the 45th Infantry Division, had been seriously mauled. Could the Thunderbirds ward off the next German smash?

As exhausted American and British fighting men, their ranks depleted by the vicious fighting of the day, were pounded by icy rains in their water-filled slit trenches that night, in the basements of battered Anzio and the wine cellars and maze of catacombs that meandered through the porous volcanic soil under Nettuno thousands of ragged, frightened, hungry and shivering Italian civilians huddled miserably.

Many of the civilians were refugees from the farms in the flatlands who, when the fighting became bitter, headed for the relative safety of the rear area, at Anzio and Nettuno. But on the beachhead, there was no rear area.

Out in No-Man's-Land, trapped in the hurricane of explosives and bullets, other civilians cringed in shallow cellars. There they clung as bombs and shells rained down on them. Earlier they could have fled to the coastal towns, perhaps even been evacuated to Naples, but it was too late now. Besides they had spent their lives on these farms; if need be, they would die on them. Many did.

From a strictly military point of view, the wretched civilians on the beachhead were a nuisance, even a hindrance to the Allied invaders. The innocent and pitiful pawns of war always seemed to be underfoot, in the path of vehicle convoys and marching columns of men.

Living conditions in the cellars, catacombs and other underground passages were utterly intolerable—but there was no recourse for the civilians. To go outside would invite sudden death. In dark underground vaults the air was putrid and a sea of packed humanity jockeyed for a few feet of living space. Women wailed. Babies cried. Fumes from gasoline flares that gave off a measure of light wafted into nostrils, causing a continuous chorus of coughing and hacking, even vomiting.

There was no privacy. Traditionally modest Italian ladies were forced to heed the call of nature in buckets placed in corners under the gaze of scores of strangers. The underground chambers reeked with the sickly smell of unwashed bodies, urine and feces.

The handful of native priests remaining on the beachhead moved from cellar to cellar, hearing confessions, administering to the sick and elderly, imparting hope and consolation.

The thousands of refugees now presented a major problem for the Allied command. Shipping space so vitally needed to bring in ammunition and supplies to the hard-pressed fighting men was, of necessity, being diverted to bringing in food for the wretched civilian population. There was only one solution: the noncombatants would have to be evacuated from the beachhead.

As fighting raged up and down the bridgehead perimeter, the monumental task of shipping out the masses of civilians got underway. The debarkation would continue for many days, often interupted by inclement weather or especially heavy shellings of Anzio and Nettuno.

In the meantime, Anzio, the once beautiful and tranquil resort where carefree Romans holidayed and soaked up sun on the glistening white sands, had been undergoing a drastic transformation in its architecture—quicker and more thoroughly than at any other period in its long history. German shelling of the town and harbor continued relentlessly, day and night.

One by one, buildings disintegrated. Here and there a partial wall remained upright. Ornate villas had elaborate cornices blown off, then the roofs went, finally the rubble was pulverized.

Naval men making the shuttle run with supplies between Naples and Anzio laid bets as to whether this sturdy white apartment or that especially lavish pink villa would be standing upon their return.

Death lurked incessantly on the streets and docks of Anzio. One of the most hazardous assignments on the beachhead fell to the military police whose lot it was to stand in the open, one ear always cocked for incoming shells, and direct convoys and individual vehicles debarking from LSTs. Many MPs were killed at their posts—eight to 10 miles from the "fighting."

Each night the airwaves over the embattled beachhead were filled with the silky voice of the lady the dogfaces and the Tommies came to call Axis Sally and her broadcast partner, known only as George. The Allied fighting men weren't too interested in what George had to say, it was the sultry Sally who drew their attention, much as a flame would attract a moth.

It wasn't Sally's "message" that intrigued the mud-caked and lonely Americans and British at Anzio. It was her "product"—sex.

For her part, Sally was not concerned with entertaining the enemies of Nazi Germany. She and George were cogs in the propaganda machine of Dr. Paul Josef Goebbels, the wiry little genius of the Third Reich. At Anzio, the Germans had hauled out every weapon in their arsenal and sought to destroy the Allied fighting man's morale with subtle propaganda barrages as well as with bombs and shells.

What better way to grab the attention of the beleaguered Tommies and dogfaces than through a steady dose of their favorite subject—sex? So each night sultry Sally and her sidekick George took to the airwaves over *Radio Berlin*.

On occasion the British soldiers would be her target. "Why are you nice Tommies wallowing around in the mud and cold of Anzio and getting killed while your American friends back in England are in nice warm beds, making love to your wives and girl friends?" she would coo in her suggestive voice. "Is it really worth it? Is that what you are fighting for—so the Americans can shack up with your women back home?"

Sally left nothing to the imagination. She would go into

intimate detail to describe a bedroom encounter back in
England involving an American soldier and the wife of a
Tommie on Anzio. Of course, Goebbels knew, even a steady
diet of sex talk would eventually bore his targeted "audience."
So Sally would play records of the popular American tunes of
the period.

Four-Fs, the classification of American men found unqual-
ified physically or emotionally for military service, were the
heavies in sultry Sally's sallies aimed at GIs on the beachhead.
In vivid detail she would describe carnal encounters between
lecherous 4-Fs back home and the willing wives and sweet-
hearts of dogfaces at Anzio undergoing the physical and mental
torments of the damned.

Perhaps it would have spoiled the diversion for British and
American fighting men on the beachhead had they known that
glamorous, seductive Sally was in reality extremely fat and
plain looking.

George's role in the nightly broadcast over *Radio Berlin* to
the Allied troops on besieged Anzio was to regale them with
tales of horror, in grisly detail, as to the unspeakable fate that
befell this Allied solider or that one. Goebbels, the master of
propaganda psychology, was careful to make sure that the
soldier was named, and that he had in reality undergone the
ordeal described.

George was perfect for his role. Like Sally, he spoke fluent
English and his tone had a sinister quality to it, yet one of
sincerity.

"Guess by now you fellows on the beachhead have heard
about Sergeant Blank of the 179th Infantry," George would say
in a voice tinged with deep concern. "Too bad. He was a nice
guy and a good soldier. Sergeant Blank had been ordered with
some of the rest of you fellows to make a foolish attack on a
German strong point. His stomach was ripped open by a
machine gun burst, and his guts fell out on the ground. He
lay there in agony for hours, calling for his mother . . .
screaming . . . pleading. It was pitiful."

During the first two days of the massive German offensive,
American and British front line troops were the targets of
thousands of leaflets printed in English and fired in containers
by German artillery. One pamphlet was directed at the British:

"In the face of unsurmountable odds, a thousand men in the

crack British Guards (had to) surrender. General (Mark) Clark certainly played a dirty Yankee trick on you! And who has got to bear the consequences?"

A leaflet fired into American lines inquired:

"Yanks, why are you fighting and dying in the mud and cold of Anzio 4,000 miles from home? You know why—to let the Jewish war mongers back in the States get even richer!"

German propagandists worked overtime on leaflets with drawings or photos of naked women, again on the theory (which had merit) that this was the way to attract the attention of Allied fighting men. Most leaflets had been hastily done and poorly crafted.

Along the British sector, leaflets were scattered which had a drawing of an extremely amply endowed naked woman in bed with an American paratrooper, who looked somewhat out of place clad in full uniform complete with necktie and jump boots. Out the window in the distance could be seen London's famed Big Ben clock.

The caption read: "Tommies! Don't worry about your women back home. Your American friends there are seeing that they're well taken care of."

"Blimey," remarked a member of the Sherwood Foresters, gazing at the voluptuous woman in the drawing. "That bloody well isn't my old woman!"

That night of the second day of the do-or-die German offensive to drive the Allies into the sea, February 17, handsome, energetic General W.R.C. Penney was up front in the darkness inspecting his troops, lending encouragement, analyzing the battle picture. It was Penney's habit to be where the fighting was the hottest.

Having completed his tour through the fluid and confused sector, the commander of the British 1st Division returned to his caravan to grab an hour or two of sleep. He had just entered his trailer when the eerie sound of an approaching shell reached his ears. Moments later there was an explosion, as the projectile destroyed Penney's caravan.

Painfully though not critically wounded, the dashing Briton had to be evacuated. The 1st Division was deprived of its leader at the precise time it most needed him.

At the headquarters of General von Mackensen that night, the Fourteenth Army commander and his staff debated the next

move. Should the assault be called off entirely? The feldgrau
first wave had suffered frightful losses attacking across the
barren flatlands for two days. The fighting strength of each
German battalion in the initial assault was down to 110 to 140
men, about the size of a company.

Von Mackensen knew it would be impossible for these
exhausted, battered battalions to force a breakthrough the
following day. But his chief of staff counseled, "If we're on the
verge of winning the battle, it would be folly to break off
now."

There was merit to that argument, the Prussian aristocrat
agreed. In addition, he felt an uncomfortable gust of air
continually flowing down his neck—Adolf Hitler's hot breath.

The decision was made: the two fresh divisions in the second
wave would jump off at 4 A.M.

Shortly after midnight storm demons shrieked over bloody
Anzio beachhead. Rain poured down in torrents. Angry winds
howled. The weather was ideal to mask German movements.
All through the black night von Mackensen maneuvered fresh
formations into position for the knockout blow.

In the flatlands (above) Colonel William Darby's three Ranger battalions were wiped out when ambushed by German armor and infantry early in beachhead fighting. It was down this road leading from Cisterna to Nettuno that General von Mackensen later sought to break through to the sea.

Maj. Gen. Fred L. Walker
36th Infantry Division

Maj. Gen. John P. Lucas
VI Corps

Colonel Reuben H. Tucker
504th Parachute Infantry

Maj. Gen. Gerald Templer
British 56th Division

Prime Minister
Winston S. Churchill

Gen. Alphonse Juin (left),
leader of French Corps, and
Lt. Gen. Mark W. Clark

Typical of treacherous terrain confronting troops trying to break
through to beleaguered Anzio beachhead. A pack mule train on a mountain path passes American engineers knee-deep in mud.

Digging in tents at Hell's Half-Acre, the evacuation hospitals near the shoreline.

Campoleone was the farthest point of advance reached in the early days when the British briefly held the town. This view looks off across the flatlands to the south.

Hunting for victims after an artillery shell plowed into "Hell's Half-Acre," the tented evacuation hospitals near the shoreline.

Site of some of the most vicious fighting on the beachhead was the first overpass above Anzio where an east-west road crossed the main road to Albano. Knocked out German tank is circled at left.

Brig. Gen. Robert T.
Frederick
First Special Service Force

Brig. Gen. "Iron Mike"
O'Daniel
3rd Infantry Division

Maj. Gen. Ernest N. Harmon
1st Armored Division

Maj. Gen. Lucian K. Truscott
VI Corps

Lt. Col. Warren R. Williams
504th Parachute Infantry

Colonel William O. Darby
Rangers

Captain Carlos C. "Doc"
Alden
509th Parachute Infantry

Field Marshal Albrecht Kesselring (facing camera) confers with Field Marshal Erwin Rommel.

General Fridolin von Senger
und Etterlin

General of Panzer Troops
Heinrich von Vietinghoff

Typical dugouts along the front lines at Anzio. Most holes were shallow, but covered with timber, doors, tree trunks and dirt.

German prisoners file by American infantry company while on their way to the rear.

General Fridolin von Senger und Etterlin assists the abbot of the monastery at Monte Cassino after the Allied bombing.

General Harold R.L.G. Alexander, 15th Army Group commander, and an aide inspect town of Anzio.

General Lucian Truscott (left), General W.R.C. Penney (center) and Colonel Chalmers discuss strategy on the beachhead during lull.

British Brigadier K.C. Davidson and Brigade Major J. C. Thomson go ashore.

Lt. John R. Martin
509th Parachute Infantry

Lt. Louis Hauptfleisch
504th Parachute Infantry

Sgt. Richard Fisco (left)
Sgt. Nick DeGaeta
509th Parachute Infantry

Sgt. William Berndt (right)
and comrades, 1st Special
Service Force

Conference aboard the HMS *Winchester Castle,* bound for Anzio. Left to right: Captain S.F Newdigate, Royal Navy, Lieutenant Colonel William P. Yarborough, commander of the 509th Parachute Infantry Battalion, and Lieutenant Colonel Roy A. Murray, leader of the 4th Ranger Battalion.

Anzio beachhead terrain (looking northeast). In the front is Anzio and to the right Nettuno.

U.S. 3rd Infantry Division troops going ashore on D-Day south of
Anzio town.

Attack on a German-held house in No-Man's-Land by First Special Service Force is shown in these two photos. Above, bazooka fired at house. Rifle fire poured into house (below) to keep Germans down.

Maj. Gen. W.R.C. Penney

Lt. Gen. Mark W. Clark

6

Test of Iron Wills

Captain James G. Evans, commander of I Company, 157th Infantry Regiment, was peering intently up the Albano-Anzio road as the first gray streaks of dawn began to pierce the cold black sky. His battered Americans were dug in around him just in front of an overpass where an east-west road crossed the main road running north to Albano.

I Company was virtually isolated. This would be the second day Evans and his men had defended this crucial position directly in the path of the main German smash to reach Anzio and the sea. The previous day I Company had suffered heavy casualties in repelling repeated frantic German infantry and panzer attacks.

For over 24 hours, Evans' wounded Thunderbirds had been lying in frigid, water-logged slit trenches within the company position. It had been impossible to evacuate them. Dead men were left slumped in their holes.

I Company had been without food and water for two days, but during the night ammunition had been sneaked up from the rear.

Captain Evans was a worried man. He knew his position was a crucial one, but he doubted if his cold, hungry, thirsty and nearly exhausted men could stand up to yet another full-blooded German assault.

Now the ears of I Company men picked up the frightening

rustle of huge shells cutting through the air toward their position. Moments later tremendous explosions along the line of slit trenches rocked the terrain.

Clusters of 170-millimeter and 210-millimeter shells blasted huge craters in the soggy terrain around the overpass. Muddy water oozed back into the blackened, ragged holes to partially cover the torn strips of uniforms and mangled pieces of flesh and bone which, moments before, had been riflemen or machine gunners.

One by one, five of I Company's officers were blown to bits. The living clung face-down on the bottom of slit trenches, faces pressed into the mud and icy water. Most prayed. The terrifying barrage raged for 15 minutes.

As suddenly as it began, the bombardment lifted. The pitiful cries and moans of I Company men mutilated by shellfire drifted across the hazy landscape. Some of those previously wounded were hit again.

Captain Evans, bearded, mud-caked, near exhaustion, raised his head to glance over the rim of his slit trench toward German lines. He called out: "Here come the bastards!"

Crossing the flatlands, charging directly toward the overpass, were waves of German feldgrau, their ankle-length greatcoats flapping grotesquely at their heels. As they neared the line of American slit trenches the Germans shouted in broken English: "At ease, I Company! Watch out, I Company! Here we come, I Company!"

A loud yell rose from the Thunderbird positions at the overpass: "Go to hell, you goddamned Kraut sons of bitches!"

As the enemy waves approached the barbed-wire rolls to I Company's front, Captain Evans' machine gunners and riflemen opened a withering blast of fire into the ranks of the Germans. Many were cut down, but others took their places and rushed onward. Trying to get through the barbed wire, their clothing caught, and I Company men poured bullets into their ranks leaving scores of dead and wounded Germans draped face down over the entanglement. Survivors of the attacking force, now under artillery fire, turned and fled.

As Captain Evans and his men tended to their wounded and braced for the next attack that was sure to come, stretched over the barbed-wire rolls to the front mutilated Germans were moaning, crying and begging for help. *Bitte! Bitte!* (Please!

Please!) a blond youth wailed, his bloody intestines spilling out.

All along the Albano-Anzio road sector that morning savage fighting raged. Von Mackensen was seeking desperately to break through with the 721st, 741st and 735th Infantry Regiments and the 29th and 309th Panzer Grenadier Regiments spearheading the assault. Supporting the foot soldiers were panzers in greater numbers than had yet been employed on the beachhead. Held in reserve to pour through a hole ripped in Allied lines were the fresh 26th Panzer and 29th Panzer Grenadier Divisions.

Out on the flatlands along the main road to Anzio smoke from tons of explosives drifted over the bleak landscape. The ear-splitting din of battle echoed across the terrain and up the sides of the heights far to the rear.

Confusion reigned. In the fog of the violent conflict, tanks were firing madly at each other, the sharp cracks of their high-velocity guns reaching above other battle noises. Sometimes, in the chaos, panzers would fire at panzers and Shermans at Shermans.

The sickly gray sky grounded most aircraft, but on occasion Focke-Wulf fighter-bombers zipped in at tree-top level to strafe and bomb American defensive positions. British Spitfires, in turn, found their way through the murky overcast to machine gun and bomb the waves of attacking Germans.

Onward came the gray-green hordes. The crushing weight of the combined infantry, artillery and panzer assault fell most heavily upon the weary and battered 179th Infantry Regiment which for three days had borne much of the brunt of all-out enemy efforts to crash through to Anzio. The broken regiment had been unable to form a continuous defensive line and was scattered about in small pockets out of contact with higher headquarters.

At mid-morning, a full-fledged crisis was on hand. The moment of truth had arrived. At 45th Infantry Division headquarters, a calm, pipe-smoking G2 (intelligence officer) told a visitor:

"Things are a bit confused at the front this morning. Maybe we'll have to write off the 179th Regiment. Nothing has come in from them for some time."

Things, indeed, were "a bit confused." Under heavy attack

by enemy tanks on three sides, elements of the 180th Infantry Regiment were ordered to pull back. Lieutenant Benjamin J. Blackmer, who had just taken command of Company G, failed to get the word.

Blackmer's depleted company was soon surrounded and under attack from all sides. There were barely 50 able-bodied men remaining. Communications to the rear had been severed, the radio was damaged, and there were no supplies. G Company men had beaten off repeated German efforts to overrun them, but by afternoon were out of grenades, mortar shells, and had only a few rounds left for rifles and machine guns.

Four of the company officers had been evacuated previously. Many of the men were suffering intense pain from early stages of trench foot, and none had had food or water for two days. Isolated in No-Man's-Land, Lieutenant Blackmer and his tiny force were pounded by both German artillery and by "friendly" gunfire.

At 2:30 P.M. Blackmer took his men some 300 yards to the rear to get out of the impact area of "friendly" artillery. But Allied spotters noted the movement of the "enemy" band, and began pounding G Company's remnants in their new position.

When G Company had pulled out of its initial position, Private William J. Johnston, a machine gunner, was left for dead by his comrades. On the heels of the unit's short withdrawal, the Germans moved in, just as the seriously wounded Johnson regained a hazy consciousness. Arduously he crawled to his gun and opened fire on the enemy, causing them to pause while Blackmer and his men dug in at their new position.

At 4 P.M. Private First Class Robert Keefe was dispatched to try to work his way to the rear through enemy lines to battalion headquarters. He reached the unit's CP and received instructions for G Company to pull back after dark—if it could. Keefe had another perilous journey crawling back through German forces, but reached Lieutenant Blackmer just before dark with the instructions.

West of the Albano-Anzio road, the 2nd Battalion, 157th Infantry Regiment, had been slowly pushed back until it had reached the wadi country. Weary, depleted in strength, low on ammunition, the battalion was soon surrounded.

The battalion commander, Lieutenant Colonel Laurence C.

Brown, was undaunted by his command's perilous predicament. Establishing his CP in one of the caves which dotted the wadi country, Colonel Brown organized his defenses facing each direction. Several platoons turned caves into fortified mini-fortresses, others dug in around the natural cavities.

Almost immediately the Germans attacked Brown's battalion, and edged in close enough to toss hand grenades at the Americans. But the attack was repulsed.

At 45the Division headquarters, the lack of any news from Colonel Brown's battalion generated a thick pall of gloom. It was presumed the outfit had been wiped out, and a gaping hole had been torn in the line.

Division HQ had not reckoned with Larry Brown's fighting spirit and that of his men. Cut off from any contact with other units or headquarters, the battalion would fight on stubbornly, refusing to be budged by a determined enemy bent on destroying it.

Late that morning, with the front lines aflame, Captain William H. McKay was piloting a Cub aircraft and observing targets for the 45th Infantry Division. McKay felt his heart beat faster as he peered into the distance behind German lines. He had spotted a force of panzers and some 2,500 foot soldiers moving south from Carroceto along the Albano road toward American lines.

In an excited voice, Captain McKay radioed the juicy target to the corps fire control center and in less than 12 minutes 224 British and American guns had been directed toward the large oncoming German force.

The beachhead erupted in an enormous roar as the 224 guns began firing. From his lofty perch, McKay looked on in delight. The ground around the marching columns and the rolling panzers seemed to literally blow up from the concentration of massed fire. When the smoke had cleared it was as though some huge supernatural force had waved a wand over the terrain. The German force had simply disintegrated.

By noon of that desperate day of Allied crisis on Anzio, February 18, it appeared that the oncoming waves of German infantry and panzers were on the verge of crashing through the positions of the disorganized and decimated 179th Infantry Regiment. Allied gun barrels on the beachhead—hundreds of them—had been kept red hot all morning pouring explosives upon the attacking Germans. Yet on they came, more tanks, new units being hurled into the assault to replace those carved up by Allied artillery and smallarms fire. Now it became a test of wills: could von Mackensen continue to shovel in new waves of feldgrau to be slaughtered on the flatlands in the hope of achieving a breakthrough before the Allies could somehow patch up their shattered defensive line and hold on?

The 179th Infantry Regiment was on the brink of extinction as a cohesive fighting force. One of its battalions had been virtually destroyed that morning, one was at less than half strength and the third was seriously understrength. Near exhaustion, bewildered, disspirited, individuals and tiny bands filtered back to the final beachhead line which VI Corps had ordered held at all costs.

Under the crushing burden of relentless crises and lack of sleep for more than 60 hours, the beleaguered regimental commander was on the verge of collapse.

Into the gloom-ridden CP of the 179th Infantry Regiment at 2 P.M. that afternoon strode an outwardly confident Colonel Bill Darby, former leader of the Ranger force destroyed outside Cisterna. Shoulders back, jaw firmly set, Darby began issuing orders in his customary crisp, staccato manner. General Lucas had sent him to take command of the regiment and try to restore order out of chaos.

In the shell-shattered old farmhouse CP as *El Darbo* arrived was the crestfallen commander of the 3rd Battalion, Major Merlin G. Tyron. His men had been overrun that morning. Only a handful had survived to trickle back to the final beachhead line.

"Sir," Major Tyron addressed Colonel Darby in a resigned tone, "I guess you will relieve me for losing my battalion."

Darby gave the dejected Tyron a friendly slap on the back. "Cheer up, son," he said, "I just lost three of them, but the war must go on."

There was nothing frivolous about the remark. The loss of Colonel Darby's beloved Rangers would forever fill his heart with grief. But these few words worked magic on the despairing and exhausted officers at the 179th Infantry Regiment CP. A new spirit of confidence and resolution, a feeling that somehow the shattered Thunderbird regiment would pull

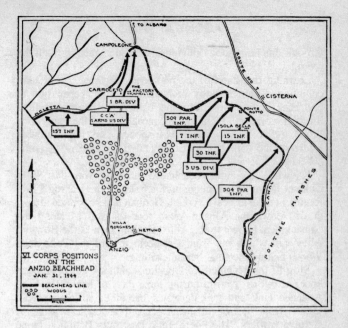

VI CORPS POSITIONS ON THE ANZIO BEACHHEAD JAN. 31, 1944

TO ALBANO

CAMPOLEONE

CARROCETO

THE FACTORY (APRILIA)

1 BR. DIV.

CISTERNA

ROUTE NO. 7

MOLETTA R.

CCA 1 ARMD US DIV.

157 INF.

509 PAR. INF.

7 INF.

PONTE ROTTO

ISOLA BELLA

15 INF.

30 INF.

3 US DIV.

504 PAR. INF.

MUSSOLINI CANAL

PONTINE MARSHES

VILLA BORGHESE

NETTUNO

ANZIO

BEACHHEAD LINE
WOODS
MILES

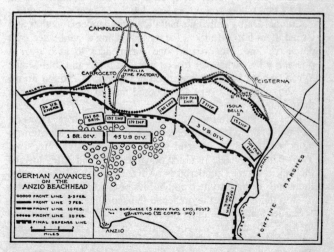

GERMAN ADVANCES ON THE ANZIO BEACHHEAD

CAMPOLEONE

CARROCETO

APRILIA (THE FACTORY)

CISTERNA

MOLETTA R.

36 US ENGRS

141 BR. BRIG.

157 INF.

179 INF.

180 INF.

509 PAR. INF.

7 INF.

ISOLA BELLA

15 INF.

1 BR. DIV.

45 US DIV.

3 US DIV.

504 PAR. INF.

MUSSOLINI CANAL

PONTINE MARSHES

VILLA BORGHESE (5 ARMY FWD. CMD. POST)
NETTUNO (VI CORPS HQ)

1 SPEC. SERV. FORCE

ANZIO

FRONT LINE 3-5 FEB.
FRONT LINE 7 FEB.
FRONT LINE 10 FEB.
FRONT LINE 20 FEB.
FINAL DEFENSE LINE
MILES

through this horrendous situation, seemed to race through the room.

Learning first-hand of the regiment's depleted and chaotic condition, Colonel Darby immediately sought permission to pull back his scattered remnants behind the beachhead final line and reorganize them in the concealment of the Padiglione Woods. "No," replied the soft-spoken and imperturbable leader of the 45th Division, General Bill Eagles, "the final beachhead line will be held to the last man."

Knowing the entire beachhead situation was desperate, Colonel Darby began plugging the holes in the leaking 179th Regiment dyke as best he could. German tanks operated almost at will down the Albano-Anzio road as well as along the embankment known to the Allied fighting men as the Bowling Alley and which ran from Carroceto toward the Padiglione Woods behind the final beachhead line.

Most of the Thunderbird Division's antitank guns had been knocked out or overrun during three days of heavy fighting. Attached tank and tank-destroyer battalions suffered severe losses while beating off what seemed an endless wave of German panzers. The 645th Tank Destroyer Battalion alone had 14 tanks knocked out in one day.

Colonel Darby called his battalion commanders together and issued them hurried orders for reestablishing a semblance of a defensive line. He ordered one commander to take over a position with "whatever troops you can find" and told Major Tyron, whose battalion had been destroyed, to "round up all the stragglers and every able-bodied man in the rear and run them into the line."

Late in the afternoon, with the 45th Infantry Division reeling, scattered and disorganized, General von Mackensen launched his most powerful punch of the massive offensive. Twelve huge panzers rumbled down the Bowling Alley toward the beleaguered Thunderbirds. Advancing behind them were thousands of infantrymen and hordes of tanks. There was little to stop them before they reached the shoreline.

Earlier that day, General Mark Clark flew into the beachhead in his Cub aircraft with a Spitfire escort. The Fifth Army commander had been forced to land on a hard-surfaced road. The Allied air strip outside Nettuno had been under heavy bombardment by long-range guns and three parked airplanes were destroyed.

A noon conference of top commanders was held at VI Corps' wine cellar in the urban shooting gallery known as Nettuno. Among those present were Generals Clark, Lucas and Truscott, as well as the Fireman of Anzio, scrappy Ernie Harmon of the 1st Armored Division.

"What do you propose to do?" Clark inquired of his beachhead commanders. General Truscott pointed to armored and infantry reserves not yet committed and wanted to "counterattack with everything we've got!"

General Harmon, peppering his remarks with salty expressions to dramatize key points, proposed that elements of his 1st Armored crash into the flank of the powerful German force attacking the 45th Infantry Division down the Albano-Anzio Road. Harmon wanted to send his tanks along the diagonal embankment known as the Bowling Alley which intersected the Albano-Anzio Road at a point considerably behind the scattered American positions along the final beachhead line.

The aggressive Ernie Harmon wanted to "knife through the Krauts and cut 'em off!"

Before General Clark arrived, John Lucas had opposed a counterattack and wanted to hold on to his reserves to plug holes in Allied defenses should the Germans break through in strength.

Now with Clark's attitude appearing to be one consistent with that of Truscott's and Harmon's, General Lucas reluctantly agreed to counterattack "with everything we've got" to halt or slow down the Wehrmacht juggernaught crashing down the road to Anzio.

Harmon's bold plan was accepted and details worked out for the counter-blow, which would be supported by every gun on the beachhead and a maximum effort from the air.

Tanks of the 1st Armored would advance up the Bowling Alley in the morning, with Harmon's 6th Armored Infantry Regiment on one side, and the 30th Regiment of the 3rd Division on the other.

Ernie Harmon, sensing a good fight, departed confidently for his headquarters to launch preparations for the morrow's slugging match. As he drove along, the sound of gunfire from

German tanks moving down the Bowling Alley reached his ears.

Later, General Clark took Lucian Truscott aside. "You'll be replacing Johnny (Lucas) in command within the next few days, just as soon as this crisis is over," Clark declared.

Truscott had been placed in a difficult position. As a professional soldier, he aspired to higher command. "I have no desire to replace Johnny," Truscott stated. "He's a personal friend."

After a moment's silence, Truscott added thoughtfully, "I think we can overcome our difficulties, and I'm perfectly willing to continue as Johnny's deputy as long as is necessary."

"I appreciate your feelings," Clark replied. "I don't want to hurt Johnny, either. Anyhow, for the present, there'll be no change."

As darkness pulled its veil over the tortured beachhead, scores of General Harmon's tanks revved powerful motors and clanked into position for the jumpoff. Most of the foot soldiers in the counterattack, as was their habitual lot, had to trudge through ankle-deep mud for five miles to reach the line of departure by dawn.

Having achieved all that he could to prepare for the morning assault, General Harmon, fully clothed and ready for action, flopped down on a cot in his renovated ordnance-repair truck to steal a few winks of sleep. At 2 A.M. he was awakened by an urgent call from VI Corps headquarters.

The Germans had nearly broken through at the overpass along the Albano-Anzio Road. Did not Harmon think it would be wise to call off his counter thrust into the German flanks and pull back his armor to head off the enemy breakthrough?

Harmon disagreed vehemently. The way to halt the German drive was to hit the enemy in the flank, just as he was about ready to do, he emphasized.

He received permission to continue as originally planned.

Barely two hours later, General Harmon was again roused from fitful slumber. Colonel Maurice W. Daniel, division artillery commander, had alarming news: a battalion of the disorganized 45th Infantry Division had, in the confusion, gotten in front of the artillery's No-Fire Line and would be slaughtered by the massive barrage to be laid down at dawn.

The No-Fire Line was to assure rounds did not fall in friendly positions.

Harmon was faced with an agonizing decision. Should he order the bombardment to proceed as scheduled, perhaps hundreds of 45th Division men in the impact area would be killed. But to call off the barrage would mean to abandon the armored assault up the Bowling Alley. And Harmon was convinced that attack was all that would save the beachhead.

After several minutes of meditation, General Harmon told his artillery commander: "Fire as planned."

7

"Doom's Day" Averted

Dawn of February 19 was just starting to break over Italy's rugged, towering Apennine mountains when the gray skies over Anzio beachhead were streaked by the jagged lightning-like flashes of hundreds of Allied guns. The enormous roar from the massed artillery echoed for miles across the bleak, blood-saturated landscape.

Eight British field artillery regiments pounded German positions along the Albano-Anzio road, while eight battalions of American artillery fired for 45 minutes on enemy assembly areas in and around The Factory.

Warships in the Anzio roadstead sent salvos screaming into The Factory and Carroceto. More than 250 fighter-bombers and medium bombers blasted German installations and possible troop concentration areas.

This was the showdown. All the cards were on the Allied table. If General Ernie Harmon's thrust up the Bowling Alley and into the German flank should fail, it well could signal Doom's Day for tens of thousands of American and British soldiers.

The mammoth concentration of Allied shells and bombs up and down the Bowling Alley and along the road to Albano sent sheets of flame and smoke rolling across the flatlands. An Almost uninterrupted crescendo of explosives caused the ground to tremble and quake.

170

Unknown to General Harmon, the barrage was paying dividends to a much greater degree than he had hoped for. Elements of a fresh German division were trekking along the Bowling Alley to launch another smash into the battered 45th Infantry Division at the precise time the American and British big guns began to thunder. Caught in the open with no place to take cover, the advancing German columns flopped to the ground and lay there as the barrage took a fearful toll. Some grenadiers, half out of their minds with fear as the endless stream of Allied shells shrieked into their ranks, ran around in circles seeking refuge from the death-dealing holocaust of steel and explosives.

Within minutes, dead and wounded Germans littered the Bowling Alley and the terrain around it. Scores of vehicles were twisted, blackened wreckages. The large German force disintegrated.

Precisely to the minute, at 6:30 A.M., General Harmon's men struck. It was do-or-die for the beachhead. Colonel Louis V. Hightower, leader of the 1st Armored Regiment, sent his tanks clanking up the Bowling Alley while the 30th Infantry Regiment, 3rd Division and the 6th Armored Infantry Regiment advanced abreast to either side of the road.

Tanks and infantry moved steadily ahead, and by 8:30 A.M. had reached a point a mile from the line of departure. There the Americans ran into a heavy concentration of Germans forming up to launch yet another full-blooded smash down the Anzio-Albano Road. As Generals Harmon, Truscott and Clark had hoped, the surprise thrust into the German flank totally disrupted and disorganized enemy forces.

Task Force Harmon, supported by artillery, steadily pushed back the enemy, now in a chaotic condition. A blown bridge along the Bowling Alley slowed the advance, but the span was quickly repaired under fire by combat engineers and the drive resumed.

Harmon's tankers raked a panicky enemy with 75-millimeter and machine gun fire, blasting the Germans from heavily-fortified stone farmhouses along the Bowling Alley.

So many German prisoners were taken in the advance that the 180th Infantry Regiment was called on to remove them to POW cages.

Aware that a large force of American tanks and infantry was

shooting up their rear areas, German formations assaulting the depleted and disorganized 179th Infantry Regiment defending the Albano-Anzio road hesitated, slowed then ground to a halt.

At 4:30 P.M., with dusk beginning to settle over a tortured battlefield strewn with dead and mutilated bodies, General Harmon reined in his rampaging task force. Its mission had been accomplished.

Task Force Harmon captured in excess of 1,700 Germans. An American prisoner who escaped in the confusion of the fighting reported seeing German dead "stacked up like cord-wood in piles of 150" along the main road to Albano. Bulldozers dug mass graves.

It had been a great slaughter.

But Task Force Harmon had also paid a heavy price. War was never totally one-sided. The company leading the advance of the 30th Infantry had been chopped down to one officer and 50 men. Pacing the 6th Armored Infantry Regiment on the other side of the Bowling Alley, a company had been badly chewed up when raked by direct fire from German Mark VI tanks.

That evening in his converted ordnance-repair truck, General Harmon learned of the fate of the 45th Infantry Division battalion which, in the fog of war, had been reported in the center of the Allied barrage impact area. Harmon felt a surge of relief to learn that it had not been a battalion but a platoon that had wandered out in front of the No-Fire Line. And the platoon had pulled back before the bombardment began.

Also that day G Company of the 180th Infantry Regiment, commanded by Lieutenant Benjamin Blackmer, reached friendly lines after fighting its way out of enemy encirclement in the darkness. Blackmer's depleted company had waded over a mile through waist-deep water of a creek to reach his regiment's defensive positions.

By some miracle, the seriously wounded machine gunner, Private First Class William Johnston, who remained behind to cover G Company's withdrawal, crawled through the black night and German positions to reach safety.

Regimental headquarters called the 2nd Battalion CP to inquire about G Company's fate. Not many were left, but those who got back were in good spirits and "Lieutenant Blackmer came out grinning," the regimental colonel was told.

Two miles to the south from where Ernie Harmon's spear-heading tankers were creating panic and confusion up the Bowling Alley, the British North Staffs and Loyals were preparing to wipe out the last pocket of Germans in front of the Albano road overpass where American Captain James Evans and his isolated band had fought off enemy assaults for two days and nights.

The German force was holed up in a large farmhouse complex just north of the Allied final beachhead line. The structures were heavily pounded by artillery and then the British Tommies began moving in. Suddenly a white flag appeared over the ruined buildings, and several Germans staggered out of the smoke with arms held high and shouting, "*Kamerad! Kamerad!*" (We surrender).

Holding their fire until the capitulating Germans reached them, the Tommies saw a much larger group charge out of the rubble with hands in air. That opened the flood gates. The feldgrau poured from the ruined buildings in a steady stream to give themselves up.

Pounded incessantly by massed Allied artillery for four days and nights, attacking dug-in American and British positions constantly, without sleep for more than 50 hours and near exhaustion, the Germans in the farmhouse complex had reached the limits of human endurance.

Assessing the Anzio battle picture that night, top Allied commanders were in agreement: the back of the German smash down the main road toward the sea had been broken.

During the four-day German do-or-die effort that drove the Allies back to the final beachhead line 5,000 feldgrau had been killed or seriously wounded. The Anglo-Americans had suffered in equal measure, also losing about 5,000 men. The 45th Infantry Division, which had been standing in the way of Adolf Hitler's ambitions, had 400 men killed, 2,000 wounded and 1,000 missing, many of the latter being captured.

Added to the heavy losses of the Thunderbird Division were 2,500 victims of trench foot, pneumonia, severe dysentery, exposure and exhaustion. These came after living through freezing days and nights in shallow slit trenches often filled with slush and ice water.

These 2,500 Thunderbirds hardly went along with the

army's official definition of their plight—non-combat casualties.

Anzio beachhead, after a month of existence, had proved to be a Devil's Inferno where men by the thousands were chewed up in the enormous meat-grinder of violence. Each of the adversaries had lost about 2,000 men, or 20 percent of the combined 200,000 men engaged in the death struggle for a strip of bleak, barren Italian real estate.

Most casualties were suffered by front-line combat forces, so both the Allies and the Germans had been ground down to impotency. Like two huge prehistoric beasts just engaged in a savage, life-or-death fight, each side lay back in almost total exhaustion, panting and licking its wounds.

While the blood-letting and the carnage were running rampant on the flatlands around the peacetime resort of Anzio, 30 miles to the north German officials were brow-beating the 80-year-old abbot of Monte Cassino Abbey, the ancient structure pulverized by Allied bombs on February 15. Dr. Paul Goebbels, the cunning propaganda chief of the Third Reich, gleefully recognized that he had in the "wanton destruction" of the revered Catholic edifice a golden tool for undermining the morale of the embattled American and British fighting men on Anzio and in front of the Gustav Line.

Indeed the Third Reich could now dramatize to the entire world the "barbarism" of the Anglo-American leaders and soldiers.

There was one hitch to Goebbels' dream: the old abbot refused to cooperate once German scheming to gain a propaganda bonanza became obvious to him.

Two days after the abbey was destroyed, the elderly abbot formed a procession with his monks and those civilians who survived the air bombardment, and carrying a wooden crucifix, led it down the mountainside to the vicinity of Piedimonte. There General Fridolin von Senger und Etterlin, German commander in the region and a Benedictine lay brother, arranged for a car to pick up the abbot and an aide and bring them to von Senger's headquarters at Castel Massimo, where the abbot spent the night.

While the exhausted and distraught abbot was asleep, General von Senger received a directive from the Oberkommando der Wehrmacht (meaning Adolf Hitler): the abbot was to be interviewed by a German reporter on the conduct of German troops and the Allied destruction of the Abbey of Monte Cassino.

Von Senger, a devout Catholic, was reluctant to ask the abbot to publicly perform on behalf of German propaganda. But the soldier in the XIV Corps commander won out—he realized the bombing of the abbey was a once-in-a-lifetime opportunity to display to the world the basic decency of the Wehrmacht as opposed to the base indecencies of the Anglo-American high command.

So General von Senger asked the abbot to give the interview, and the elderly monk agreed, believing he was merely to discuss the monastery and events there. As a movie camera ground, a German lieutenant read the introduction to the carefully orchestrated scenario:

> The Abbey Monte Cassino is completely destroyed. A senseless act of force of the Anglo-American Air Force has robbed civilized mankind of one of its most valued cultural monuments.
>
> Abbot Bishop Gregorio Diamare has been brought out of the ruins of the abbey under protection of the German Armed Forces . . .
>
> The old abbot, who today is 80 years old, found here a place of refuge and recovery after the days of horror which he, his monks, and numerous refugees, women, children, old men, crippled, sick and wounded civilians had to undergo because of an order by the Allied Supreme Commander . . .

The camera and sound recorder switched to a "voluntary discussion" between Abbot Diamare and General von Senger which continued for five minutes and concluded with the bewildered cleric declaring:

"Even today the German Armed Forces provides for us and for the refugees in model fashion . . . I thank you and the German Armed Forces for all the consideration given to the original abode of the Benedictine Order both before and after the bombardment."

To protect Abbot Diamare from further harassment by German officialdom, Senger bundled him into his car and with one of the general's most trusted aides as an escort sent him to a Benedictine monastary in Rome. The abbot there was a lifelong friend of von Senger.

Outside the gates of Rome, the small car was intercepted by a contingent of German SS troops. They dragged the weary old man to a radio station in Rome where he was neither fed nor allowed to rest.

Here he was given a specially prepared script on the difference in the behavior of German and Anglo-American troops and forced to read it over the air.

Disillusioned at being made the unwitting tool of others, Abbot Diamare was still allowed no rest. Now German Foreign Minister Joachim von Ribbentrop got into the act, not wanting to be outdone by his hated rival in Nazi government, Dr. Goebbels. Tired, hungry and dejected, the old abbot was dragged to the German Embassy in the Vatican, where he was asked to sign a statement that bristled with propaganda against the Allies.

But von Ribbentrop had miscalculated the staying power and resolution of the old monk—he refused to sign the document.

Minutes later Abbot Diamare collapsed, and was later released from his captivity. Whatever may have been his true feelings toward the Anglo-Americans with regard to the destruction of his abbey, the elderly monk had no intention of implying through his testimony that he was favorable toward the Axis.

When General von Senger learned from his military aide of the kidnapping of Abbot Diamare by the SS and his subsequent treatment by fiefs of Goebbels and von Ribbentrop, he was furious. He promptly called Field Marshal Kesselring direct—bypassing the Tenth Army chain of command—and protested vehemently.

Kesselring's only comment was that he had nothing to do with the episode.

Nazi propagandists were not connected with such technical-ities as to whether the abbot refused to sign the document denouncing the Allies. Within 24 hours leaflets were printed with the abbot's testimony over his "signature" and German artillery fired them into American and British lines at Anzio and along the Gustav Line.

An estimated 20 percent of the American fighting men in

Italy were Catholic, Goebbelss' minions were quick to point out to their superiors. The abbot's testimony of the "barbarity" of top Anglo-American leaders would plummet Allied morale on Anzio and at the Gustav Line, they declared.

Nazi efforts to undermine American and British morale in Italy were in vain. Each man who carried a gun and beachhead nurses who daily were battered with shells and bombs accepted the destruction of the Abbey of Monte Cassino in good faith.

Although the maximum German effort to break through to Anzio and the sea had been halted, heavy fighting continued on parts of the bridgehead. The 2nd Battalion, 157th Infantry Regiment, 45th Division, was still surrounded and fighting for its life six days after von Mackensen's rush down the Albano-Anzio road had forced it into a series of caves in the wadi country several hundred yards west of the road.

The "doomed" battalion's commander, Lieutenant Colonel Laurence Brown, had turned each cave into a miniature fortress and defied the Wehrmacht to root his men out.

At one point the Germans attacked and worked their way up close to the caves. Colonel Brown, knowing that his men in the caves and burrowed into the ground around them were safer than the Germans out in the open, called for friendly artillery fire on his own position. Soon shells from Allied guns were screaming into the area around the caves, and the German attackers withdrew, leaving behind many dead and wounded.

On the night of February 21 the Queen's Royal Regiment jumped off with the mission of rescuing the trapped American battalion which had been beating off persistent enemy attacks for five days and nights. The Germans opened heavy artillery fire on the approaching British force, and it suffered over 70 casualties before fighting its way through to the caves.

Hardly had the Tommies of the Queen's Regiment begun to take over positions from Colonel Larry Brown's men than the Germans attacked once again. Closing in under the cover of darkness, the enemy grenadiers edged up to the caves and showered the defenders with potato-masher grenades and sprayed them with machine-pistol fire.

Captain George O. Hubbard, artillery observer for the 2nd Battalion, once more called for salvos directly on the American-British positions in and around the caves. The first volley was on target, and the German force scattered.

The weary, hungry and decimated American battalion prepared to pull out at dawn and turn the cave strongpoints over to the Tommies who had come to their relief. But two companies of German infantry waded through the wadi country to resume the battle.

All day fierce hand-to-hand fighting raged around the caves. At 1:30 A.M. Colonel Brown assembled his men for the break-out. They silently slipped out of the caves and headed south for the black-top road which was the final beachhead line.

Captain Peter Graffagnino and several medics volunteered to remain with the large number of wounded, who had to be left behind.

Stealing through the dark night in a column of companies, Brown's battalion was halfway to the relative safety of the final beachhead line when suddenly heavy bursts of machine gun and rifle fire raked the Thunderbirds. Flopping face downward, the Americans hugged the ground or crawled for cover as streams of tracer bullets criss-crossed the black air just above their heads. The heavy firing was coming from a group of houses.

In the confusion of the nighttime firefight that erupted, the column became split. Colonel Brown and the first half of the battalion column pushed on safely, but the others became scattered.

During the early hours of daylight, individuals and tiny groups in the cut-off portion of the column filtered through to the black-top road.

There Brown took a head count. Some 650 men had been in the battalion when it was first struck with great violence by powerful German forces rushing down the Albano-Anzio road. Now only 225 men had reached the final beachhead line—and 90 of these survivors were hospital cases.

For seven days and nights the 2nd Battalion of the 157th Infantry Regiment had undergone a nerve-shattering ordeal of nearly constant combat. They had had little or no food and were pounded relentlessly by German artillery and mortar fire. Some men had lost their hearing. Others were unable to walk. Large numbers had bloody, mud-caked bandages—the walking wounded. All had nearly reached the end of human endurance.

Now the Germans turned their attention toward the Tommies

who had taken over the caves from Colonel Brown's men. The Queen's Regiment was in bad shape. The Germans had once again cut in behind the caves, and the British fighting men found themselves surrounded, running out of ammunition, and unable to evacuate the large number of wounded that was piling up.

Shortly after dawn on February 23, enemy grenadiers, supported by several panzers assaulted the cave positions. Two companies of the Queen's Regiment were overrun and destroyed and other Tommies had to withdraw into the caves for a last-ditch stand.

After dark, the remnants of the British regiment were formed into groups of 12 to 15 and tried to infiltrate out of the trap. Few made it.

After eight days and nights of relentless effort to seize the terrain around the embattled caves, the Germans finally succeeded. But it was too late. The powerful Wehrmacht smash down the Albano-Anzio road had been turned back, and the caves were now but a hollow prize.

On the morning of February 22, Lieutenant Jack C. Montgomery, a platoon leader of Company I, 180th Infantry Regiment, was angry. For seven days he and his Thunderbird comrades had been fighting for their lives in defensive warfare. Now Montgomery wanted to strike back—even if it meant launching a one-man assault.

Two hours before daylight the young officer detected enemy soldiers moving into No-Man's-Land directly in front of his platoon's position. Armed with a rifle and several grenades Montgomery crawled up a ditch for nearly 75 yards. He froze in place as he heard German voices to his front.

Crawling on up the dark and water-logged ditch for some 20 yards, the lieutenant paused again. He could hear the muffled sounds of digging. The Germans were setting up four machine guns and a mortar.

Clutching his Garand rifle tightly, Montgomery sprang to his feet and raced a few yards to a low knoll. There he raised his weapon and raked the enemy position with bullets and pelted it with grenades. Eight Germans were killed in the surprise one-man onslaught, and the remaining four surrendered.

Lieutenant Montgomery returned with his prisoners. He informed an artillery observer of a thick-walled stone farmhouse which he thought was where the main German force was concealed, then grabbed a carbine and a few more grenades and started back up the cold, wet ditch.

Now it was daylight, and little concealment was available to the one-man army. He continued on until reaching another German outpost, where he knocked out two machine guns, killed three of the enemy and took seven prisoners. Returning once more with his captured grenadiers, Montgomery replenished his carbine ammunition and grenades and up the ditch he went. Now his attention turned to the house strongpoint which was being shelled as he neared it.

Waiting for the barrage to lift, the lieutenant rushed the formidable stone building, but before reaching it he paused— 21 stunned and weary Germans came out of the smoking ruins with hands raised in surrender.

It had been a productive morning for Lieutenant Montgomery. Alone he had killed at least 11 enemy soldiers, knocked out or captured six machine guns, had taken 32 prisoners, and left behind an undetermined number of German wounded.

In the bomb- and shell-racked town of Anzio on the twenty-second, U.S. Army engineers were digging feverishly into a large heap of ancient ruins half buried under a mound of recently pulverized rubble. American officers had heard that the Emperor Nero centuries before had built an underground aqueduct between Rome and his villa at Anzio.

Maybe this was a way to get behind German lines without firing a shot. Some were fascinated by the thought of sending a battalion or a regiment, even a division, trekking through an ancient and long-forgotten tunnel to surface in the Eternal City 30 miles away.

The engineers found the passage leading from Nero's villa. They also found that it ended 29 1/2 miles short of Rome.

8

Life (and Death) on Mussolini Canal

While the attention of both the Allied and German high commands had been focused first on the Wehrmacht's breakthrough effort down the Albano-Anzio road and next on the sector in front of Cisterna where the U.S. 3rd Infantry Division had been struck, a nasty, no-holds-barred, bizzare, often clandestine kind of warfare had raged along a water barrier known as the Mussolini Canal. It was not the type of fighting that generated bold newspaper headlines in London, New York or Berlin. But it was brutal, even barbaric on occasion.

The *Canale Mussolini* guarded the right flank of the Anglo-American beachhead. Almost since the initial landing, the U.S. 504th Parachute Infantry Regiment and the First Special Service Force, a mixture of Americans and Canadians, had been holding the line along this sector. Each unit was thinly spread, but the canal and its 28-foot-high banks formed an ideal defensive barrier, particularly against tank attack.

The canal had quickly turned into one of the hot spots in the Devil's Cauldron of Anzio.

A few years previously, the Italian premier, Benito Mussolini, had launched a massive agriculture project in this area. The Pontine Marshes had been drained and model farmhouses built. These farms were supplied with excellent farm equipment and stocked with hogs and cattle, then Fascist families in good standing were moved in to live there.

Cutting through this model farm settlement was the canal built by the bombastic Italian premier, which he modestly named in his own honor. Into the thick, wet banks of this waterway American paratroopers and the men of the Special Service Force had burrowed, like hundreds of moles seeking refuge from the lurking dangers of a hostile environment.

The earthen embankment along the Allied side of the canal resembled a massive dirt-moving operation which would have been the envy of large commercial excavation contractors back home. Feverish digging continued relentlessly. An American or Canadian would excavate a deep hole that satisfied the safety requirements of his keen and experienced eyes. Then the banks would be pounded by artillery and mortar salvos, several men would be killed or wounded, and the "moles" would emerge to deepen their holes.

When the holes reached a point where water was seeping in and eventually covered the bottom, the individual excavation work had to cease. Then another barrage would pound the canal, and paratroopers and Forcemen would scavenger the neighborhood and lug huge timbers to place across their holes.

Two to three hundred yards behind the canal company and platoon headquarters had been established in stone farmhouses. Most of the "mole men" along Mussolini's waterway spent their days in these houses, leaving a strong outpost line along the canal. When the Germans attacked, the paratroopers and Forcemen in the houses sprinted hell-bent to take up firing positions along the banks.

Sharp-eyed German observers on the heights inland soon became aware that the Americans and Canadians were occupying these houses in daylight, so the sturdy structures came in for their share of artillery and mortar barrages. What had once been Benito Mussolini's ideal farmhouses before long deteriorated under constant enemy shellfire into batterd shambles which had to be patched up daily by their occupants.

However humble and torn were their farmhouse homes, the Allied fighting men along the canal, suffering through an endless night in water-logged, frigid, cramped holes and buffeted by thick sheets of rain, howling winds and enemy shells, counted the minutes until a merciful dawn allowed them to scamper off to the relative comfort of the farmhouses.

Fully manning the canal line was mandatory during darkness. An enemy attack across the flatlands could be upon the banks before there was time to rouse the sleeping men in the farmhouses and for them to scramble to the canal to help repulse the assault.

Outposts were established some 200 yards out on the enemy side of the stream, each one having a telephone connected to the "moles" burrowed into the waterway banks. There was a considerable distance between outposts, so that often German patrols would pass through the outer positions. When an outpost spotted the dim silhouettes of an enemy patrol stealing through the tar-black night toward the canal, the German force would be allowed to continue unmolested.

But the outpost would telephone the main line of resistance along the waterway about the approaching patrol. As the hostile force neared the embankments the men along the canal would fire flares into the sky, bathing the vicinity in iridescence and trapping the German patrol naked in its frightening glare. Paratrooper and Forcemen machine gunners and riflemen then would mow down the frantic enemy grenadiers.

It was a deadly and bloody war along the *Canale Mussolini*, but also a sort of personal and private one during those days and nights of the all-out German effort to break through to the sea down the Albano-Anzio road and in front of Cisterna. The canal war was uniquely different in character from the bitter fighting taking place elsewhere in the bridgehead. Part of this uniqueness, in addition to the static mission, resulted from the resourcefulness of the gladiators of the First Special Service Force and the 504th Parachute Infantry Regiment.

To the Forcemen and the parachutists, war was a throwback to medieval days where warriors took great pride in their professional skills (killing other men swiftly and in considerable numbers), daring and courage. Something of a tongue-in-cheek rivalry had developed between the American parachutists and the Forcemen. Each unit was shelled so often that ducking enemy barrages had become a way of life along the *Canale Mussolini*.

"What the hell's going on?" a Forceman would inquire loudly of his comrades. "The paratroopers got shelled 21 times yesterday and we got it only 18 times. The goddamned Krauts *owe* us three shellings."

It was the grim battlefield humor of men who lived by the
minute with the specter of sudden death constantly hovering
over them. Against incoming mortar and artillery shells, the
parachutists and the Forcemen could not pit their exceptional
individual skills and resourcefulness. It was merely a case of
clinging to the bottom of a hole during a barrage and hoping for
the best. Their fate was in the hands of the gods, who would
select those to live and those to die.

Sitting in place and waiting for the enemy to come to them
was not in the nature of either of the units holding the
Mussolini Canal line. Nightly they launched daring raids deep
into German territory, terrorizing the enemy, bringing back
prisoners, raising merry hell in general. In this type of Indian
warfare the American paratroopers and the SSF (Special
Service Force) were in their element. It was what they had been
trained to do—and they came by it instinctively, with boldness,
cunning and ingenuity.

In the First SSF, where the common denominator was
toughness and courage, the commander had already become a
living legend among his men. Before the war would end,
Brigadier General Robert Frederick would receive four Distinguished Service Crosses and would be wounded eight times.
He was loudly touted by his idolizing warriors as "the toughest
man on the beachhead," a designation disputed by numerous,
if not all, other Anglo-American outfits.

Yet if the real General Frederick were cast by a Hollywood
director for the role of General Frederick in a movie, the
unfortunate director would have been fired on the spot. Bob
Frederick's appearance and mannerisms were almost precisely
opposite to the stereotyped image of a two-fisted fighting man.
He was spare in build, pale in complexion and a small
moustache gave him the look of a mild-mannered bookkeeper.

On occasion during lulls, soldiers from other units on the
beachhead would call at the SSF headquarters to get a look at
the presumably fire-breathing, rip-snorting, hell-for-leather
legend whose feats had repeatedly made the rounds of the
beachhead. On having Bob Frederick pointed out to them, the
visitors were convinced they were being spoofed.

Men serving under the SSF leader swore that he was without
fear. Yet Frederick told a reporter on the beachhead, "When I
get in the front lines I'm scared to death, but I know I mustn't

show it. So I light a cigarette as calmly as I can, and my boys say, 'Well, if he can do it, I can too!"

Despite his mild appearance, General Frederick spoke rapidly and decisively. He was indefatigable, skilled in his profession and possessed an indefinable talent for instilling confidence among those who served under him—even in "hopeless" situations.

The Forcemen had occupied a number of farmhouses on the German side of the canal as outposts and as bases from which to launch night raids. Staff Sergeant D.J. McLachlan, a Canadian, and several of his men were ordered to take over and hold a house across the stream which was in a particularly exposed position. The next morning a friend went forward to visit the house taking the customary concealment procedures to reach the outpost.

There he saw Sergeant McLachlan striding up and down the road in front of the exposed house, under the gaze of Germans to the front and on the heights. It was as though the closest enemy soldier were in Rome. His visiting comrade pointed out that he was needlessly exposing himself to sudden death. But McLachlan calmly explained that the road to that point belonged to him and he wanted the Germans to know it.

A short time later Sergeant McLachlan was killed on a night patrol far out in No-Man's-Land.

Lieutenant Taylor Radcliffe was surprised and captured while on a night patrol. By his blackened face, the Germans knew they had seized one of the infamous (to the Germans) Black Devils of Anzio. They bound and gagged Radcliffe, dragged him off to a command post to be interrogated.

A German officer sought Allied dispositions along the beachhead. Lieutenant Radcliffe suggested that the interrogator perform an impossible sex act upon himself, a response that so infuriated the frustrated German that he struck the Forceman a heavy blow across the face with a large stick.

A provident Allied barrage on the CP sent the enemy personnel scurrying for foxholes in the yard, leaving one unlucky German to guard the recalcitrant prisoner. The guard made the mistake of turning his back momentarily, whereby Radcliffe picked up a board and knocked the German unconscious.

The SSF officer dashed into the next room where he freed

several other bound American prisoners, then fled the building and two days later returned to friendly lines. A few nights afterward, Lieutenant Radcliffe was back on patrol.

General Frederick, wearing a cloth cap and face blackened, often accompanied these nocturnal patrols into German real estate. He had simplified the purpose of the nightly bold raids by the SSF—kill Germans and capture prisoners for interrogation. On one of the raids in which Frederick participated, his patrol wandered into a minefield in the inky blackness, then was raked by automatic weapons while trying to get out.

Many Forcemen were cut down, including a stretcher bearer. The surviving bearer was left with a wounded man. Frantically, he shouted to the dark figure of a comrade, "Goddamn it, don't just stand there. Grab hold of the other end of the litter!" After the two Forcemen carried the wounded soldier out of the minefield under a torrent of machine gun fire, the stretcher bearer caught a glimpse of the comrade he had ordered loudly to help him. It was General Frederick.

Battlefield guile was not a monopoly of the Forcemen. The Germans had become aware that Frederick's men habitually used a draw while leaving on nightly raids and planted a large number of diabolical devices known as *Schu* mines, so called after the German inventor. (Allied soldiers thought they were called "shoe" mines because they were designed to blow off feet and legs.) The devilish explosive contrivances were cased in plastic containers which defied mine-detectors.

An SSF patrol set out through the draw and in moments started detonating mines. As explosives rocked the draw the Americans were raked by machine gun fire. Thirty-two of Bob Frederick's men lost feet or legs in that brief encounter.

Grim-faced Forcemen vowed revenge for the bloody disaster in the draw. The next night a strong combat patrol pounced on a known strongly-held position far out into No-Man's-Land and wiped out the Germans to a man.

During this period, the Norwegian-born intelligence officer of the Force, Lieutenant Roll Finn, learned that his father had just been murdered by the Nazis in Oslo. Each time after that when Germans were captured on Anzio, the big blond lieutenant would take them to the second level of a building and order them to "talk"—that is, give wanted information. If they refused, Lieutenant Finn tossed them over the balcony. First he would ask a prisoner if he had ever been in Norway. If the answer was Yes, the unfortunate German might be tossed from the balcony several times.

During an SSF company-size raid against a German-held village, a husky SS sergeant was captured during house-to-house fighting. A Forcemen found a young woman's photo on the German and contemptuously tossed it to the ground after a pointed reference to her alleged "profession." Infuriated, the German offered to fight. The Forceman eagerly accepted, laid down his Tommy gun and began slugging it out with the German. Minutes later the SS man was kayoed, after which the American fisticuffs victor and a few watching comrades resumed firing weapons at the enemy.

The antics of the SSF soon became known throughout the Allied world, as news reporters sent back stories on "The Wild Men of Anzio." Summed up one correspondent: "These men are crazy as hell." It was an expression of awe and admiration for the Forcemen's almost reckless bravery and battlefield ingenuity.

Side by side with Frederick's men along the canal, Colonel Reuben Tucker's 504th Parachute Infantry Regiment had been enduring a similar miserable existence of cold, wetness, constant shelling, nighttime raids and sudden death. The 1st and 2nd Battalions of the 504th were defending a portion of the canal. The 3rd Battalion had been transferred to help the British beat off do-or-die German efforts to break through Allied lines along the Albano-Anzio road.

Colonel Tucker, known to fellow officers as Rube, was short in physical stature, extremely long in heart. Barrel-chested and intense, Tucker spoke rapidly with a deep, booming voice. If he was not the toughest man in the battle-tested parachute regiment, then he ranked among the elite in this respect. Tucker lived to fight.

The Germans opposite the American paratroopers soon grew to fear them. "We're ready to fight," a captured enemy soldier told a parachutist, "and we can handle your regular infantry. But you sons of bitches are crazy!"

During this period, a tall, thin, curly-haired member of the 504th Parachute Infantry Battalion became a legend on the beachhead. Private Ted Bachenheimer was 20 years old, had the facial features of a choir boy and aspired to be an opera singer. Soft-spoken, friendly, liked by his comrades, Bachenheimer was something of a mystery man in the regiment. It was known that when Ted was about 10 his parents fled their native Germany to escape Nazi oppression and the family eventually settled in California.

Private Bachenheimer made no outward display of emotion concerning his feelings for the German enemy. Inwardly, he detested all the Nazi regime stood for. His specialty was one-man raides into and behind German lines, and before long the Wehrmacht knew by name the American paratrooper who had become a constant irritating—and often deadly—menace.

Bachenheimer's battalion commander, Lieutenant Colonel Warren Williams, himself a rugged and experienced fighting man, was among those awed by the youth's battlefield exploits. Watching Bachenheimer apply soot and dirt to his face before departing on a sojourn behind enemy lines, Colonel Williams inquired, "Ted, tell me the truth, aren't you sort of scared on these missions?"

"Well," the trooper replied thoughtfully, "I'm a little nervous when I leave friendly lines and have to piss a few times out in No-Man's-Land. But after that I'm not bothered."

Bachenheimer liked to make his night forays alone, figuring that others would be a hindrance. On one particularly dangerous mission, he was persuaded to take along three comrades. Out between the lines, a flare shot into the air and the four-man patrol was raked with automatic weapons fire. The three others, reasoning that their mission was to locate German positions, returned to friendly lines. Before departing they noticed that Bachenheimer had continued toward German lines.

Soon there was the angry rattle of machine gun and rifle fire in the darkness to the front, followed by silence. Ted's comrades speculated if he had been killed.

A half-hour later, an outpost on the "German side" of the canal called back, "Bachenheimer's just passed us. He's got a Kraut sergeant in tow."

Brought to Colonel Williams' battalion headquarters, the enemy soldier was sullen and haughty. He boasted that he had been a sergeant with the famed *Afrika Korps* of Field Marshal Erwin Rommel, but had been "busted" for striking an officer and "demoted" to a regular infantry outfit

Williams showed the prisoner an aerial photo of the sector and demanded that the German point out troop dispositions. He refused, declaring that he was a professional soldier loyal to *Der Fuehrer* and would give only his name, rank and serial number.

Through Bachenheimer, who spoke flawless German, Colonel Williams began to taunt the prisoner. "No wonder the *Afrika Korps* got the shit kicked out of it if you are an example of their noncoms," Williams declared. "You're such a dumb son of a bitch you don't even know where your outfit is positioned!"

The German's face turned red with anger and a degree of wounded pride. Williams continued to bore in: "And you are such a poor fighter that you allowed this kid, 10 years your junior, to capture you and bring you into our lines!"

The bewildered German broke down. He pointed out his unit's dispositions on the aerial photo and gave other damaging intelligence information.

His professional honor at stake, the prisoner insisted on telling Colonel Williams how he had been captured by "the kid 10 years his junior." He said that an outpost, nervous because American paratroopers had been infiltrating almost nightly, opened fire at "a movement." The German sergeant went forward to investigate, heard a voice call out in German: "Here are the Americans, we've got them!" He walked toward the voice and an American (Bachenheimer) with a pistol pointed at his stomach instructed him to "come with me or you're dead."

On another night Bachenheimer was prowling around German lines when he spotted an enemy soldier in a slit trench. The American sat down near him and the two engaged in friendly conversation. Ted told him he was from an adjacent Wehrmacht unit. Convinced that no other German was nearby, Bachenheimer tired of his game and shoved a pistol in the startled man's stomach and ordered him to be quiet and come along with him.

A German laying quietly in a nearby hole heard the conversation, raised up and shot Bachenheimer through the left hand. Bachenheimer killed both Germans, then returned to his own lines, disappointed that his prisoner-for-the-night had eluded him via sudden death.

On the way back, Bachenheimer had stuffed dirt into his

hand wound to stem the bleeding. On reaching 1st Battalion headquarters, to which he was assigned, the young master scout was confronted by Colonel Williams who told him he would be evacuated to Naples. Bachenheimer protested strongly, declaring that the nasty-looking penetration of his hand was "only a scratch."

Williams relented and told the trooper to get his hand repaired at the regimental aid station. "But at the first sign of infection you're going to Naples!" the battalion commander stressed.

Bachenheimer never left the beachhead until his regiment was pulled out.

It was by no means a "one man war" for the 504th Parachute Infantry Regiment in the cold, dreary and miserable days along the *Canale Mussolini*. Each day paratroopers died in an unspectacular manner—by artillery or mortar fire while huddled in water-logged holes. Feet and legs were blown off when men on night patrols stepped on *Schu* mines which had been sown by infiltrating Germans. In a major probe of enemy lines, 50 troopers of the 1st Battalion were cut off, surrounded by panzers (against which they had no means to resist) and had to surrender. A large-caliber shell made a direct hit on a shed where 14 replacements sought protection from the cold and rain, blowing bits and pieces of bodies to the four winds.

At the 504th Parachute Infantry Regiment CP during this period, Colonel Tucker and his aides were looking at a translated entry found in a German officer's diary:

American parachutists—devils in baggy pants—are less than 100 meters from my outpost line. I can't sleep at night; they pop up from nowhere and we never know when or how they strike next. Seems like the black-hearted devils are everywhere . . .

PART THREE
Churchill's Stranded Whale

1

"We're Holding This Beachhead!"

Exactly one month to the day after the Anglo-American landing at Anzio, General John Lucas' head "fell in the basket," as he had earlier predicted to his diary.

General Mark Clark, a long-time friend of his VI Corps commander, on February 22 gave Lucas the expected news—he was being replaced by General Lucian Truscott, effective immediately. It was a painful task for Clark, who was quite fond of the friendly, pipe-smoking Lucas.

Almost since D-Day at Anzio, criticism of General Lucas' handling of beachhead operations had been growing steadily.

In far off London, Prime Minister Churchill, increasingly angry and frustrated over failure of his Anzio "baby" to rapidly drive the Wehrmacht north of Rome, had been relentlessly exerting pressure on Allied leaders to replace the methodical General Lucas with "a bold thruster."

Churchill's protege, General Harold Alexander, the suave commander of 15th Army Group, concluded that Lucas had become unequal to the physical demands of the Anzio stress, that he had a "harried look" and "would not be able to stand up to the hard, long struggle which . . . it was clear the Anzio operation would involve."

General Jacob Devers, American deputy to British General Jumbo Wilson at Allied Force Headquarters in the Mediterranean, had for some time been beating the drums for Johnny

Lucas' relief. Devers felt after visits to the beachhead that Lucas was "tired."

Clark, who had daily been closely involved with Lucas, was convinced that the white-haired VI Corps commander was "worn out physically and emotionally" from his arduous months of command in Italy's chamber of horrors, first in the drive to the Gustav Line and now on Anzio.

General Truscott, who was deeply anguished over replacing a good friend who had been removed from his post, had confided to a few close aides for a period of time that in his view Lucas was "exhausted."

Johnny Lucas departed the beachhead a broken and bitter man. He felt that he had performed as well as anyone had the right to expect. A secure beachhead had been established, tons of supplies were ashore, and a maximum German effort to drive him into the Tyrrhenian Sea had been thwarted in bloody fighting.

Lucas was "kicked upstairs" to the newly-created and hollow post of Deputy Fifth Army Commander.

In Truscott, Clark had the ideal man for the job. Bold, decisive and vigorous, the new VI Corps commander, unlike the unfortunate John Lucas, looked and acted like a two-fisted fighting man. At this point in the death struggle on fire-swept Anzio beachhead, that was a vital prerequisite.

Lucian Truscott had another redeeming attribute—he got along well with his British contemporaries on the bridgehead. On quiet nights, British Generals Penney and Templer had often driven to Truscott's 3rd Division CP where the three exchanged informal toasts with spirits "bootlegged" onto the beachhead, rehashed the day's fighting and discussed plans for the morrow.

On the other hand, nearly two weeks had passed since D-Day before General Lucas had visited a British headquarters, and he had admitted to his diary that "I wish I understood the British better."

During the period of the behind the scenes clamor to sack General Lucas, the rotund shadow of Winston Churchill was thought by many to be behind a move to not only replace the VI Corps commander with a British general but to bring in an entire British corps headquarters to direct operations. This proposal threatened to shake the foundations of inter-Allied solidarity. The implication was clear: not only had an American general "failed" but an entire American corps headquarters also had "failed."

In London, General Dwight Eisenhower, although he no longer held authority over the Mediterranean Theater, was deeply disturbed by the British proposal to replace Lucas and/or VI Corps with Britons. On February 18, Eisenhower had written his superior and mentor, Chief of Staff George Marshall, in Washington and expressed his alarm over the British proposal for the switch of command at Anzio.

"It is absolutely impossible in an Allied force to shift command of any unit from one nationality to another during a period of crisis," Eisenhower stressed. He suggested that the command question be thrashed out among Allied military leaders in the Mediterranean, and added that he would be willing to dispatch General Patton to Anzio to take temporary command on the beachhead.

General Marshall heartily agreed with the inadvisability of a nationality shift in corps command at Anzio. He promptly fired off a signal to General Devers at Allied Force HQ: "Let nothing stand in the way of procuring leadership (of VI Corps) of the quality necessary."

Jakie Devers, as his fellow generals called him, did not need his 30 years of military experience to discern his boss' wishes—Lucas' successor better be wearing an American uniform.

Meanwhile in London, General George Patton already had his bags packed. He was always eager for a fight and had long maintained that his destiny was to "lead men in a desperate battle." Patton had been in Eisenhower's dog house since the previous fall when it became publicly known that he had slapped a soldier in Sicily, and in the Anzio situation Patton saw a golden opportunity to redeem himself in the eyes of his superiors and the American public.

In Italy, General Clark was far from enthralled on learning of high-level discussions concerning a role at Anzio for Patton. Clark and the silver-haired, ramrod-straight armored leader had been friends since boyhood. But the Fifth Army commander, while recognizing Patton's qualities as a combat leader, may have harbored gnawing inner concerns as to his ability to establish a workable rapport with the explosive, independent-minded George Patton.

Truscott, Clark had noted, "is with me all the way."

On the same day that General Lucas' head "fell in the basket," Winston Churchill was addressing the House of Commons in London. Adolf Hitler, The Prime observed, had "decided to defend Rome with all the tenacity he had mustered at Stalingrad." The fuehrer's decision to send "something like a half-million German troops" into the south of Italy was a decision "not unwelcomed" by the Allied high command, Churchill declared.

In January the Oberkommando der Wehrmacht had intended to shift five of its crack paratrooper and panzer divisions from Italy to the English Channel coast in anticipation of the impending Anglo-American assault there, but when the Allies landed at Anzio the procedure was reversed, Churchill pointed out to the Commons.

As the entire concept of the Italian campaign had been to draw off German forces from France where they would oppose the massive operation known as Overlord, Churchill's grand strategy, he intimated, was bearing fruit. The Prime had long been the prime mover in expanded Allied operations in the Mediterranean.

With the command situation on Anzio resolved by General Truscott's appointment, Mark Clark's attention returned to the battle picture. That same day, February 22, he sent a signal to General Eisenhower in London: "The Boche has shot his wad today."

Now that the energetic, decisive Lucian Truscott was in charge, a subtle yet almost tangible wave of new hope swept through all ranks on frigid, wet and bleak Anzio beachhead. Truscott inspired confidence. Unlike Johnny Lucas, who seldom left his wine cellar command post, the new corps commander constantly strode briskly among his fighting men, an impressive figure in his lacquered helmet with two large silver stars, cavalry boots, riding breeches and leather jacket.

War correspondents met with General Truscott shortly after his appointment. Most were impressed by his honesty and forthrightness.

"No, everything here is not for the best," he declared.

"We're going to have a hell of a tough time for months to come."

The new corps commander paused briefly, thrust out his jaw, and rasped: "But we're going to hold this beachhead, come hell or high water!"

Truscott rapidly plunged into the immediate task at hand—preparing his battered defenses for the new all-out German smash he knew was bound to come.

On the other side of the line, Field Marshal Albrecht Kesselring and Fourteenth Army commander Eberhard von Mackensen were reshuffling forces and bringing up more supplies, ammunition and reinforcements. They indeed would strike again, although their professional instincts told them that the February 19 attack down the Albano-Anzio road, which missed by an eyelash of breaking through, was the Germans' high-water mark on embattled Anzio.

In their hearts, Kesselring and von Mackensen were bitter over the failure of the drive. They laid the blame at the feet of one man—Adolf Hitler. From his lofty perch in his chalet in the Bavarian Alps overlooking Berchtesgaden, the fuehrer had issued orders for the attack down to the most minute detail.

By insisting that the Wehrmacht mass its assault troops and panzers and attack down a narrow corridor (the main road to Anzio) the feldgrau was slaughtered by the firepower of hundreds of Allied artillery pieces and warships.

At his Bavarian retreat, Hitler was little concerned over the massacre inflicted on the flower of German youth on the bloody killing grounds at Anzio. He brushed off mild protests from his field commanders in Italy and demanded that a new attack be prepared—immediately.

The Anglo-Americans on the beachhead were battered, confused and reeling like a punch-drunk boxer, the fuehrer declared. He demanded that Kesselring and von Mackensen summon up the steel will power to launch one more blow for the knockout.

This time the German Fourteenth Army would employ different tactics and strike at another sector. Von Mackensen recommended to Kesselring on February 22 that the attack be launched from the Cisterna area and strike the U.S. 3rd Infantry Division at several points on a much wider front instead of massing forces as was done in the drive down the Albano-Anzio road in the just-concluded five-day battle.

Von Mackensen would employ the Hermann Goering, 26th Panzer and 362nd Divisions in the assault, with the 29th Panzer Grenadier Division held in reserve to exploit a breakthrough. Jump-off would be at dawn on February 28.

General von Mackensen promptly began shifting his forces from in front of the 45th Infantry Division to the Allied right flank in front of Iron Mike O'Daniel's 3rd Division. To mask his true intentions, the Fourteenth Army commander directed the 1st Parachute Corps along the Albano-Anzio road to make extensive night raids and create heavy vehicular movement to indicate the Germans would strike there again.

Meanwhile, Kesselring and von Mackensen were determined that the Americans and British on Anzio would get no rest, even when resting. True to their word, German artillery, including the monstrous 280-millimeter Anzio Express, pounded every portion of the beachhead day and night. There was not one minute of respite for any man or woman in VI Corps. In the front lines or at the shoreline, it didn't matter— Death was always only an instant away.

As General Truscott and his men braced for the next German onslaught, Lieutenant Colonel Warren Williams, commander of the 1st Battalion of the 504th Parachute Infantry, early one morning went to the regimental CP. On entering he saw an older gray-haired man wearing only "long johns" (full-length woolen underwear) getting up from a cot in one corner.

"Who's that old bastard?" Williams inquired of a staff officer, nodding toward the figure in the long johns.

"Oh, that's Iron Mike O'Daniel, the new commander of the 3rd Division," was the reply.

Williams, having thought the general was an Italian refugee, was thankful that he had kept his voice down.

General O'Daniel and an aide had left his headquarters in a jeep in the tar-black night to check on forward positions. They became lost and were halted by a sentry of the 504th Parachute Infantry. The alert paratrooper challenged the two men in the jeep, and neither O'Daniel or his aide knew the countersign.

The sentry was unmoved by O'Daniel's fervent explanation that he was the new commander of the 3rd Infantry Division.

At gunpoint, the general and his aide were taken to the 504th Parachute Infantry CP.

There Iron Mike O'Daniel was quickly recognized. But the general decided it would be foolhardy to wander around longer in the blackness, so decided to spend the remainder of the night in the paratroopers' CP.

Colonel Williams and his fellow parachutists could not help but feel sorry for the crestfallen aide. He should have known the password and countersign.

On the night of February 27, a 30-man patrol from the 2nd Battalion, 504th Parachute Infantry Regiment, under Lieutenant William Navas, slipped across the Mussolini Canal and headed for a group of four houses about one mile toward German positions. The patrol's mission was to seize prisoners that night and remain in the houses the following day to observe German movements.

It was 9 P.M. and the front was dark and quiet. Stealing up to the four houses, the patrol neared a wooded area. Lieutenant Navas divided the patrol into two sections, leaving one under his command and assigning the other to Sergeant Rod Rodjenski.

The parachutists had just entered the woods when a trooper set off a trip flare. It shot into the air, illuminating the area. The men froze in place, hardly daring to breath.

Ahead in the darkness Navas and his patrol heard the scurrying of feet in and around the houses. Suddenly, a frightening noise: the revving of a tank or self-propelled gun motor. Moments later, swissshhh—CRACK! A shell exploded among the paratroopers. Swissshhh—CRACK! Swissshhh—CRACK! Two more shells.

Navas led a rush toward the dark farmhouses and the flame-spitting enemy gun. Almost immediately there was another explosion under the lieutenant's feet. He had run into a minefield. He fell to the ground, writhing in agony. Several other troopers following their leader also set off mines. The remaining troopers, caught in a lethal spiderweb of explosives, clung to the ground.

One parachutist fired a rifle grenade at the tank, which promptly pulled back behind a house. Leaping to his feet, Sergeant Rodjenski called out in the darkness, "Let's go!" and rushed the house. He and his men were met by a torrent of machine gun and rifle fire.

Clearly, the cluster of houses was a heavily manned strongpoint, too formidable for a decimated patrol to capture. Rodjenski ordered the remnants of the patrol to withdraw. Reaching its own lines, the patrol was found to have had eight wounded. Lieutenant Navas and three troopers were missing.

Sergeant Rodjenski took seven men and went back to the woods in search of the four missing comrades. The little patrol located all four, who were wounded and unable to navigate. All were brought back safely.

Many patrols prowled through the eerie and black No-Man's-Land that night. Like Lieutenant Navas' patrol, they reported considerable German activity to the front of the 3rd Infantry Division.

Based on intelligence reports, General Truscott concluded that the next German offensive would not be down the Albano-Anzio road but would strike from the direction of Cisterna. Like a cunning, fast-footed boxer warding off a blow from his opponent, Truscott hurriedly transferred guns, tanks and foot soldiers to the threatened area. When von Mackensen struck, General Truscott would be ready.

On February 27, one day before the scheduled attack toward Nettuno, General von Mackensen contacted Kesselring: could the offensive be postponed one day, until the twenty-ninth? The Fourteenth Army commander explained that the rainy weather had made it impossible to get his units, particularly panzers and artillery, into position to jump off.

Kesselring had no alternative. He agreed to the 24-hour delay. Then, hopping into his staff car, the field marshal drove through torrents of rain to visit his assault troops. There Smiling Al was buoyed by the welcome he received from his frontline soldiers. They were spirited and confident. Maybe, just maybe, Kesselring thought as he drove back to Monte Soratte, the next day's attack might succeed. After all, the bad weather would make it difficult for Allied tanks to maneuver, for enemy artillery observers to see and for the powerful Anglo-American air fleet to get off the ground.

Kesselring was once again his customarily optimistic self. Still, there were nagging doubts trying to steal into his mind . . .

On February 28, indications grew that the Wehrmacht was about ready to strike the 3rd Infantry Division. The division headquarters duty officer recorded in the daily log:

"4 P.M. Call from Divarty (division artillery): Report of three enemy tanks. 'We're firing on them.'"

"5:45 P.M. Call from VI Corps: 'PW (prisoner of war) said there was quite a few tanks coming into Cisterna and the attack would come very shortly.'"

"8:07 P.M. Call from VI Corps: '77th Field Artillery (spotter plane) reports trains running in and out of Velletri. Smoke-screen laid on front and troops moving up. Personnel running around there all day.'"

At 9:30 P.M. Iron Mike O'Daniel, commanding general of the 3rd Division, felt an enemy smash was at hand. He telephoned his regimental commanders: "Be especially alert. Send out patrols."

About two hours later on the left flank of the 3rd Division, Sergeant Richard Fisco of the 509th Parachute Infantry Battalion and two comrades were lying in the pitch-black darkness some 100 yards in front of the main body of Company C. Fisco and his men were a listening post to warn of a German attack.

Suddenly the troopers in the outpost heard muffled digging sounds to the front. Fisco had heard the ominous scraping noise many times before in North Africa and southern Italy: Germans were digging in, probably machine guns or mortars.

The 509th Parachute Infantry Battalion was thinly spread between the 3rd and 45th Infantry Divisions. For seven days and nights the men of C Company, weary, hungry, bones aching, nerves on edge, had held a small knoll a mile northeast of the village of Carano. Another company of the parachute battalion was in the second line of defense and a third company was in reserve.

Holding this low hill had been a nightmare. The pressure and physical discomfort had been so intense that even the tough, veteran paratroopers could endure only a week there. Companies had to be rotated every seven days. Many men departed the hill shaking violently from their ordeal.

The low knoll was barren and under constant view of the enemy. Even at night the Germans watched by flare light. The knoll protruded out like a sore finger from the main line of resistance. The troopers there could not leave their holes or even stand or sit upright briefly to stretch stiff joints for fear of attracting a heavy mortar or artillery barrage. They were forced to lie in icy water that continually seeped into their slit trenches or foxholes and to urinate in C-ration cans and pitch out the contents after dark. Frozen rations served as sustenance.

Added to the constant shelling on the barren incline was the gut-wrenching psychological impact of being incessantly under the gaze of enemy observers on the heights to the front, knowing that one brief careless movement could be fatal.

That evening of February 28, the men of C Company were counting the minutes. After dark they were to be relieved by B Company, commanded by 23-year-old Lieutenant John R. Martin.

The relief was completed about midnight—except for one man. Lieutenant William McMasters, an assistant platoon leader of the machine gun platoon of C Company, refused to depart with his comrades to the relative "safety" of a reserve position. McMasters insisted on remaining on the hill with John Martin's company.

"I think McMasters wants to die," one of his men whispered to a comrade.

Lieutenant McMasters was something of a mystery man in the 509th Parachute Infantry. He was not even a paratrooper, but an Air Corps officer who had joined the airborne unit just before it sailed for Anzio. The popular opinion was that he had become bored with a desk job and had gone AWOL to join a fighting outfit.

As C Company pulled out, Sergeant Fisco and his men withdrew from their listening post. Stopping briefly at Lieutenant Martin's CP (a slit trench) Fisco said, "I think you're going to get hit at dawn. The Krauts have been laying smoke out in front all afternoon, and about an hour ago we heard them digging assault positions about 50 yards from our listening post."

Throwing the strap of his Tommy gun over a shoulder, Fisco added: "Well, good luck!"

2

Death of a Parachute Company

It was cold, wet and miserable at 2 A.M. on February 29 as the B Company paratroopers on the barren little knoll were pounded periodically by artillery and mortar fire. Several men in Lieutenant John Martin's reserve platoon were killed or wounded.

At 2:30 A.M. Martin was visited at his CP on the knoll by Lieutenant Peter Gaich, who had joined the battalion only a few days previously and was in the front lines for the first time. Gaich was with the reserve platoon.

"We're catching hell from the Krauts' mortar fire, and we've already lost several men tonight," the new officer told the company commander. "Is it okay if we move the platoon into those caves along the creek just behind us?"

Martin pondered the question momentarily. He knew every man might have to start fighting at any minute. Yet there was no point in letting the reserve platoon be chewed to bits by shell-fire before the German attack struck.

"Okay," Martin replied. "Go ahead. But have your guys back in position no later than 5 A.M."

At about 3:30 A.M. Martin received a call from Lieutenant Colonel Bill Yarborough, commander of the 509th Parachute Infantry:

"John, corps headquarters has just intercepted a Kraut message. They're going to hit you at around 5:30 A.M."

The battalion commander added that corps artillery would pound the Germans at 5 A.M. in an effort to break up the looming attack.

"Good luck, John," Yarborough said as he rang off.

It flashed through Lieutenant Martin's mind that he would need a lot of "luck." He had taken over the low hill a few hours before with only 97 men and several of these had already been lost to shellfire. And his company was spread thinly over a 1,200-yard front. But the order from on high was for no unit on the beachhead to give up a yard of ground, so the little band of paratroopers would have to stand and fight it out—come what may.

Promptly at 5 A.M. the dark sky behind Martin's parachutists broke out in lightning-like flashes as nearly every Allied gun on the beachhead erupted and poured shells into the German Infantrymen just as they left their positions and were advancing toward American lines. The enormous bombardment slowed but did not halt the enemy assault troops.

Now German artillery opened a thunderous barrage of their own, and shells began screaming into the knoll held by the 509th Parachute Infantry Battalion. It was against this stretched-out line of paratroopers that von Mackensen would make an all-out effort to break through.

The German barrage was so heavy that the knoll shook and quivered as though an earthquake were in progress. Thick clouds of black smoke covered the knoll, and the pungent odor of cordite fumes filled nostrils.

The Americans huddled in foxholes, mouths dry and perspiration dotting foreheads and palms. Many were praying, some out loud and others to themselves, as the crescendo of shells burst around them. Above the din could be heard piercing screams as white-hot shell fragments hacked off a paratrooper's arm or the side of his face. To the 509th men clinging helplessly to the bottom of their damp and cold foxholes, the barrage seemed to last a lifetime.

Suddenly, the thunderous German bombardment lifted. The moaning and cries of seriously wounded paratroopers was drowned out by the menacing roar of enemy tank motors to the front. Peering over the rims of their holes, the dazed parachutists who survived the savage barrage viewed a frightening scene in the dimness of a gathering dawn. Rumbling toward the low knoll over the bleak flatlands was a swarm of German panzers and hundreds of enemy infantrymen—all heading toward the little knoll.

From his foxhole CP, Lieutenant Martin put in an urgent radio call for artillery fire to his front. But there were more German voices on his frequency than there were American, so his desperate appeal for help was never understood.

Onward came the German attackers. When less than 100 yards from the thin line of American paratroopers, the enemy grenadiers broke into a trot, shouting oaths and battle cries, firing rifles and Schmeisser machine pistols into Martin's men. The parachutists returned the fire at the onrushing Germans, and enemy bodies began piling up at the mouths of American machine guns. Still the mass of gray-green figures surged forward.

Now the enemy infantrymen charged into the line of paratroopers' foxholes, and at point-blank range raked the Americans with machine pistols and showered them with grenades. Outnumbered four to one, the B Company men fired their Tommy guns and rifles until they were empty, then hurled the weapons at Germans leaping toward their holes. Paratroopers whipped out trench knives and grappled with their adversaries in bloody face-to-face death struggles. Some of Martin's men grabbed their rifles by the barrels, swung the weapons as clubs. Others used fists.

In the semi-darkness, confusion reigned as bodies thrashed about and grenades exploded at random. It was impossible to tell friend from foe. One band of Germans pounced on Lieutenant Martin and his staff, who were furiously firing rifles and Tommy guns at oncoming silhouettes. Sergeant George Fontenesi emptied his rifle clip, then clobbered a lunging German with the butt of the weapon. Corporal J.R. Cross, Martin's radio operator, was struck in the chest by an exploding grenade and collapsed in a bloody heap. His radio was shredded, ending any hope for communications with the rear.

The overwhelming German force swept on past the knoll, and for a few minutes an eerie calm hovered over the scene of the carnage. Only an occasional cry from a mutilated American or German pierced the tranquility. A few of the B Company men who had survived the onslaught began to withdraw down a creek bed. They were confronted by a furious Lieutenant

John Martin. "Get the goddamned hell back up there and fight the bastards!" he roared. The confused men returned to their holes among the scores of dead and dying.

Minutes later a second wave of Germans, singing and shouting curses in broken English, charged up the gentle slope of the knoll through shell-torn barbed wire and pounced on the few remaining paratroopers of Company B. Again a nose-to-nose fight erupted. Bodies locked together thrashed about on the muddy terrain. There were grunts as trench knives plunged into fragile flesh. Curses and screams rang out. Grenades exploded. Rifles cracked.

A force of about 30 Germans pounced on Lieutenant Martin and a few of his staff and another savage melee erupted. The tiny command group was forced back into a creek bed where they were showered with grenades. Firing his rifle at the figures in the gray-green overcoats, Martin felt a searing pain rush through his body as a grenade exploded next to him. He lost consciousness.

An indeterminate amount of time later, the company commander regained his senses. He was vaguely aware that a comrade, also wounded, was dragging him out of the water and onto the bank. Martin's jump-suit was saturated with blood. Minutes later a German force approached and took the lieutenant and several of his wounded men prisoner.

Shortly after dawn that morning, Lieutenant Bernard Berman of A Company of the 509th Parachute Infantry was drinking hot coffee in his platoon's CP, a battered farmhouse with only one crumbling room still standing. Berman had been up all night in a shed across from the CP watching the front. The shed was filled with farm equipment, and Berman's view was through the spokes of a large wagon wheel. The wheel reminded him of cowboy films he had seen back home as a boy.

Berman had come to Anzio only a few days before as a replacement officer with the 509th Parachute Infantry. Some 12 hours before the massive German smash against the paratroop positions, the new officer had been sent forward to join A Company in the second line of defense. Just as Berman approached a hole to take over for another lieutenant, a salvo of shells screamed into the position. Berman flopped to the ground.

When the smoke cleared, Berman saw that the officer he was going to replace in the shallow hole had received a direct hit. Only bits and pieces remained. It was a grisly baptism of fire for the new man.

Already he agreed with the cynical view voiced a few hours before by a seasoned parachute officer: "Berman, you picked a hell of a time to get your feet wet!"

Now as Berman was sipping coffee on the twenty-ninth, he heard a fear-tinged voice call out, "Lieutenant Berman! Lieutenant Berman!" The officer dashed outside and saw a B Company man staggering toward him. Being new to the battalion, Berman was puzzled as to how a trooper from another company knew his name.

The distraught man was covered with mud, and his uniform was crimson-stained. He was without rifle and helmet. His legs wobbled as he moved.

"B Company's been overrun!" the man blurted. "They're all dead! . . . The Krauts came out of the smoke . . . Hundreds of them . . . They jumped all over us . . . We didn't have a chance . . ."

Berman dashed across the road to the shed observation post. Through his field glasses he gazed across the flatlands to the little knoll and could see green-gray clad figures milling around, taking a handful of American paratroopers prisoner.

Berman hurriedly called the battalion commander, Colonel Yarborough, and told him "B Company's apparently been wiped out." He then relayed the circumstances as he knew them from the survivor who had staggered into his CP and what he had viewed through his field glasses.

"Get ready," Yarborough replied, "They'll be after you next!"

Indeed the Germans would be "after" A Company next. Having broken through Lieutenant John Martin's company by sheer weight of numbers and concentrated firepower, the 1st Battalion, 1028th Panzer Grenadier Regiment, which led the assault, swung southwest across open fields toward the west branch of the Mussolini Canal—and hopefully a clean breakthrough toward Nettuno and the sea.

With the scent of victory in their nostrils, the enemy grenadiers were closing in on the paratroopers of A Company who were in water-logged slit trenches along a road below the village of Carano and some 600 yards to the rear of the little knoll.

Lying in freezing water in his shallow hole, Lieutenant Dan A. DeLeo peered out across the fields and was astonished by what he saw. The oncoming Germans were in battalion formation as though on parade.

"Get that goddamned Kraut antiaircraft gun ready to fire!" DeLeo called out.

In a previous action DeLeo's company had captured the high-velocity weapon and a large supply of ammunition. Now the gun was going to be turned against the Germans.

"All set!" called out Sergeant Nicholas DeGaeta, one of those manning the gun.

At 7:35 A.M. Colonel Yarborough tried to get a call through requesting fighter-bomber support to slow down the rampaging German force. His line to the rear had been cut by shellfire.

The 7th Infantry Regiment on the right of the beleaguered paratroopers sent a platoon of tanks to help out. The Shermans became bogged down in the muddy fields.

It was left to the artillery, the mortars and the 96 men of Lieutenant DeLeo's A Company to halt the German breakthrough.

From his observation post in the shed full of farm equipment, Lieutenant Bernie Berman of A Company peered through his binoculars and saw the parade-ground formation of feldgrau heading his way across the flatlands. He went along his platoon's row of slit trenches and told his men, "Don't shoot 'til you see the white of the bastards' eyes!"

The parachute battalion's commander, Colonel Yarborough, had gained contact with the artillery fire control center, and now hundreds of shells started falling on the German battalion advancing across the open fields. The paratroopers' 81-millimeter mortar platoon and several 60-millimeter mortars plastered the enemy force with telling effect. Gaps were torn in the gray-green skirmish line. But on they came.

Now the Germans were so close the parachute mortarmen ceased firing and reached for their rifles. All along the thin line of A Company a withering blast of machine gun and rifle fire erupted, sweeping the closely-packed ranks of feldgrau.

The thump-thump-thump of the captured enemy antiaircraft gun rang out over the din of battle. Each time the paratroopers fired the weapon a wide swath of shoulder-to-shoulder Germans toppled over. The sight reminded Lieutenant DeLeo, in his ice water-filled slit trench, of some huge supernatural force wielding a giant scythe on the advancing enemy formation.

Only 100 yards short of the 509th Parachute Infantry Battalion's second line of defense, the assault wave slowed, halted, then scrambled for the relative safety of ravines and irrigation ditches. Sprawled out in grotesque contortions of death and mutilation were scores of German grenadiers. It had been but a short time before that many of these had been singing loud battle songs as they stormed Lieutenant John Martin's outmanned and outgunned paratroopers on the knoll.

Pounded by mortars and artillery, ranks riddled by machine gun and rifle fire, the Germans began to withdraw. That afternoon the 2nd Battalion, 30th Infantry Regiment, and a platoon from C Company, 509th Parachute Infantry, launched a counterattack which drove the depleted assault force of the 1028th Panzer Grenadier Regiment back past the little knoll where Lieutenant Martin's paratroopers had made their stand that morning—literally to the last man.

It was about 2 P.M. that day when a badly wounded John Martin was lying along a railroad embankment some 1,300 yards in front of American lines. He had been hit twice in the nose-to-nose fight with German grenadiers, then after his capture and before he could be moved from the knoll he was wounded again—this time by "friendly" artillery fire. American observers knew that B Company had been wiped out and were pounding Germans on the knoll.

Although wounded in the foot and two other places, Martin had walked all the way to the German lines at the embankment, assisted by two of his lesser injured men. In his hazy condition from shock and loss of blood, the B Company commander was only vaguely aware that 16 of his captured men were with him, including Lieutenant Gaich and Steve Hannon who had joined the parachute battalion only a few days previously and were involved in their first combat.

Meanwhile, at the 509th Parachute Infantry Battalion aid station, alarming word was received: B Company had taken heavy casualties on the knoll.

"I'm going up to John Martin's company," Captain Carlos Alden, the battalion surgeon hurriedly remarked to his assistant doctor, Captain Harry Stone. "They've had the hell kicked out of them it appears, and they'll need some help, if we can reach them."

As he grabbed his Tommy gun, stuffed grenades in his bulky jump-suit pockets, and headed for the door, Alden added, "That is if Martin's wounded are not behind Kraut lines by now."

Taking several medics with him, the parachute surgeon raced for the site of that day's bloody disaster for the paratroopers. The scene of American carnage on the knoll was the worst Alden had viewed during his heavy combat experience.

Several of the parachutists, still in their holes, had had their heads blown off during the thunderous enemy artillery barrage. Many other dead were strewn about the premises where they had been fighting hand-to-hand with swarms of Germans. Still other paratroopers had arms and legs blown off and were barely alive. Others had been bayoneted in their holes. Some were gasping for breath with bullet holes through their lungs.

A shell fragment had sliced the face off one trooper, leaving the front of his head a ghastly mask of blood and tissue. One B Company man lay dead with two stumps for legs. He apparently had tried to continue the fight in that condition, as two trails of blood, one from each leg stump, led toward the attackers.

The grisly scene brought tears to Doc Alden's eyes, a combination of pride for what these comrades had achieved and heart-gnawing grief over the disaster that befell them.

"They never gave a goddamned inch!" the paratrooper surgeon muttered to one of his medics.

Captain Alden began to work feverishly among the seriously wounded, who had been lying there in excruciating agony for hours as the savage fight ebbed to and fro around and over them. Alden had known most of these dead and wounded and loved them all, but he had to read identification tags around the necks of many to know who they were—particularly those whose heads had been blown off—so mutilated were the bodies.

All that day, Doc Alden's aid station, as with others along the 3rd Infantry Division sector, had been overflowing with patients. Wounded paratroopers of the 509th had been brought in on stretchers, their jump-suits bloody, wet and caked with mud. They were ashen-faced and wearing that haunted look of men who had just escaped the Black Angel of Death.

Most of the wounded were shivering and shuddering from the cold February weather and the debilitating effects of their ghastly wounds. Hasty emergency bandages, applied by medics under fire in the front lines and once immaculately white, were stained with blood and dirty-brown wet earth.

Many were unconscious when carried in, mainly those with head wounds, and only their heavy snoring and deep, struggled breathing identified them from the corpses. Others arrived dying in the care of medics, there being no hope for them except to possibly ease the intense pain of their last few minutes on earth.

Still others were carried in, uttering not a sound but staring fixedly into space. These were the ones with intestines hanging out, whose unbearable pain had been diminished by morphine shots but were in deep shock.

Some were carried in hacking and coughing, spitting up blood and gasping for breath. They had been shot or bayoneted through the lungs.

Late that night, the exhausted surgeon of the 509th Parachute Infantry, Doc Alden, had finished patching up his final patient, as the front had quieted. He took out his weather-beaten pocket diary and scribbled:

It has been the saddest day ever for me. A gruesome day. We brought out bits and pieces of bodies all afternoon and evening. Our men were outnumbered, pinned down by artillery, assaulted by infantry, then tanks. But our guys *stopped the German attack!*

3

Bad News for the Fuehrer

While the main weight of the German effort to break through to Nettuno fell on the 509th Parachute Infantry Battalion, General von Mackensen hurled spirited attacks at other points along the defensive sector of the 3rd Infantry Division and its attached units.

To the right of the paratroopers, German grenadiers, shouting battle cries, stormed the positions of I Company, 30th Infantry Regiment. The feldgrau became entangled in barbed wire rolls just to the front of the Americans. The defenders opened fire on the Germans in the wire, killed an officer and several others. Twenty-one of the attackers surrendered.

A short time later the Germans hit I Company again. It was a repeat performance. The assault force became caught in the barbed wire, many were cut down by machine gun fire at nearly point-blank range and 18 survivors threw up their hands.

Sergeant William Bolich of the 751st Tank Battalion was standing in the turret of his Sherman, concealed in a crumbling farmhouse, when German infantry and panzers advanced against L Company, 30th Infantry. An enemy shell struck the house and Bolich was stunned when struck a heavy blow in the back by a large piece of concrete. Another chunk of masonry damaged the elevating mechanism of his Sherman's 75-millimeter gun so that the muzzle could not be sited.

Despite his intense pain, Sergeant Bolich pulled himself out of the turret, propped up the gun barrel with timbers and chunks of concrete to permit the gunners to fire. The impromptu action was taken just in time. Three Mark IV tanks rumbled into view in support of attacking German infantry. The makeshift firing arrangement worked. The three panzers were knocked out by Sergeant Bolich's gun and the assault was broken up.

On the right flank of the 3rd Infantry Division sector Kampfgruppe (battle group) Schindler, composed of bits and pieces of the 715th Infantry and Hermann Goering Panzer Divisions, attacked to gain a bridgehead across the Mussolini Canal. Many of the assaulting kampfgruppe were young boys under fire for the first time.

General Bob Frederick's enterprising men of the Special Service Force crossed to the German side of the canal before the assault reached their positions and laid a trap for the oncoming enemy. When the inexperienced German force walked into the trap, the American-Canadian soldiers opened fire and the enemy grenadiers scrambled for a nearby cluster of houses.

Artillery was called in and when the houses were heavily shelled the confused Germans scattered. Many were cut down by the Forcemen and four German officers and 107 men were captured.

Early that morning, Private First Class John B. Silva, his machine gun crew and 12 riflemen were tensely watching the front from their position in a battered house in the tiny village of Ponte Rotto, so insignificant that it was not even posted on maps. Control of the hamlet was essential to operations in the sector, and Lieutenant Colonel Jack Toffey, commander of the 2nd Battalion, 15th Infantry Regiment, ordered Silva and the others to "hold at all costs."

Through the haze and mist of the cold winter morning, Silva and the others looked across the flat fields to see a German force of about 100 men advancing toward their house. Silva waited until the feldgrau were within 50 yards, then opened fire, cutting down many Germans and causing others to scramble for cover.

Two enemy machine guns peppered the barricaded window which Silva was using for a machine gun position. Germans rushed to within a few yards of the house and tossed potato-masher grenades. Silva kept firing and the enemy force pulled back.

Two hours later the little knot of Americans in the house saw a Mark VI tank rumble into an irrigation ditch only 100 yards away. The tank fired several rounds with its 88-millimeter gun at point-blank range, and the house tumbled down on Silva and his companions in a shower of timber, rock and masonry.

Still at his gun but half-buried by rubble and suffering from cuts and bruises, Private Silva dug himself free, then frantically began removing debris which had covered his automatic weapon. Swiftly he began cleaning and checking the weapon as German grenadiers, believing the gun had knocked out the position, advanced steadily toward Silva's house.

The machine gunner dragged his weapon to the corner of what had been the house and in a mass of rubble set up the gun. He began raking the attacking force which again scattered.

Soon Silva ran out of ammunition. But he dashed back into the rubble of the house and located four boxes of bullets, returned to his weapon and resumed firing.

Throughout the day the young machine gunner continued to fire his weapon as the enemy force sought desperately to seize the house. At dusk he exhausted his communication for the second time, but grabbed a carbine and resumed firing.

After dark a force slipped up to Silva's position to relieve him. For 13 hours he had held off repeated German efforts to dislodge him. Some 30 Germans were sprawled in death in the flat fields to the front of his machine gun.

When the Germans struck that day, Private First Class Frederick Vance, a BAR (Browning automatic rifle) man and his gunner, Private First Class Eugene Procaccini, were manning an outpost of Company I, 30th Infantry Regiment. In the face of the German onslaught Vance and Procaccini refused to budge.

The Germans pounded the outpost with artillery and mortar fire, then about 60 enemy grenadiers charged forward in short rushes, reaching within 20 yards of Vance and Procaccini.

A short time later, Staff Sergeant William C. Beeson, at the main line of resistance some 100 yards to the rear of the outpost, spotted Vance wriggling along on his stomach at as fast a pace as that mode of movement would allow. Enemy mortar shells were exploding about the crawling man as he headed toward Beeson. Vance was without a rifle. He had left it at the outpost for Procaccini to ward off the attackers, as the pair had exhausted their BAR ammunition.

Captain Maurice Rothseid, commander of Company I, told Vance that "you have done your job, it's time to abandon the outpost."

Vance turned a deaf ear to the order of his company commander and continued to stuff two sandbags with BAR ammunition. He picked up a BAR from a dead comrade and started crawling back to the outpost. Halfway to the BAR position, a German machine gun on the flank raked Vance with a long burst, two of the bullets ripping through the pack on his back.

Vance aimed his weapon at the enemy gunners, who were some 70 yards away, and squeezed off a burst, killing both Germans. He resumed his arduous crawl until he reached his comrade.

Meanwhile, Procaccini had been holding off the enemy force with fire from Vance's rifle, defying enemy efforts to kill him.

Now, with a pair of Browning automatic rifles and adequate ammunition, Vance and Procaccini became a major menace to the ambitions of the assaulting force. The two stubborn Americans were raking Germans on their flank who were attacking the main body of Company I, causing the confused grenadiers to halt their advance and take cover.

In the meantime, the Germans moved a high-velocity self-propelled gun into place. A round hit the besieged outpost, killing Fred Vance and Gene Procaccini instantly. Eighteen dead Germans dotted the marshy field to their front, four of them sprawled within 10 feet of the emplacement.

Murky skies and heavy squalls of rain had grounded the Allied air forces that morning. But in the afternoon the weather cleared for brief periods and 247 fighter-bombers and 24 medium bombers knifed in over the killing grounds to bomb and strafe German infantry, panzers and assembly areas.

The barrels of 1,200 Allied guns, most aimed toward the 3rd Infantry Division sector, were kept white-hot all day as tens of thousands of shells rained down on the attacking Wehrmacht.

On the ground, the fighting men of Iron Mike O'Daniel's 3rd Division and attached units had suffered heavy losses, but except for a dent here and there in the lines had hardly budged from their defensive positions. Out of the barren, flat fields as dusk began to gather hundreds of feldgrau lay mute in death. About 25 German tanks were strewn about, now only burned, twisted wreckage.

During the following day, General von Mackensen continued to funnel in foot soldiers and armor against the 3rd Division. But ranks sapped by horrendous casualties, disorganized and dispirited, the enemy attacks lacked the power of those of the day before.

The one thing von Mackensen and his exhausted feldgrau around the beachhead did not want to occur took place on March 2—the skies cleared. Early that morning fighting men locked in a death struggle down below heard the familiar humming sound of massive formations of Allied aircraft approaching. Soon the hum turned into a roar which echoed across the marshy flatlands and up the heights inland from the shoreline.

Allied airplanes were out in force to administer the *coup de grâce* to the battered Wehrmacht. Flying majestically in precise formation, the early morning rays of the sun glinting off wings and fuselage, 241 Liberators and 100 Flying Fortresses opened bomb-bay doors and rained thousands of bombs on German infantry, tanks and gun positions.

Then 113 graceful, twin-beamed Lightning and 63 Thunderbird fighter-bombers swept over and saturated with fragmentation bombs the areas around Cisterna, Velletri and Carroceto. Next swarms of medium bombers pounded positions just behind the German front lines.

It was an awesome display of Allied airpower which buoyed the spirits of hard-pressed and battle-weary Tommies and dogfaces, and at the same time drained the slight remaining residue of German morale and willpower. Even the most fanatic feldgrau on the beachhead knew that it would no longer be possible to drive the Allies into the sea.

Yet the following day, March 3, General von Mackensen, sensing Adolf Hitler peering over his shoulder from his far-off retreat at Berchtesgaden, ordered his depleted and exhausted forces to strike once more. The big guns roared on each side and several savage fights broke out along the 3rd Infantry Division sector. All the local assaults were repulsed.

The steam had been taken out of the German juggernaut which had rolled forward four days before with high hopes for smashing through the 3rd Infantry Division and reaching the sea at Nettuno.

At a conference that same day, Kesselring and von Mackensen arrived at a painful but obviously necessary decision: plans would be abandoned, at least for the time being, for further major offensives at Anzio.

The third all-out assault to wipe out the beachhead ended in costly failure for the Germans. In five days of heavy fighting the Wehrmacht suffered in excess of 3,500 battle casualties and the loss of large amounts of equipment. Minor penetrations made in 3rd Infantry Division lines were wiped out by counterattacks.

But on the other side of the line, American and British fighting men had also reached the point of exhaustion after six weeks of savage fighting while under almost incessant shelling and air bombardment. A heavy toll had been taken in 3rd Division ranks. The 45th Infantry Division was still licking its wounds after the terrible pounding it had taken in mid-February to halt the do-or-die German drive down the Albano road.

In the British sector on the left flank of the beachhead, the 56th Division was strengthened on March 2 with the arrival of 660 fighting men of the elite Royal Marine Commandos. But the 56th Division was weak from the battering it had absorbed, and the 5th Division was en route to Anzio to relieve it.

Now it was clear not only to Kesselring and von Mackensen but to Fifth Army commander Mark Clark and 15th Army Group commander Harold Alexander that one side was as exhausted as the other and incapable of further offensive action—perhaps for weeks to come.

With the six-week battle of attrition on Anzio ending with both sides laying back and panting like a foxhound at the end of an all-day chase, Kesselring had inherited a monumental problem which defied logical solution: who would tell the supreme warlord of the Third Reich, Adolf Hitler, that the offensive which he had personally ordered had crumbled?

Whoever would be the unfortunate individual saddled with that unpleasant chore, his task would be made doubly difficult: he would also have to inform the fuehrer that his Fourteenth

Army at Anzio now lacked both the strength and the spirit to strike again.

The wily Kesselring knew that Hitler had for a period of time been living in a dream world of his own in the lofty environs of Berchtesgaden, conjuring up fanciful plans as to how his "secret weapons" and his own scintillating generalship would turn the tide against the Western Allies and at the same time crush the Russian "barbarians." Now any mention of the true situation at Anzio would evoke a towering explosion from the fuehrer.

Kesselring was aware that written reports from the battle-fronts had been simply brushed off by Hitler. What was needed was someone to inform the German warlord face to face of conditions along the flaming beachhead south of Rome. Chosen for the hazardous mission was Kesselring's young and capable chief of staff, General Siegfried Westphal.

Leaving at once for Berchtesgaden after being carefully briefed by Kesselring on what to tell the fuehrer, Westphal arrived at the Bavarian retreat on March 5, one day after heavy fighting had died down on Anzio. He first called on General Alfred Jodl, chief of the operations staff of the Oberkommando der Wehrmacht, who for more than four years had been constantly at Hitler's elbow—and ear.

A nervous Jodl, one of the fuehrer's most trusted confidants, knew that an explosion was about to erupt. He firmly cautioned Westphal to stay out of Hitler's presence until Jodl had had the opportunity to pave the way for the catastrophic news being carried by Kesselring's emissary. As he waited, General Westphal's thoughts turned to the ancient days of the Roman empire when innocent messengers carrying bad news to an emperor were summarily beheaded. Could this be repeated in the twentieth century?

Jodl long had been the one selected by fellow generals to bear bad tidings to the fuehrer. The operations chief possessed a gift for eliciting a lesser outburst from Hitler on these occasions.

As expected, on hearing of the Wehrmacht failure at Anzio, Hitler broke into a towering rage, spluttering, turning purple with anger. Even Jodl's customary soothing approach failed. "Where is the man who is slandering my troops?" he shouted at Jodl. The fuehrer refused to believe that the offensive he had ordered had fallen short—far short—of its objective. Therefore whoever made that statement had to be a liar bent on disparaging his valorous feldgrau.

Hitler in his wrath issued an order of a type never made at any other time during the war: 20 average German soldiers from the front lines in Anzio were to be flown to Berchtesgaden immediately to be questioned by him as to the true conditions on the battlefront.

On the following day, "the man who had slandered" the fuehrer's troops, General Westphal, was ushered into Hitler's office. Unlike some generals who quaked in the presence of the Third Reich dictator, Westphal for two hours explained to a sullen Hitler that there was no longer the possibility of driving the Anglo-Americans into the sea at Anzio.

Perhaps conditioned to accept the Wehrmacht's failure at the beachhead by his interviews with the 20 feldgrau who had been battered by artillery and from the air for weeks, the fuehrer slowly began to realize that what General Westphal was saying was true. Before Westphal departed, Hitler even summed up praise for the "valor" of Fourteenth Army at Anzio. Still, the fuehrer was deeply disappointed.

As an emotionally relieved Westphal prepared to return to Italy, he was approached by Field Marshal Wilhelm Keitel, who along with Jodl was the fuehrer's most trusted aide. "You are lucky," the aloof, stiff Keitel told Westphal. "If we idiots here (at Berchtesgaden) had said half as much to him, he would have had us hanged."

Adolf Hitler was not the only strategic leader disillusioned with the turn of events at embattled Anzio. In London, Winston Churchill early in March was grumbling over what he considered timidity by Allied generals to fully exploit the marvelous opportunity presented to them through The Prime's brainchild, Anzio.

He had grown sarcastic. How many vehicles did the Anglo-Americans have at Anzio? Just over 18,000 was the reply of General Jumbo Wilson, the Mediterranean commander. "We must have a great superiority in chauffeurs," Churchill noted.

The Prime in recent days had also found it necessary to lecture his protege, 15th Army Group commander General Alexander. "I have a feeling that you may have hesitated to assert your authority because you were dealing so largely with

Americans," he wrote ". . . You are however quite entitled to give them orders."

Deep concern over Churchill's Great White Whale of Anzio stretched to the far corners of the Allied world. An alarmed Field Marshal Jan Christian Smuts, the highly regarded South African statesman, had written the British prime minister to determine if reports were accurate: "(I understand) an isolated pocket has now been created . . . which is itself besieged instead of giving relief to the pressure against us in the south."

Churchill replied that "in all his talks with me General Alexander envisaged the essence of the battle was the seizure of the Alban Hills with the utmost speed . . ." Toward this goal, The Prime continued, "I was able to obtain from the United States their 504th Parachute Regiment, although at the time it was under orders to return (to England) for Overlord."

He concluded his lengthy explanation with the obvious: "The whole operation (has become) stagnant."

Far from London, American and Allied soldiers at Anzio came to regard their inhospitable and perilous isolation on a bleak strip of Italian real estate as detached from the rest of the world. Most forgot that they were a part of Fifth Army, which had been butting its bloodied head against Gustav Line to break through and rescue the stranded VI Corps on the beachhead. Men on Anzio, fighting desperately for their lives, had been only vaguely aware that an ancient building known as the Abbey of Monte Cassino had been pulverized by Allied bombers and that Americans had suffered heavy casualties trying to force a crossing over a river known as the Rapido. These events took place in the "outside world."

Now, early in March, Anzio took on a new complexion, a throwback to the bloody, muddy static trench warfare of World War I at Ypres, the Somme, Passchendaele and Verdun.

4

A Strange Kind of Lull

As the ensuing days and weeks passed at Anzio, war weariness settled in on both sides. Like two gigantic prehistoric monsters, bleeding, exhausted and gasping for breath after a savage fight in which there was no winner, both Allied and German forces spent their time licking hideous wounds and digging in for an extended stay. Tens of thousands of fighting men on each side were forced into static warfare.

There would still be deaths from shelling and small, sharp clashes, mainly by patrols, along the 21-mile perimeter, but the stalemate resulted in a unique atmosphere and way of living for American and British troops. Nearly 100,000 Allied fighting men, plus some 200 nurses at evacuation hospitals along the shoreline, in addition to their supplies, vehicles and equipment, were confined on a tiny "island" stretching out in each direction from the peacetime summer resort of Anzio.

The static battle lines extended from the Moletta River in the British sector on the left flank in a huge arc around to the eastern embankments of the Mussolini Canal on the right, a distance of 16 miles along the shoreline. But forward positions along the Albano-Anzio road were only seven miles from the sea, and in the U.S. 3rd Infantry Division sector in front of Cisterna it was only nine miles to the water line. These were the extreme distances. Most of the bridgehead lay within three to four miles from German artillery positions.

221

Perched comfortably on the surrounding heights, enemy observers with high-grade binoculars and artillery range-finders were able to view nearly every foot of ground, and an American or British soldier could hardly make a move without a shell being fired at him. It became a way of life—and death—for Allied soldiers penned up on the beachhead.

Some days it was worse in the front lines, other days the danger was more acute at the harbor. Wounded lying on cots in tented evacuation hospitals received clusters to their Purple Hearts when they were hit again by fragments from German shells or bombs. Nurses received Purple Hearts right along with patients.

Living underground was the norm, from General Truscott to infantrymen on forward outposts, to military policemen directing traffic near the Anzio docks, the nurses tending to patients. Elaborate dugouts were constructed in the sandy soil. Overhead were placed timber, boards or doors, on top of which were shoveled several feet of dirt. Only a direct hit could kill the occupants.

Curiously, headlights and batteries began to disappear from the thousands of Allied jeeps and trucks on the beachhead, only to mysteriously reappear as reading lamps in scores of dugouts. A paratrooper in the 504th Parachute Infantry explained the presence of headlights and batteries in his underground chamber: "It was dark when I spotted this GI truck. How did I know it was brand new? I could have sworn it had been knocked out by gunfire. So I borrowed the headlights and battery to save the army the cost of hauling them away."

Gasoline cans were utilized in the dugouts as stoves, and the brass artillery shell casings served as stove pipes. The heavy cardboard containers for shells were converted into excellent wall coverings to help keep out the wetness and cold. Ornate Italian vacation villas along the beach and other houses abandoned by their owners suddenly were without rugs which found their way to the floors of Allied dugouts.

Looking at a beautiful Oriental rug in his underground chamber, a member of the 509th Parachute Infantry Battalion told visitors: "I put it here for safekeeping. There's a lot of goddamned thieves running around the beachhead and one of them might have stolen it from that Eytie house."

As the tedious days rolled by, it began to appear to American and British fighting men that they would spend the remainder of the war—or perhaps their lifetime—on bleak Anzio beachhead. American soldiers put their unexcelled scrounging techniques to work and soon distilleries popped up at hundreds of spots. These consisted of gasoline cans and tubing from wrecked airplanes, of which a good-sized number had been shot down over the beachhead. Out of these improvised apparatuses flowed a liquid concoction the men called Kickapoo Joy Juice, a phrase extracted from a popular stateside comic strip, *Lil' Abner*. Cut with grapefruit juice "liberated" from unit stores, thirsty GIs were able to get the drink down—and in most cases, keep it down.

Along the perimeter there were only shallow slit trenches in the sandy soil. To dig deeper would invite a torrent of water rushing into the hole. Even though shallow, most of these trenches filled with water anyhow and, as it was dangerous to move out of the excavations in daylight, the riflemen on the line had to exist in cold weather with their feet almost always wet. This constant dampness resulted in hundreds of cases of trench foot which usually resulted in evacuation of the victim, depriving his commander of a trained soldier in a situation where each man was sorely needed.

In an effort to hold down the incidence of trench foot, a painful swelling and discoloration of the member, dry socks arrived daily in the front lines. But an infantryman would put on a pair of dry socks and in minutes his feet would again be wet.

There were only four ways for American and British soldiers to get out of the hell-hole known as Anzio—by being killed, wounded or captured or by trench foot. The latter served as a means for eluding the first three. Allied surgeons and medics on the beachhead had to be alerted that some soldiers were seeking escape by claiming to have trench foot. A simple test determined the issue. A man's foot was placed in hot water. If the member swelled up, he did indeed have trench foot. Otherwise the soldier was promptly dispatched back to his duty post.

Suspects did not always prove to be malingerers. Lieutenant Kenneth Shaker, a platoon leader in the 509th Parachute Infantry Battalion, had spent several days in an exposed frontline position with his feet in constant pain, although they did not display the customary symptoms of swelling and discoloration. Finally he could endure it no longer, so he caught a ride to his battalion aid station for treatment.

Shaker had been involved in extensive fighting in North Africa and in southern Italy and was regarded by comrades as one of the most fearless among them. But on entering the tent which served as an aid station Captain Harry Stone, who had just joined the outfit as assistant surgeon, suspected Shaker of being a malingerer. The lieutenant had been in such an exposed outpost that he was not wearing insignia, and Captain Stone had not been around long enough to recognize many members of the battalion. He did not know that Shaker was an officer.

"Give him the test!" a suspicious surgeon barked to a medic.

Lieutenant Shaker's feet were plunged into hot water—and promptly mushroomed in size. He was tagged for treatment, no longer under a cloud of suspicion.

As the cold, damp, tedious days of March inexorably crawled forward on a beachhead crammed with humanity, with men living like moles and always in danger of sudden death from an isolated shell or a sniper's bullet, American and British soldiers became victims of extreme nervous tension. The human constitution could absorb only a certain amount of relentless punishment, then shattered nerves and taut minds would snap. Nervous tension symptoms abounded. Americans joked of "Anzio Anxiety" and "Nettuno Neurosis," but their laughs were hollow. Each knew he could be the next to crack.

They joked about being afflicted with the "Anzio Crouch" whereby a soldier, always aware that the Germans on the heights were watching his every move and that a shell could blast him into powder at any second, constantly walked in a slightly stooped manner, subconsciously presenting a smaller target.

The men wisecracked about these conditions, but for many they were only too real. A large number of soldiers had to be evacuated to Naples due to extreme nervous tension. Some under the relentless pressure had taken total leave of their senses and had to be strapped to stretchers.

American fighting men coined another succinct name for those who were not stricken so severely by endless days and nights in the Devil's Cauldron of Anzio—"The Shakes."

"Old Joe's come down with the goddamned shakes!" a

soldier would remark to a comrade. Ordinarily a day or two of "rest" at an aid station, out of the rain and with some warm food to eat, would be sufficient to return to duty a soldier inflicted with The Shakes.

Men died hourly on both sides of the lines. But the urgent sense of desperation which had almost tangibly blanketed the beachhead for weeks had vanished into thin air. An almost eerie mode of living (or existing) replaced it.

A Catholic chaplain in the First Special Service Force (some said he was as tough as the fighting men) held Sunday Mass from a portable altar positioned on the banks of the Mussolini Canal. Each time he announced to his kneeling "congregation" that in the event of a sudden enemy artillery barrage he could be reached for spiritual consultation in the nearest foxhole.

A soldier in Iron Mike O'Daniel's 3rd Infantry Division fought an extended bout with a quantity of Kickapoo Joy Juice—and came out second best. Putting on a black civilian top hat and jauntily swinging a cane on one arm, he staggered across No-Man's-Land and into the arms of German grenadiers manning an outpost line. These particular Germans were among those caught up in the certain benign spirit which had infected both sides due to the greatly reduced casualty rate in the stalemate. After talking casually with the American for an hour, the enemy grenadiers turned him around and, with top hat still in place, sent him reeling back to American lines.

The 3rd Infantry Division set up a "rest camp" some five miles to the rear of the front lines. A company at a time was brought to the camp, with only the occasional interruption of a salvo of artillery shells marring the relaxation of the war-weary combat soldiers. Despite the blackout, an outdoor movie theater was set up and troops sat on the ground and K-ration boxes to gaze—and hoot—as the handsome Hollywood matinee idol wooed and won his fair lady.

American and British combat surgeons, with fewer casualties to treat, found time to visit farmhouses to deliver Italian babies. Many of the new offspring would be named after the delivering doctor by grateful parents.

Beachhead meals showed marked improvement during the lull, as succulent steaks often were available to Allied soldiers who had existed for weeks primarily on cold K-rations. Although there was a standing Fifth Army order against shooting cows, many of the bovines appeared to be suicide-prone and would stick their heads in front of a dogface's or Tommie's rifle just as he was shooting at an enemy soldier. Obviously, the unfortunate cow was no good to anyone due to its fatal accident, so why not hustle its carcass back to the unit cook?

When it became obvious that the German Fourteenth Army would be incapable of large-scale offensive action for some weeks to come, 10 percent of Allied personnel were allowed to go by LST to Naples on a three-day pass. Strolling the streets of the Sin Capital of Italy (as the GIs called it), some fighting men of Anzio, mud-caked and with uniforms torn, were arrested by nattily-dressed military policemen and tossed in jail for "being out of proper uniform."

Hearing of his men being jailed, General Ernie Harmon on the beachhead was furious. "I'm going to leave half of the 1st Armored to fight the Germans and take the other half to go back to Naples and kick hell out of those rear area bastards there!" he thundered.

The Allied situation at Anzio developed a camaraderie never found elsewhere during the war. There was a pervasive feeling: "We're all in the same boat!" Axis Sally unwittingly contributed to this warm glow among Allies by cooing over *Radio Berlin:* "Hello, out there, boys and girls at Anzio. How does it feel to be cooped up in the world's largest self-sustaining prisoner-of-war camp?"

The one common denominator at Anzio was that there was no "rear area." Staff officers of VI Corps were killed by shells as they emerged from their underground headquarters at Nettuno. Quartermaster soldiers were cut down by artillery fire that whistled into the docks while unloading supplies. Nurses were killed and wounded while feeding blood plasma to patients or assisting in surgery. Cooks, clerks, truck drivers and stevedores, who had never been in combat, had been handed rifles and rushed to the front lines to help beat off General von Mackensen's all-out offensives.

It soon became known to front-line fighters that the areas along the shoreline were what they called "death traps." The cluster of tents serving as field hospitals had been dubbed by Allied combat soldiers as Hell's Half-Acre. The latter was to be avoided at all costs, due to the regular visits of 700 pound shells from the Anzio Express, heavy bombings by the Luftwaffe, particularly at night, and periodic pounding by field artillery.

Tough Allied fighters, such as paratroopers, Special Service Forcemen and Commandoes, often refused to report minor wounds to avoid being sent back to Hell's Half-Acre, also known to frontline soldiers as The Plague.

A company of the 504th Parachute Infantry was told that it was going to go into reserve about two miles to the rear. There, the paratroopers learned, they would be bivouacked near to artillery, which was always a prime target for big German guns and even the Anzio Express. A chorus of vicious and prolonged profanity erupted. The battle-tested parachutists preferred taking their chances on the front lines.

General Ernest Harmon, leader of the 1st Armored, was mildly chastised by his boss, General Mark Clark, for having his converted ordnance-repair truck command post too near the front lines. "Hell, Wayne," Harmon responded, calling the Fifth Army commander by his middle name, a common practice, "it's a lot safer up there than it is back farther!"

Clark shrugged his shoulders. Not a foot of ground on the beachhead was "safe," each knew.

Maintaining what the army called discipline was always difficult in extended battle situations. On Anzio, it was nearly impossible during heavy actions. Now, with a lull, General Truscott ordered that troops pulled out of the front lines for "rest" be given close-order drill and personal-weapons inspections and to hear lectures on military courtesy. It was a galling experience. The men turned the sky blue with their violent curses. But the "chicken shit," as fighting men termed such activities, continued.

Recreation was largely created by the fighting men themselves; often it was bizarre in nature. The men of the Special Service Force were addicted to horse racing. They rounded up several sturdy steeds, usually in nocturnal forays of Italian farm stables. A strip of ground was marked off as a track, the horses were lined up with mud-caked Forcemen aboard, and a rifle shot into the air sent the ponderous farm animals racing, more or less, over the track. The SSF men had heavy bets laid on these races, a factor which resulted in vocal cheering—and a periodic fistfight when a winner was disputed.

Only a heavy enemy barrage would break up these races; an occasional shell was ignored. In their balcony seats on the heights, the Germans may have also been laying bets on the same races.

Racing was also the rage in the British sector—beetle-racing. It was a simple manner to locate contestants. All a Tommie had to do was to scoop out a shallow slit trench and in minutes the bottom was lined with beetles. A soldier would display great ingenuity in conducting tests to determine which one among his collection was the fastest beetle. This he would enter in The Great Race.

The beetle of each soldier was painted a different color and all the race contestants were placed in a jar. The jar was put in the center of a ring some six feet in diameter, and as excitement rose among the onlookers, the starter lifted the jar. Wild cheering and shouts of encouragement rang across the bleak landscape as the beetles scurried about. Pride was involved in the rabid rooting, but money played a role. Like the American SSF, the Tommies put down large bets on their favorite.

The first beetle to cross the circle line was declared the winner.

A particular beetle won so often over the days and weeks that he was pronounced the Grand Champion. Unfortunately his sudden fame was short-lived. Someone accidentally stepped on the Grand Champion.

In the 45th Infantry Division sector, two companies in reserve went at it tooth and nail in a football game. The contest was concluded under a cloud of foul-play charges by the losers. The winning touchdown had been scored on a 60-yard run by a rifleman wearing mud-clogged combat boots. But the losers declared he was "unfairly inspired" to greater speed by a shell that whistled in nearby during the course of his broken-field gallop.

Wits drew up ground rules for a softball game held in the American sector and billed as the World Series of Anzio. One of the rules proclaimed that it would be legal to replace a base runner if he were struck by a shell. Another declared that a batter could carry no more than one hand grenade to the plate.

The term "recreation" on Anzio had different meanings to different men. Sergeant Nick DeGaeta, of the 509th Parachute Infantry Battalion, had a poshly furnished personal dugout near the front lines. Into this subterranean chamber DeGaeta smuggled a beautiful young Italian lady who was either attracted by the paratrooper's good looks or his large horde of food supplies. Undoubtedly the latter, his comrades chided. For seven days and nights, with shells periodically screaming into the vicinity, Sergeant DeGaeta and his young lady held a lover's tryst in the front lines.

Beachhead boredom was an ever-present ogre. It seeped relentlessly into the fighting man's being, like cold water oozing into his slit trench and through his clothing. Anything that would momentarily relieve the tedium was pounced on by the soldiers like a dog would pounce on a bone.

One day a German ME-109 flew over the bridgehead and was shot down by antiaircraft guns. The pilot managed to bail out of his burning craft and parachute to earth between the lines of the 504th Parachute Infantry along the Mussolini Canal and the German front. As he scrambled out of his chute, an American paratrooper stood up and signaled for the pilot to come in his direction. The confused airman ran a few steps, then halted abruptly as German infantrymen in the distance shouted at him.

As the Luftwaffe man started dashing back toward his own lines, a paratrooper fired a rifle shot at him, not to kill him but to frighten him. The German flopped down into a depression in the ground. There he remained all afternoon during which 60-millimeter mortarmen of the parachute regiment periodically sent shells toward the harassed enemy pilot to see if a bull's-eye could be scored.

Each time the German leaped to his feet to continue his dash toward his own lines an American would fire a few rounds at his heels, sending him to earth again. Finally the beleaguered pilot reached his comrades.

The German's parachute was draped over bushes just over halfway toward enemy positions, but a few Americans decided they wanted it as a souvenir. After dark a couple of paratroopers from the 1st Battalion crawled out to grab the chute. They knew it had probably been booby-trapped, but were determined to get it. As expected, the parachutists found a wire attached to the shute, cut the wire, gathered up the silk cloth and took out at a run for American lines.

The two men had gone but a short distance before the

Germans opened fire on them. In turn, paratroopers along the canal sent a fusillade of bullets into enemy positions. Moments later the souvenir hunters burst into their own positions unscathed, triumphantly waving the German parachute over their heads.

During the lull, Captain Carlos "Doc" Alden boldly drove his ambulance right up to the front lines and filled it with trench foot cases. The 509th Parachute Infantry doctor liked to do his own driving. There were no windows in the back of the ambulance, which did not bother the evacuees. There was nothing out there they wanted to see. Soon this viewpoint would be altered.

Alden had driven the ambulance only a few hundred yards across the barren, flat landscape when the evacuees heard a sharp crack near the vehicle. Their trained ears and battle instinct told them the source of the loud report—German observers had spotted the red-cross-marked ambulance and had taken the mercy vehicle under fire.

"What in the hell was that, Doc?" Corporal Charles Doyle, a trench foot victim called out, voicing the question on each man's mind. All knew it was an explosion, but cooped up in the windowless vehicle it was human nature to want a first-hand observation on this latest peril to their existence.

"Only an 88 shell," Alden replied calmly. "Hit about 20 yards to our right. Wasn't even close."

The injured men silently disagreed with Doc Alden's remark that 20 yards was not "close" for an exploding shell. Seconds later another loud crack rocked the ambulance.

Wehrmacht gunners, seeing the ambulance in the front line, apparently believed it was hauling ammunition, a trick the Germans used on occasion.

"Keep telling us what's going on, Doc," a nervous Corporal Doyle called out. "We can't see a damned thing back here."

"Affirmative," the surgeon replied, puffing on a cigarette. "For openers I would say Jerry is definitely sniping at us with his 88."

Another loud explosion. "That one hit just to the right of us," Alden announced in a soothing voice untinged with anxiety. "It's kicked dirt into the air. At least 15 yards away."

The men in the rear "white-knuckled" their stretchers. The German gunner was now getting the range.

Crrraaaccckkk! Another explosion.

"Now they're getting closer," Alden announced. "That one struck right in front of us."

He added: "Went right over the roof. If this rig had been a foot higher, you fellows would now be riding in Anzio's first open-aired ambulance."

To Charlie Doyle and others lying on stretchers and unable to see, Captain Alden sounded like a radio play-by-play announcer, the kind they once heard broadcasting World Series baseball games.

The surgeon continued to drive the ambulance over the open terrain in full view of the Germans, and after several more rounds exploded near the vehicle the enemy gunners apparently tired of the cat-and-mouse game and ceased firing.

Reaching his aid station, Captain Alden hopped out of the ambulance and opened the back doors. "I always knew the Krauts were lousy shooters," the unruffled doctor observed to his cargo of trench foot patients. "Hell, the bastards should have blown us apart with their first shot!"

Always there was the threat of the Luftwaffe. During the day, swift Focke-Wulf fighter planes would dart in over the beachhead, usually "skimming along the deck" of the flatlands to strafe unwary Allied soldiers. One Special Service Force sergeant's timing was faulty on just such an occasion. He had moved to a "sanitary trench" to heed an urgent call of nature, and was straddling the narrow excavation when two German fighter planes came zipping toward him with machine guns spitting. There was no place to take cover—except in the sanitary trench he was straddling. As bullets hissed past him, he deftly dropped into the excavation.

Slithering back out of the trench, the SSF sergeant was covered with feces. For many days, until new uniforms reached the front, the unfortunate fighting man was largely shunned by his mates who demanded that he keep his distance.

Technical Sergeant William H. Berndt, a Kansas farmer and original member of the SSF, was racing down a road to Nettuno on a captured German motorcycle whose original owner had died suddenly. It was daylight and Berndt and a comrade rider were on an urgent mission—to "liberate" sugar for making Kickapoo Joy Juice.

Above the roar of the cycle's motor, the two SSF men heard

the chilling sound of low-flying aircraft and turned to see a pair of enemy fighter planes zooming toward them with all guns blazing. Streams of bullets zipped past the motorcyclists. Although the vehicle was traveling 35 to 40 miles per hour, the SSF men leaped off and scrambled into a roadside ditch. The cycle continued to speed on down the road as though its riders were still aboard. Berndt and his comrade escaped with numerous cuts and bruises.

Except during the most inclement weather, Luftwaffe bombers paid calls on the front lines almost nightly. The SSF and the 504th Parachute Infantry Regiment caught the brunt of these bombings, as the Mussolini Canal provided an easily visible landmark for German bombardiers to locate American front lines. The routine was always the same. First the distinctive throbbing of engines in the black sky, then the bright illumination of flares followed by the staccato of explosions from anti-personnel bombs.

Artillery shells rustled constantly through the skies. Death often struck suddenly in unexpected ways. An American pilot and artillery observer lifted off in a light plane from the beachhead airstrip. Moments later aircraft and passengers disintegrated in mid-air—hit by a "friendly" shell being fired toward German positions.

A touch of gaiety swept through American ranks when a German shell plowed into a supply dump and destroyed several hundred crates of K-rations, the battlefield sustenance detested and long cursed by fighting men. "Someone ought to award the Kraut gunner a Silver Star!" a soldier called out to his comrades on hearing the news.

The Great Lull was especially exasperating to the aggressive General Ernie Harmon. He considered his Sherman and light tanks to be iron-plated modern-day cavalry whose purpose was to dash through the enemy and around his flanks. Now most of the 1st Armored Division tanks lay mute and immobile in the Padiglione woods, with huge mounds of wet dirt piled around them to thwart large chunks of shrapnel. The static warfare had the general, in the words of a staff aide, "chewing on the rug."

Still, Harmon refused to accept entirely a passive role. Often he would send a few of his tanks rumbling out of the woods to fire a barrage, after which they would return to their enormous holes to wait . . . and wait some more.

The Germans knew the 1st Armored was congregated in the Padiglione woods. So did Axis Sally. "We know you boys in the Armored are in the woods," she would purr in her sultry voice. "It must get lonesome there. So we'll give you a little shelling today."

Coordination between Axis Sally and frontline gunners was precise. Later that day the ground would rock as big German guns pounded Padiglione Woods. Several of Harmon's men were killed and others wounded. And Axis Sally's credibility soared.

5

House Warming in No-Man's-Land

It was about 10 P.M. on March 9 as four figures carrying a small boat and explosives were slipping through the darkness near the village of Fossa Incastro, 13 miles south of Rome, heading for the nearby beach. The men were highly-trained saboteurs and agents of the dreaded German Gestapo who had been assigned an important and perilous mission by their bosses in the Eternal City—murder the Allies' two top commanders in Italy, General Harold Alexander and General Mark Clark.

The murder plan, as outlined by the Gestapo, was for the assassination team of Italian Fascists to sail south along the Tyrrhenian coast, circle widely around No-Man's-Land at Anzio, and come ashore on the beachhead near the mouth of the Moletta River, behind Allied lines and only a half-mile from British positions. From that point the saboteurs were to work their way inland to advanced Allied headquarters where, after determining that both General Alexander and General Clark were present, to blow up the facility—along with the two commanders.

The insurgents should have little trouble reaching Allied headquarters, the Gestapo believed, as all were Romans who knew the region well. Wehrmacht intelligence would flash word to the murder squad when Alexander and Clark were present.

As the saboteurs shoved off from Fossa Incastro, a young one-armed man named Michelle Coppola insisted on steering the boat, despite his physical handicap. The others did not protest; Coppola was too highly regarded by the Gestapo chiefs in Rome and was recognized as one of the more zealous agents with a deep hatred for the Americans and British.

Curiously, instead of hugging the shoreline as planned until reaching No-Man's-Land, Coppola steered the little craft in a sweeping arc, almost as if he were trying to run into Allied ships known to be on regular patrol. The other three were growing uneasy. Had it not been for Coppola's stupidity in guiding the boat off-course, the sabotage team would have been on land by now. Fortunately, no Allied patrol boats were encountered.

The vessel burrowed on through the night. "When are we going to land?" the other three began asking Coppola with increasing regularity.

"Soon," was the recurring reply. "Very soon."

Now the others had grown mutinous. The idiot, one-armed Coppola was lost and would get them all captured and executed, they were convinced.

Coppola was aware of the cresting anger and alarm. He reached into a pile of ammunition, grabbed a grenade, pulled the pin, and announced to his startled comrades that he was an Allied agent, loyal to the King of England, and that he intended to head for shore and turn himself—and the other three—over to the Allies.

Coppola had long been working for the British underground in Rome and had connived his way into the confidence of the Gestapo and became one of its most trusted agents.

Furious and frightened over the turn of events, the three assassins, cursing and ranting, began edging toward the one-armed man. In a firm voice Coppola called out: "One more step and I'll blow us all to hell!"

As his comrades muttered threats, Coppola laid the grenade beside the tiller and steered the boat toward shore and up onto the beach at the appointed spot near the mouth of the Moletta River. After ordering the others to unload the explosives, Coppola tossed the grenade into the distance where it detonated with a roar that echoed for a great distance across the black landscape. Moments later several shadowy figures carrying rifles and wearing the pieplate helmets of British soldiers advanced out of the darkness and took the four saboteurs prisoner.

For two weeks, Allied intelligence had been aware of the impending Gestapo plot to murder Generals Alexander and Clark. Coppola, at great personal peril, had managed to slip off from the Gestapo on a pretext after learning of the saboteurs' mission, had warned his confederates in the Allied underground in Rome and they, in turn, had alerted Fifth Army by secret radio. The Gestapo chiefs in Rome were in a quandary for weeks trying to determine what had become of their murder squad—it had simply vanished.

Meanwhile, Allied vessels lying off Anzio town continued to be pounded by the Luftwaffe on an almost daily basis. Bustling, vibrant Anzio, once the idling grounds of the rich, had been transformed into the world's seventh largest port. One day a German bomber winged in over the port, dropped its big radio-controlled bomb, started to guide it toward the Allied supply ships squatting helplessly in the water like ducks on a farmer's pond.

The vessels below tossed up a fountain of flak, trying to explode the electronic missile. Suddenly the bomb slowed in mid-air, twisted into a crazy loop, started straight back toward its parent plane. The Luftwaffe pilot banked wildly to avoid it, but the radio-beam mechanism had evidently been knocked out of kilter, for the bomb swung gracefully around and again chased the aircraft. Down below sailors and dock workers cheered. When last seen, the bomber was high-tailing over the horizon, its rocket bomb in hot pursuit.

Despite the relatively quiet atmosphere that hovered over the beachhead in the month of March, the Germans continued to edge up closer to Allied lines at many points. The sturdy stone farmhouses dotting the flat terrain were fortified centers of resistance. When Allied artillery or tank guns destroyed one of these miniature fortresses, the debris covered the premises to furnish natural camouflage and firing positions.

Each house had a concrete oven in the yard which provided natural protection for machine gunners. Manure piles and bound bundles of hay strewn about the premises served as ideal cover for automatic weapons. Booby traps, mines and barbed wire abounded.

Static conditions permitted Anglo-American intelligence officers to pin-point each house around the perimeter with a numerical designation. Hence, a division commander's briefing on a given morning would be:

"General, houses Number 5 and 6, northwest of Carano, are in German hands. Houses Number 1, 2 and 3—or at least their debris—remain in our possession. House Number 3 is, however, on the rim of our outpost line and might change tenants at any time. House Number 4 is in No-Man's-Land and we usually occupy it by day and the Krauts set up housekeeping in it at night when our outpost pulls back. As for House Number 7 . . ."

On March 12, Lieutenant Colonel William Yarborough, commander of the 509th Parachute Infantry Battalion, received orders: assault, seize, outpost, and hold Houses 5 and 6. For weeks the German inhabitants of those two heavily-fortified strongpoints had resisted efforts to evict them by force. Once before a platoon of the 509th had attacked House 5, only to be driven off under withering bursts of automatic-weapons and tank gunfire. This time, Yarborough was going to make certain that Houses 5 and 6 were seized and held—he would send two companies into the attack.

Company C, commanded by Captain Erven E. Boettner, would make the main assault with Company A brought up in case it was needed. After 43 days of contact with the enemy on Anzio, both companies were depleted in strength; C Company had 112 men and A Company, commanded by Lieutenant Dan DeLeo, had 110 actives.

On the night of March 13–14 the parachute battalion's 60-millimeter mortar and machine gun crews slipped stealthily into No-Man's-Land to within range of Houses 5 and 6. For the rest of the night they dug in their weapons and hauled up ammunition, being careful to muffle all sounds. They spent the entire following day in slit trenches, not daring to move for fear of being detected by the nearby enemy.

Companies A and C moved out of their reserve bivouac at 9 P.M. on March 14, followed by Colonel Yarborough and his command group. The battalion commander wanted to be close by in the event urgent decisions were required. The moon was not due for two hours. The ground was muddy and slippery, and muffled curses punctured the night air as soldiers took awkward spills. Progress in the pitch blackness was slow and difficult, but the assault elements edged into jumpoff positions at 11:30 P.M., just as the moon was beginning its ascendancy.

The attack plan called for a C Company platoon led by Lieutenant Justin McCarthy to advance to the northwest along the road leading from Carano, and another platoon commanded by Lieutenant Herbert Rose was to move northward up a deep drainage ditch which ran close to House 6. McCarthy's platoon was to act as a decoy to draw German fire, while Rose's men would make the main effort.

Now all was ready. The paratroopers, grim-faced and silent, waited for H-Hour. They knew this would be a nasty job. Several rounds of German artillery shells screamed into A Company's reserve position along the deep ditch Fosso del Carano, killing two men and wounding two. Was the enemy already aware that the Americans were about to attack?

Several streaks of greenish-white tracer bullets from the direction of Houses 5 and 6 passed over the heads of the waiting parachutists. The men lay in the mud like statues as the moon climbed. The hands on the watch of Colonel Yarborough ticked onward toward H-Hour.

At 1 A.M. Yarborough flashed the word by radio to Lieutenant McCarthy's platoon: "Go!" McCarthy's men scrambled to their feet and moved forward, their silhouettes ghost-like under the intense gaze of the moon.

Thirty minutes after jumping off, McCarthy's men ran into a buzzsaw. Three German machine guns around House 5 spouted fire. Private Innocent DeFabbo, a bazookaman, was spun around by a slug which ripped through his shoulder. The others flopped to the ground as bullets thudded into the mud around their tense faces.

On hearing the rattle of German automatic weapons and seeing the streaks of tracers being fired at McCarthy's platoon, Lieutenant Rose, as planned, waved his men forward. They advanced well spread out, a squad on either side of the irrigation ditch and the third squad bringing up the rear as flank protection.

A stream of tracers from House 7, some 300 yards to Rose's left front, hissed into the advancing squads. German artillery and mortar fire began to burst near the platoon. As Rose's line of skirmishers neared House 6, it was raked by machine gun fire from Houses 5, 6 and 7.

From positions along a railroad track 1,000 yards to the front, jagged white flashes lighted the sky as shells from two Nebelwerfers (multi-barreled mortar) batteries arced high into the air, their fiery comets' tails visible for several seconds for miles across the barren flatlands. It looked as though 50 projectiles were in the sky at one time. Moments later they began to crash with a deafening roar and ground-shaking impact—in the area just passed by C and A Companies.

Colonel Yarborough put in an urgent call for artillery to pound the Nebelwerfers, but 155-millimeter Long Toms could not knock out the huge mortars. Four German 81-millimeter mortars opened fire on Rose's men and were promptly silenced by shelling.

A miserable, drizzling rain began to fall. The mud was turned to soup. The moon was now veiled, and the night seemed blacker than ever. All around streams of tracers from both sides raced through the darkness. Artillery and mortar bursts, German and Allied, periodically lighted the night with fountains of flame. Paratroopers, naked in the flatlands, were cut down with regularity. Still they edged forward toward the spitting machine guns of Germans protected by thick stone walls of the houses and the concrete bake ovens.

In Rose's sector, troopers were approaching a small concrete bridge spanning the irrigation ditch up which they had been advancing. Suddenly one of the riflemen, Manley L. Crumley caught his pants on something which ripped and tore them— concertina barbed wire. He threw himself downward on the roll of sharp-pointed wire and urged comrades to race forward by stepping on his back.

One of the new men was hesitant. "Over your back?" he called out in wonderment.

"C'mon, for Chrissake, get going!" Crumley shouted. "Do you bastards think I'm doing this for my health?"

Under the bridge, a German machine gun was positioned. It fired a burst toward the attackers. Crumley grunted as seven or eight pairs of paratrooper jump-boots cut into his back as the men raced across the barbed-wire roll.

A German under the bridge tossed a grenade which struck Sergeant William H. Simmons in the eye. The missile did not explode, but caused Simmons great pain and temporary loss of sight in the eye. He was more angry than anything, and had to be restrained by comrades from charging under the bridge and taking on the German machine gunners head-on.

The platoon bazookaman fired a round at the enemy gun under the span. It plowed into the mud next to the weapon and failed to detonate. Another bazooka rocket was fired. It did not go off either. Cursing loudly, the bazookaman tried once more. This rocket exploded among the German gunners, and the weapon fell silent.

Perhaps elated over his eventual success, the bazookaman tripped over an entanglement and fell face downward in the mud. His temperamental tube-like weapon plunged into the mud with him, jamming the bazooka with the soupy muck. Furious, the trooper got to his feet cursing loudly despite the tracer bullets whipping about the area, slammed his useless bazooka into the mud and continued onward.

In the face of heavy machine gun fire, Rose's platoon worked its way forward, and by 8 A.M. the Americans were in possession of three corners of House 6. The fourth was being swept by an automatic weapon in the bake oven in the backyard. Grenades were running low, the platoon's bazooka was *hors de combat* so an ancient Springfield rifle with an attachment was used to fire fragmentation grenades at the oven. Loud screams came from the concrete oval, and the gun barked no more. At 4:30 P.M. all four corners of House 6 were in American hands.

The paratroopers took heavy casualties. A stream of German prisoners carried American wounded to the rear. Rose put out outposts and braced for the inevitable counterattack.

A radio message was sent to 3rd Infantry Division headquarters where an operations officer altered his map to show House 6 had new tenants.

While the action on the left was flaming, Lieutenant McCarthy and his men had been engaged in fierce fighting in their role as decoys. During the night McCarthy's men had continued to creep and crawl forward in the cold, soupy mud, pounded by rain, mortars and artillery, raked regularly by machine guns. They had to overcome barbed wire entanglements, booby traps and mines.

As the men of C Company edged forward, Alexander Peters

heard a voice call out above the loud bark of enemy machine guns sending tracers just overhead, "Come on, goddamn it, we can't live forever!" Peters reflected that he did not want to live forever, only a few more minutes would be adequate for the present.

Now as the fight raged around him, Lieutenant McCarthy was peering over a pile of rubble at House 5. He was suffering from several shell fragments which had lodged in his back. Up ahead a German machine gun chattered and a slug ripped away the left side of McCarthy's already battered helmet, taking with it the tip of the lieutenant's ear.

McCarthy's platoon had wiped out supporting positions around House 5, but one stubborn machine gun inside the building was firing through an archway. The parachutists were nearly out of grenades and bazooka ammunition was gone. The platoon had been cut down to about half-size.

In a quandary as to what to do next, Lieutenant McCarthy learned that a Sherman tank had moved in behind House 3. The parachute officer crawled there and pleaded with the tank commander to plaster House 5. The tanker refused.

"It'll give away my position," the armored man declared.

"What the hell about my goddamned position?" shouted McCarthy in a rage, slamming his half-helmet to the ground. The tanker was adamant.

Three paratroopers muscled a captured German 20-millimeter gun into position near House 3. Some 10 or 12 rounds were fired into House 5, but the German machine gun kept firing. Moments later there was a loud explosion near the 20-millimeter weapon. A German flat-trajectory round made a direct hit on the gun. But the three paratroopers manning it escaped with minor injuries and continued in the fight.

Now Platoon Sergeant Joe Fite and Corporal William H. Davis worked their way up to the south wall of the house, apparently undetected. They stood rock-still for several minutes listening for movement inside.

Suddenly two German egg grenades flew over the house from the other side. Fragments hit Davis in the arm. Fite and Davis had to hurriedly withdraw from the exposed position.

The machine gun from the archway continued to spray the surrounding landscape. Private Harold D. Metzger slipped up near the spitting weapon, tossed several WP (white phosphorous) grenades toward it, then cautiously poked his Tommy gun around a corner and emptied a clip in the direction of the gun. The response was immediate. The automatic weapon shot the stock off Metzger's Tommy.

House 5 obviously had plenty of ammunition. It was dying hard and daylight was about to arrive, a decided advantage to the Germans as the Americans were out in the open with minimal cover or concealment.

Lieutenant Rose in House 6 put in a radio call: "Request artillery fire 300 yards north of House 6. Enemy is forming for counterattack."

Moments later Rose again put in a call: "Also need fire on Houses 7 and 8. Enemy counterattack estimated at two platoons moving toward us on left flank."

In less than five minutes an inferno of flame and smoke mushroomed on Rose's left flank.

Captain Boettner got on his radio after viewing the shelling. "That's *bono!* (great)" he exulted. "Give it to the bastards again. I'll tell you when to stop!"

For five minutes the 105's and 4.2-inch mortars poured rounds into the attacking Germans. The parachute company's 60-millimeter mortar barrels were red hot. Nothing could survive such a concentration of fire. The enemy scrambled backward, leaving behind a large number of figures in gray-green overcoats sprawled in the cold mud.

Shortly after dawn a platoon from the 30th Infantry Regiment, as planned, relieved Rose's depleted platoon in and around House 6, as the battered paratroopers were moving back. Corporal Boggs G. Collins brought up the rear as the platoon's survivors moved down the irrigation ditch. Collins suddenly halted and pointed a muddy finger toward House 7 and called out to a comrade: "There they are again! Look at the bastards come!"

Collins and Private Edwin C. Hicks began firing at the oncoming Germans, picking off seven of them, one at a time. Four Germans reached the irrigation ditch farther north and leaped in for cover. The rest fled. Collins and Hicks went up the deep canal after the four grenadiers, but the fight had been taken out of the Germans. The four surrendered.

The 3rd Division platoon that was to have relieved Lieutenant McCarthy's decimated platoon never arrived. Thirty-eight men had followed McCarthy into the assault. There were now eight left. The paratroopers remained around House 5 all day, and were subjected to periodic bursts of machine gun fire from under the archway and relentless shelling directed by observers looking down on the scene from the Alban Hills.

At 9:30 A.M. a white flag on a pole was thrust out from a south door and a German emerged to ask an armistice to remove wounded to the rear. McCarthy, who had been wounded twice in the savage fight, was in no mood for such leniency. "Hell, no!" he barked. "If you goddamned bastards

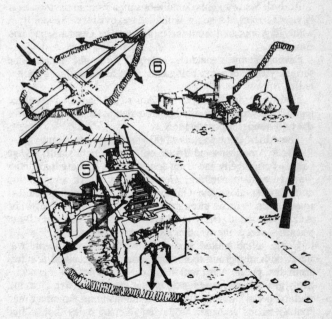

Drawing Shows Houses 5 and 6 which were captured by C Company of 509th Parachute Infantry Battalion in bloody two-day fight. Arrows indicate inter-locking fields of fire by German machine guns.

want to move your wounded, the way to do it is to give up!"

The grim-faced German spun on his heels and returned to the house. Moments later the machine gun chattered and paratroopers fired small arms into the building. Then silence descended on the area around House 5. The day wore on. The Germans inside were still as mice.

Meanwhile, Lieutenant McCarthy had been evacuated due to his several wounds.

Late in the day, Colonel Yarborough called Lieutenant Hugh P. Shaw, who commanded the demolitions platoon in the rear area: "Shaw, make up some pole charges. Bring some bangalore torpedoes along too—and one of our flamethrowers."

At dusk Shaw and his demolitions men were in position near House 5, ready to go in with their explosives. Suddenly, a white flag appeared from the building. The Germans had had enough.

Seven enemy grenadiers emerged from the house, one seriously wounded and being carried in a camouflaged shelter half.

Houses 5 and 6 were in American hands. Fifty-three paratroopers had been killed or wounded in the savage fight for the two nondescript structures.

The Allied front was now 500 yards closer to Rome.

As the Americans and British on Anzio fought small, savage battles periodically laced by long periods of boredom under almost constant shelling, General Mark Clark and his top commanders along the Gustav Line were preparing another major effort to break through the Cassino area and drive for the Anzio beachhead. Early in March all was ready for the all-out assault—except the weather would not cooperate.

Clark, as he waited anxiously for the skies to clear, was beset with numerous minor irritations. He received a signal from the public information officer at General Alexander's army group headquarters stating that Prime Minister Churchill had "ordered" that in future communications American and British troops at Anzio would be referred to as the "Allied Bridgehead Force" instead of Fifth Army forces. Clark protested. He pointed out that such a designation would not help the morale of either American or British soldiers, as it would imply that the Anzio force was cut off and isolated from the rest of Fifth Army.

There was a flurry of signals and Churchill finally agreed to
General Clark's proposed compromise—The Fifth Army Allied Bridgehead Force.

The British prime minister again involved himself in minor
details of the Italian campaign a few days later. Clark's
headquarters received an order from British Administrative
Headquarters in the Mediterranean stating that in the future all
messages sent personally to the prime minister should not
spell the American "theater" but rather the British spelling
"theatre."

On the morning of March 15, the murky Italian skies cleared
sufficiently to launch the attack on Cassino to link Fifth Army
on the Gustav Line with the Anzio beachhead. Burrowed into
the rubble that was once the town of Cassino were resolute
members of the elite German 4th Parachute Regiment. Knowing an assault was about to strike his men in the pulverized
town, Colonel Graf von der Schulenburg, commander of the
paratroop unit, issued an order of the day: "We will die before
moving from our positions in Cassino."

Von der Schulenburg knew, as did Allied commanders, that
Cassino blocked the entrance to the Liri Valley, up which
General Mark Clark hoped to send his tanks racing to join up
with beachhead forces. But first a hole would have to be
punched in German lines by seizing Cassino.

At 8:30 A.M. the first wave of Allied bombers approached
the besieged town, shimmering down below in the early
morning sun. Bomb-bay doors opened and hundreds of missiles began spilling out into the blue sky. The aim was
accurate. The heart of Cassino seemed to go up in sharp, angry
flames of orange, followed by gushers of smoke and debris
shooting skyward. By the time the second wave of bombers
arrived, the town was invisible, covered by a thick blanket of
smoke and dust.

The second wave of American Flying Fortresses dropped its
explosives into the pall of smog and the ground for miles
around reverberated with convulsions. It went on like that until
nearly noon, wave after wave.

The Allied bombers received virtually no flak, nor did
Luftwaffe fighter planes appear. The bombs hit so close to
friendly forward positions that "shorts" killed 75 Allied
soldiers and wounded 250 more. When the last bomber flew

off into the distance, the rubble of Cassino had been converted to powdered masonry.

Now Allied artillery opened up with a tremendous roar, and in two hours sent more than 200,000 rounds into the battered positions of the 4th Parachute Regiment. Nearly two companies of German paratroopers had been wiped out by the deluge of bombs and shells. But others took refuge in deep cellars, steel and concrete pillboxes and caves and survived the rain of explosives. When the 6th New Zealand Brigade, supported by the 19th New Zealand Armored Regiment, reached the outskirts of the town they found the tenacious German paratroopers, or at least the remnants, reorganized and waiting their arrival behind endless barricades of rubble.

The streets were impassable to New Zealand tanks due to the enormous amount of debris from the bombing and shelling. Savage fighting among the rubble continued for three days at which time the New Zealanders had captured two-thirds of Cassino. Still the German airborne fighting men battled from one pile of rubble to the next, often launching local counterattacks to recapture key locations the New Zealanders had paid a high price in blood to seize.

While the bitter fight was raging in the valley, the 4th Indian Division attacked up the steep slope of Monte Cassino and fought its way to an exposed terrain feature known to the Allies as Hangman's Hill. There, within 300 yards of the pulverized Abbey, the Indian fighters were halted.

For a week, the New Zealanders continued efforts to capture the Cassino rubble pile. The determined Germans held fast. On March 20, General Alexander called a conference that would decide whether to abandon the operation or make one more all-out effort to seize Cassino and the Abbey debris high above.

The day before the conference, General Clark visited the headquarters of the New Zealand division. Clark was in a pessimistic mood. "I think you and the Boche are both groggy," the Fifth Army commander remarked to General Freyberg. The New Zealand Division leader bristled. He declared his men were not groggy and expressed the opinion that he could break through.

At Alexander's conference, Freyberg argued to keep going. Alexander and Clark agreed. On March 22, reinforced by a fresh infantry battalion, the New Zealanders launched another assault to wipe out German strongpoints in Cassino. The attack soon ground to a halt.

The German paratroopers had suffered heavy casualties in following Colonel von de Schulenberg's order to "die before moving from Cassino." But the attacking New Zealanders were nearly drowned in a sea of blood. From March 15 to 23, the New Zealand Division and attached units had 1,594 men killed or wounded.

Allied progress had been nil. Cassino and the shell- and bomb-pocked ridges of Monte Cassino still blocked Fifth Army's road to Anzio—and to Rome.

6

Controversy in Allied High Command

Far from the shell-pocked landscape of Anzio and the bomb-battered ridges around Cassino on April 11, a United States Army Air Corps transport plane touched down at Bolling Field outside Washington D.C. It was 3 A.M., a time when spies presumably were catching up on lost sleep.

Stepping off the plane in the blacked-out airport was an angular figure wearing the three stars of a lieutenant general on his shoulders and a green silk scarf, symbol of his army command, around his neck. After an absence of two years, General Mark Clark had returned to the nation's capital—slinking in like a thief in the night.

Clark's trip had been cloaked in extreme secrecy. He was in Washington to discuss the bogged-down, bloody Italian campaign and plans to break loose for Rome with his boss, Chief of Staff George Marshall. Secrecy was vital. Had the Germans learned of Clark's presence in Washington they would have rightly deduced that a major push in Italy was in the works.

General Clark had been advised by Marshall that this trip was to be top-secret, but was astonished at the extreme lengths to which the chief of staff went to conceal the Fifth Army commander's visit. Even Clark's mother, who lived in Washington, was not notified. His wife Renie (Maurine) was allowed to be at the airport, but her car had drawn drapes and she entered the gates as a woman veiled in mystery.

An aide to General Marshall met Clark, took him to the curtain-draped vehicle for a hurried reunion with his wife, then advised Clark that he could not go home. Instead the aide whisked the general and his wife to Marshall's home at Fort Myer near Washington.

Next morning, in Marshall's office in the awesome-sized new Pentagon, Clark was permitted to write his mother a letter, to be delivered by special courier, advising her to meet the general, Renie and daughter Ann at the airport. The chief of staff, with the enormous burden of a global conflict on his shoulders, asked that Clark read him the letter aloud to make sure he did not reveal too much.

After a hurried reunion at the airport, the Clark family flew to White Sulphur Springs in West Virginia. Marshall insisted that Clark could do with a few days' rest after months of intense duty in Italy. The family stayed in a guest cottage, and meals were served there in order that General Clark would not be seen.

A few days later Clark, his wife and daughter flew back to Washington where Marshall reluctantly allowed the Fifth Army leader to spend the night in the family's apartment. There an aide whisked Clark to a basement door in the rear and put him in an elevator on which a Secret Service agent had taken the place of the regular operator. By now General Clark was beginning to feel like a prisoner of war.

During his visit, Clark met with both President Roosevelt and Congressional leaders, as well as with Marshall—all sessions were held under strictly secret circumstances. He described his plans for breaking the Italian logjam and seizing Rome. Roosevelt and Marshall each stressed the political, psychological and military advantages if Clark could capture Rome before the Allies stormed across the English Channel against Northwest France in early June.

Before leaving Washington, General Clark was approached by the wife of the chief of staff. Mrs. Marshall asked him if he could take a couple of packages and letters to her two sons, Captain Clifton Brown and Lieutenant Allen T. Brown, both of whom were serving under Clark in Italy. Clark happily agreed. He would have done the same for the mother of an obscure private. The Fifth Army commander had no way of knowing that a month later he would have to perform one of the saddest duties of his life: informing the Marshalls, who had always been extremely kind toward Clark and his family, that Allen had been killed in action while leading an attack from the turret of a tank. Personal grief had struck at the very top of the United States Army.

Clark was whisked to Bolling Field under cover of night. As his airplane lifted off for Italy, the general had a bit of home at his side—the family's pet cocker spaniel, Pal.

As the uneasy lull hovered over both Anzio and the Gustav Line 60 miles to the south, Field Marshal Albrecht Kesselring saw no indications of Allied plans to launch an offensive, so he allowed a number of his top commanders to go on leave to Germany. General von Vietinghoff, leader of Tenth Army defending the Gustav Line, left for home. So did General von Senger und Etterlin, the corps commander along the crucial Cassino sector. Also taking off for the homeland was Kesselring's chief of staff, Siegfried Westphal, who had been ill.

But Kesselring continued with his customary vigor. More than 12,000 Italian laborers were hard at work under the direction of German army engineers constructing a defensive position between the Anzio beachhead and Rome. Known as the Caesar Line, the fortifications consisted of a continuous stretch of barbed wire, gun emplacements, trenches and assorted man-made and natural barricades. Kesselring was convinced that if the Allies broke out of Anzio, he could halt them at the Caesar Line.

Meanwhile during the lull, extensive shuffling of troop dispositions was taking place on both sides. On Anzio, the U.S. 34th Infantry Division, a veteran outfit, replaced the 504th Parachute Infantry Regiment and the 509th Parachute Infantry Battalion, and the British 56th Division arrived to take over for the battle-weary British 1st Division. Late in April General Ernest Harmon's 1st Armored Division was brought up to full strength with the arrival of his Combat Command B. The latter force for weeks had been coiled up behind the Gustav Line waiting for a chance to race up the Liri Valley toward Anzio once a hole had been punched in German defenses. Now Combat Command B had arrived at the beachhead—by sea in LST's.

General Alexander meanwhile was reorganizing his forces along the Cassino sector in preparation for an all-out spring offensive to break through to Anzio and then on to Rome. Clark's Fifth Army was shifted westward to a narrow zone only 13 miles wide along the Tyrrhenian Sea coast, and the British Eighth Army, commanded by General Oliver Leese, was brought over from the Adriatic Coast to replace Fifth Army in the Cassino-Liri Valley sector.

The shifting of Allied troops into a relatively confined zone west of the rugged north-south Apennines aroused deep suspicions in Mark Clark's Fifth Army headquarters. Nationalistic goals were involved, most there believed. The Eighth Army, at the mouth of the Liri Valley, would now make the main effort to reach Rome, while the Fifth, after months of savage fighting and great blood-letting in the Cassino sector, would be shunted aside to a supporting role in the looming massive offensive.

To General Clark and his top American commanders, it appeared that the British had connived not just to join hands with Fifth Army in a rush to capture the crown jewel of the Mediterranean—Eternal Rome—but to lead the Allied race for the capital. Clark had no intention of allowing what he considered this blow to American military prestige. He was determined that Fifth Army would be the first into Rome.

Whatever the true purpose behind the massive Allied reorganization, the troop shifts were conducted with such skill that the alert German intelligence apparatus was unaware that this powerful force had been concentrated along the western coastline.

While bitter controversy was beginning to simmer in the upper echelons of Allied command, those carrying the ultimate burden, the combat soldiers, were occupied with more primitive concerns—staying alive and avoiding mutilation. On the beachhead, the Anzio Express, the gigantic 280-millimeter railroad gun, was continuing to inflict deep physical and psychological destruction to those caught in, as Axis Sally had described it, "the world's largest self-contained prisoner of war camp." Many on the bridgehead for weeks had tried to joke about the Anzio Express—but it was no joking matter.

A number of efforts had been made to locate and knock out the gun, which was mounted on a flatcar so that it could be moved rapidly from place to place. Even advanced scientific technology and mathematics were used to try to knock out the long-barreled menace with its 700-pound shells. With a booster charge, the rifled gun was capable of firing a projectile 50 miles.

Brigadier General Aaron Bradshaw, Fifth Army antiaircraft officer, had created a procedure by which night-flying Beaufighters would circle the suspected locale until they picked up gun flashes. Then the swift aircraft would fly directly for the spot and radar would pick up the lines of the planes' flight. Where these intersected, that was where the Anzio Express was supposed to be. It was a fine theory; it did not work.

The reason it did not work was because the Germans kept the huge weapon in a tunnel, rolled it out at night or during periods of bad weather when Allied planes were grounded, fired one or more rounds on a pre-determined target, then hustled it back into the tunnel.

As time neared for the breakout from Anzio, a deception plan, involving finely honed play-acting, was implemented. In mid-May beachhead artillery early each morning would pound a certain sector. The Germans would rush troops and panzers there to halt the expected attack—but nothing happened. At noon the next day Allied artillery would again roar, and the enemy would hurry reinforcements to the zone of impact to head off an assault. Again nothing else occurred. Finally, the Germans decided the British and Americans were merely "getting their jollies" out of these daily barrages and ceased reacting to them.

Now General Ernie Harmon's tanks got into the deception act. Each night and early morning Shermans would clank out of the Padiglione Woods, rumble up to the front lines, fire off a load of ammunition, then turn and head back. At first, the Shermans drew heavy artillery fire, but soon the Germans decided crazy Americans were simply prowling around all night and wastefully shooting off ammunition. After that the enemy ignored the nightly forays by the American iron monsters.

When time for the breakout approached, the Shermans would again go through their nightly shenanigans. Only then few tanks would return. Most would camouflage themselves in depressions in the ground, their crews remaining stone-still but ready to spring forward on a signal.

The attack out of the bridgehead, when it came, would be on the right flank in the direction of Cisterna, where Colonel Bill

Darby's Ranger battalions had been wiped out weeks before. But enemy observers perched on the heights took increasing note of the swarms of Allied tanks assembling on the left flank, along the Albano-Anzio road. These tanks were camouflaged in a careless manner. They were actually inflated balloons, so cleverly manufactured that a German peering through field glasses from a long distance could not distinguish them from real tanks.

Generals Alexander and Clark and their aides decided late in April that the Fifth and Eighth Army offensives on the southern front should kick off first, and then General Truscott would launch his troops out of the Anzio beachhead to link up with the main bodies coming up from the south, to seize the Alban Hills and to cut Route 6 leading to Rome, thereby trapping German forces fleeing toward the Eternal City.

Meanwhile General Truscott had prepared four alternative plans for the impending offensive, each with an exotic code-name: *Crawdad*, *Buffalo*, *Turtle* and *Grasshopper*. The beachhead commander's boss, Mark Clark, after extensive discussion, had approved the plans, one to be implemented depending upon the battle situation at the time.

On May 5 General Alexander visited Truscott on the beachhead. Proudly the American general rolled out his four schemes for the breakout, each having required hundreds of hours of intricate staff work and delicate timing. Truscott said that he could launch any one of the plans on 48 hours' notice.

The 15th Army Group commander stated, "The only worthwhile plan is *Buffalo*."

Buffalo called for Truscott to push northeast from Anzio, through battered Cisterna and Cori, and move south of the Alban Hills to Valmontone. This would place VI Corps troops astride Route 6, the road leading from pulverized Cassino to Rome, blocking the path of Germans retreating before the British Eighth Army driving up the Liri Valley.

"This is the plan I want and I reserve for myself the decision as to the time for launching it," the British general told Truscott.

The following day General Clark arrived on the beachhead. He was infuriated on learning that Alexander had bypassed the American chain of command and had gone directly to Clark's subordinate, Truscott.

"Apparently Alexander has decided to move in and run my army!" the angular young general exploded.

Now he became convinced of one factor: there was a devious plot afoot to deprive Fifth Army of its hard-earned glory of capturing Rome. The name of Winston Churchill popped up regularly at Fifth Army headquarters on Clark's return from the bridgehead.

General Clark promptly telephoned his chain-of-command boss, Harold Alexander. He told the Briton firmly but politely that he was surprised to learn that Alexander had bypassed him, gone directly to a Clark subordinate to issue orders contrary to those given Truscott by Clark. The Fifth Army commander had told Truscott to be flexible and ready to launch any of his four breakout plans, depending upon the situation at the time.

Alexander told Clark that he understood and had no intention of interfering directly with the operations of Fifth Army.

In one respect, General Alexander did involve himself in Truscott's beachhead plans. Late in April, he had instructed Clark not to use the two British divisions on Anzio in the looming breakout, except for minor actions. An England depleted of young men by four years of all-out war was finding it nearly impossible to provide replacements for Anzio units decimated by weeks of hard fighting. The breakout would be solely an American operation.

Despite the high-level squabbling, all Allied commanders were united in one view—the Anzio breakout would be a difficult, bloody operation. General Eberhard von Mackensen had five and one-half first-rate divisions in his beachhead noose and the 26th Panzer Grenadier Division was posted just south of Rome and could be rushed to the action on an hour's notice.

Sixty miles south of Anzio the night of May 11 was misty. A drizzling rain had fallen earlier in the evening. But the stars were flickering in the dark sky and the moon promised to shine down in a few hours on the gladiators far below.

As soon as it was dark tens of thousands of Fifth and Eighth Army troops, representing 14 nationalities, began slogging into position. Efforts were made to have the Allied front along the Gustav Line appear as normal as possible. Patrols were sent out. Some artillery was fired. It was precisely like the previous evening and for many evenings prior to that. All was relatively quiet.

Suddenly, the silence was shattered. At 11 P.M. nearly 1,100 big guns, lined up between the Tyrrhenian shoreline and Cassino, roared and flamed, the enormous sound echoing up mountainsides and far out to sea. German grenadiers, settled down for the night in their dugouts and foxholes, were taken completely by surprise by the tremendous rain of steel and explosives that engulfed them. Wehrmacht intelligence had been totally bamboozled. It had advised front-line troops that no attack could be expected along the Gustav Line until May 24 at the earliest.

After pounding German positions for 30 minutes with tens of thousands of shells, Allied artillery lifted. An eerie silence fell over the killing grounds. Grim-faced Allied infantrymen moved forward to close with the enemy.

As predicted, the massive Gustav Line assault turned into a bloody slugging match. Veteran German grenadiers, fighting in long-prepared positions fortified with every known kind of lethal device, resisted savagely. There would be no quick Allied breakthrough. General John Lucas, the sacked Anzio commander, had summed up the situation in his diary weeks before: "Magical breakthroughs occur only in story books."

Polish troops, imbued with a cold hatred for the enemy that had brutally ravaged their homeland, stormed up the steep slopes of bomb-pocked Monte Cassino, only to be driven back in a sea of blood after a bitter 12 hour fight.

At the entrance to the Liri Valley, the English fought their way across the swift-flowing Rapido River, but the bridgehead was too tiny for succeeding forces to exploit. Along the coast the Americans of Major General Geoffrey Keyes' II Corps made little progress in three days of fierce fighting.

Field Marshal Kesselring and General von Vietinghoff, the Tenth Army commander, kept throwing in reserves. The constant battering was taking a fearful toll on the tenacious Wehrmacht as the Allies kept up the pressure. The mountainsides and the valleys and the fast-flowing little streams ran red with blood—German and Allied.

On the Anzio beachhead, General Truscott and his staff were devouring every report and scrap of rumor that poured into VI Corps headquarters from the Gustav Line. Truscott's force was like a star open-field runner sitting on the bench in a crucial football game straining at the leash for a signal from the coach to leap into the fray and dash for a touchdown. The hours and the days inexorably crawled by, but the brutal slugging match to the south continued to rage. To Truscott and other commanders on Anzio, the breakout seemed as far away as ever. Perhaps Axis Sally had been right—Truscott and his men would be trapped on this thin slice of bleak Italian real estate for the rest of their lives.

As a certain despondency began to seep into the Anzio command, spirits suddenly soared. Allied intelligence reported an exciting discovery: a nervous Field Marshal Kesselring had dispatched his two crack divisions being held south of Rome to help head off the potentially disastrous and looming Allied breakthrough along the Gustav Line. At the beachhead, a violent protest by General von Mackensen over depriving him of these two first-rate formations went unheeded.

After six days of bloody fighting on the Cassino front in which Allied gains were measured in feet, the French Expeditionary Corps on the right flank of Clark's Fifth Army broke the Gustav logjam. Paced by fierce, knife-wielding Goumiers from North Africa, the French scrambled over the rugged Aurunci Mountains behind the Garigliano River, penetrating 10 miles until General Alphonse Juin's men were west of Cassino.

Uninterested in such modern accoutrements of war as artillery and air support and complex maneuver plans, the mountain-bred Goumiers relied on the knife and rifle, and were at home with mule trains along the narrow, treacherous mountain trails. Now the French stood at a point where they could move down into the Liri Valley behind Germans battling the British Eighth Army. For the first time in months, the Wehrmacht found itself in a precarious battlefield situation.

Sparked by the Goumier-led French advance, the Americans pushed forward along the Tyrrhenian coast, the British enlarged their bridgehead over the Rapido River and advanced up the Liri Valley until they outflanked pulverized Cassino and the Abbey above, and the Poles, who were fighting for revenge and honor, suffered heavy casualties as they clawed toward the pile of rubble which was once a world-famed monastery.

On the night of May 17, Kesselring gave a fateful order: withdraw at once from Cassino and the Abbey. The resolute German 1st Parachute Division, pounded relentlessly from the sky and ground for weeks and decimated to skeleton size, protested the order to yield. The parachute remnants did so only when Kesselring personally intervened.

After daybreak, the Poles under General Wladyslaw Anders, who had been captured by the Russians in 1939 and held for months in a Moscow jail, took over the monastery rubble pile and raised the flag of Poland over it. Anders had lost nearly 4,000 men in the Cassino operation.

By May 21, the Germans were in full retreat all along the southern battlefront. Some seven to 10 miles behind Cassino, Kesselring had hurriedly constructed the Adolf Hitler Line in recent weeks. When it became apparent that this fortified position would not halt the rampaging Allied tanks and foot soldiers, it was quickly renamed the Dora Line. The fuehrer's honor would be salvaged even if the battle was not.

Gloom had settled in at the German Tenth Army headquarters. "The situation doesn't look too good," the chief of staff, Colonel Fritz Wentzell, observed to a Kesselring aide, Colonel Dietrich Beelitz. The latter responded: "Christ, I didn't know the Allies would be that strong!"

"You don't know the French colonial troops (the Goumiers)," Wentzell declared. "They're a bunch of cut-throats!"

The French had plunged ahead for 20 miles and cut the main lateral highway connecting Highways 6 and 7 leading to Rome. With the Allies only 40 miles from Anzio, another controversy erupted between American General Mark Clark and British General Harold Alexander. Alexander told Truscott on the beachhead to prepare to launch Operation Buffalo on May 21. Clark violently disputed the order as premature. He pointed out that only the French Corp had reached out for 20 miles, that the British Eighth Army was lagging far behind General Juin's fighting men in the Liri Valley.

The Fifth Army commander told Alexander he did not believe the "Go!" signal should be flashed to General Truscott on Anzio until the British had advanced at least as far as the Dora Line, formerly the Adolf Hitler Line. Privately, Clark held that the British were making no real effort to advance, but were permitting the French to clear a path for them up the valley. Unless the Eighth Army pinned down the Wehrmacht in the valley, Truscott's VI Corps would not be able to break through von Mackensen's Fourteenth Army on the beachhead, Clark stressed.

On May 21, an American infantry battalion climbed into a small flotilla of "Ducks" (amphibious trucks) at the just captured harbor at Gaeta and sailed 12 miles up the coast where they landed unopposed at Sperlonga. Less than 10 miles farther up the shoreline was Terracina, the last defensible point where the Germans could make a stand below the Pontine Marshes at Anzio beachhead.

Now the intra-Allied jockeying at the upper levels got into high gear. At stake was the honor of being the first army in 15 centuries to seize Rome from the south. General Clark made no bones of the fact that he intended to be first into the Eternal City. He felt that Fifth Army deserved the recognition and that capturing the capital city would make up to a certain extent for the heavy bleeding and suffering Fifth Army had endured in keeping the pressure on the Germans all winter.

Clark had already dispatched the 36th Infantry Division to the beachhead. General Fred Walker's veterans would pass through the 3rd Infantry Division after battered Cisterna was captured and help lead the "Buffalo charge" to Rome.

The long-awaited breakout from Anzio was set for dawn on May 23.

Arrayed along the Allied beachhead from the left were the British 5th and 1st Divisions, the U.S. 45th and 34th Divisions, and the American-Canadian First Special Service Force. Held in reserve were the 1st Armored, 3rd Infantry and 36th Infantry Divisions.

Across No-Man's-Land the Germans were dug in behind formidable fortifications with five veteran divisions in the line. The 4th Parachute was behind the Moletta River, facing the British, and the 65th was astride the Albano-Anzio road, up which von Mackensen expected the Allies to attempt the breakout. The 3rd Panzer Grenadier Division was in the center, the 362nd Division in front of Cisterna, and the 715th spread out along the Mussolini Canal facing the First Special Service Force.

General von Mackensen had to contend with a factor that brought a chill to the heart of any commander—he had no reserves behind the front. If the Allies broke through, the nearest reinforcements were far north of Rome where Kesselring expected another Anglo-American seaborne landing.

7

"We're Shooting the Works!"

Veterans of General Iron Mike O'Daniel's 3rd Infantry Division instinctively sensed that Something Big was up. Bivouacked in reserve in a gloomy pine woods, for several nights O'Daniel's men could see gun flashes dancing in the clear Italian skies to the south where Fifth and Eighth Armies were advancing from the Gustav Line.

A curious mixture of elation and foreboding surged through the beings of the men of the 3rd. Anything would be better than spending one more day in the hell-hole of Anzio beachhead. Yet each combat-wise fighting man knew that the Germans would resist fiercely and that blood would flow freely.

Late in the evening of May 21 there were shouts of "saddle up, we're movin' out!" ringing though the pine woods. There was a rustling of gear being strapped onto bodies and soon thousands of 3rd Division men were filing out of the forest, heading for jumpoff positions at the front.

It was a balmy evening and still daylight. In the green fields which fronted the protective wooded area, sheep were grazing peacefully, unmindful of the holocaust about to erupt. A handful of shabbily-dressed sheepherders glanced at the passing helmeted figures with casual disinterest.

On a mound beside the main road which skirted the forest, the 3rd Division band had taken up position. As the marching men came into view the musical group broke out with the division's rousing theme song, "Dogface Soldier." Immediately a chorus of voices from heavily-burdened fighting men moving into battle joined in:

"I wouldn't give a bean, to be a fancy-assed marine, I'd rather be a dogface soldier like I am . . ."

A few miles ahead were the bomb- and shell-pocked front lines where men had struggled and died for four months. The men of the 3rd Division were marching toward their bloodiest fight of the war.

Along the Mussolini Canal, the Black Devils of Anzio—the fighting men of General Bob Frederick's First Special Service Force—were quietly preparing for their role of protecting the right flank of the 3rd Division. Faces were blackened. Bayonets and knives were sharpened. Patrols probed into the blackness of No-Man's-Land for last-minute intelligence.

Frederick's tough, confident fighters had no intention of returning to the hated *Canale Mussolini* where they had spent nearly four miserable, bloody months. Their eyes were on Rome—and they intended to get there. The entire Force would move out with the attack. Provisions even were made for carting "Anzio" by truck to the Eternal City. "Anzio" was a black colt whose mother had been killed by shellfire and the Forcemen had adopted as a mascot. "Anzio is black," an SSF man explained. "So he belongs with the Black Devils."

The massive forward movement of tens of thousands of troops and tons of supplies for the VI Corps' assault took place during the two nights before H-Hour. All activity had to be made under a mantle of darkness as German observers could view nearly every foot of the flat terrain. The monumental logistics task was carried out without a hitch. So delicately timed was the operation that some battalions did not edge up to jumpoff positions until 30 minutes before H-Hour.

A light drizzle pelted the beachhead as a gray dawn arrived on D-Day. Mostly it was quiet along the semi-circular perimeter. Suddenly, the silence was shattered. At 5:46 A.M. more than 500 American and British guns roared and for 45 minutes pounded German positions with a deluge of death and destruction. The beachhead shook and quivered incessantly from the thunderous bombardment, as though an earthquake were in progress or the gods of war were' angry. In the misty sky 60

American medium bombers plastered already pulverized Cisterna, VI Corps' initial primary objective.

Their barrels red-hot, the big Allied guns fell silent. A few moments of eerie quietude returned to the smoke- and haze-covered battleground. Then the loud, grating chatter of American machine guns, the crack of rifles, the hoarse cough of mortars. Through the pall could be heard the thunder of powerful motors as American tanks rumbled forward. Thousands of grim-faced foot soldiers climbed out of their water-logged slit trenches and began advancing across bleak, open flatlands.

The timing of the assault had caught the Germans by surprise. Some enemy soldiers were captured at bayonet-point in dugouts while still in their underwear. A few were enjoying the company of Italian girl friends.

But the Germans, although thrown off balance, recovered quickly and began resisting with customary tenacity, raking advancing American dogfaces with withering automatic-weapons fire from strongpoints in thick-walled stone farmhouses. Enemy mortar and artillery shells began to explode among the attackers. Early on, it was evident that the breakout would be difficult and bloody, just as the Allied high command had predicted.

The 2nd Battalion of the 15th Infantry, 3rd Division ran into a hornets' nest at a patch of trees named Chateau Woods by the Americans. Dug in along the front of the woods were German infantry, machine guns and tanks, supported by heavy artillery fire. E Company, leading the battalion assault, was badly chewed up, but it quickly reorganized under heavy fire and an order rang out above the din: "Fix bayonets!"

On signal, the men of E Company scrambled to their feet and charged across the flat terrain, screaming and yelling. Fifteen Germans were bayoneted in their holes, 81 were captured, and a number fled back through the woods.

One company of the 30th Infantry had reached a road junction when it came under intense flat-trajectory fire from a mobile 88-millimeter gun and three machine guns. The men were pinned to the ground, unable to move. Staff Sergeant Cleo A. Toothman heard a voice call out above the din: "Toothman, I'm going to get that 88 bastard with my heater!"

Toothman recognized the voice of Private First Class John Durko. He invariably called his BAR a "heater."

Before Toothman could reply, Durko took off across the flatland like a frightened jack rabbit, racing directly toward the German gun. Machine gun bullets thudded into the ground around him, and two shells exploded nearby. After dashing for about 100 yards, Durko dived into a huge shell crater.

Sergeant Toothman, reflecting that he had never seen such heavy fire in such a small area, knew that Durko could go no farther. But a few minutes later the American BAR man scrambled from the crater, ran in a wide circle to within a few yards of one machine gun. He hit the ground and tossed a grenade, killing both crew members.

Hardly pausing, Durko leaped to his feet and moved toward the 88-millimeter gun. Some 10 yards away he let off a burst from his BAR and wiped out the five Germans manning the lethal weapon. Then he spun around and killed the crew of the second machine gun.

Now the young soldier was raked by the third machine gun, only 20 yards away. Several bullets tore into his body. Durko staggered, but continued toward the spitting automatic weapon. Like a wounded beast, he slowly charged the machine gun, firing his "heater" from the hip. Both German gunners were killed.

When Durko's company continued the advance, they found the BAR man sprawled dead across the enemy machine gunners.

By evening of D-Day for the breakout General Ernie Harmon's 1st Armored Division, on the left flank of the heavily-engaged 3rd Infantry Division, had fought forward for 4,000 yards, cut the Cisterna-Campoleone railroad and captured much of the German artillery in its sector. Bad weather had curtailed planned air support that morning, but by noon the skies had cleared and Allied bombers and fighter-bombers were out in force in front of Harmon's tankers.

General Harmon was in the thick of the action all day, feeling that he had been given a reprieve by the Creator. During the night he had moved to a forward foxhole to be ready for the attack and a German artillery concentration had demolished his converted ordnance-repair truck parked in the Padiglione Woods, killing or wounding several headquarters personnel.

Only later would a German map be found with a large "X" drawn on the precise spot where Harmon's vehicle sleeping quarters had been dug in for weeks.

Despite the substantial advance by 1st Armored, Cisterna, only two miles from American jumpoff positions, remained in German hands as darkness enfolded the battleground. The 3rd Infantry Division had suffered 995 casualties that day, one of the heaviest single-day's toll by an American division during the war, and Harmon had lost 116 tanks and tank destroyers, mainly to mines. Frederick's First Special Service Force had moved forward along the Mussolini Canal and met determined resistance.

On the left flank of the Allied bridgehead, the U.S. 45th and British 1st and 56th Divisions had conducted such successful holding attacks along the Albano road and in The Factory area that General von Mackensen refrained from shifting his forces to meet the breakthrough threat at Cisterna until it was too late. At the end of the first day American forces were on three sides of that battered town.

The Germans had also taken a terrific beating. The 362nd Division in front of Harmon's tankers had lost 50 percent of its effectives, and two regiments of the 715th Division were badly mauled by elements of the 3rd Division and the First Special Service Force. Some 1,500 German fighting men had been taken prisoner and hustled back to cages at Anzio and Nettuno.

At dawn the following day, the twenty-fourth, VI Corps continued the assault. Harmon's 1st Armored drove ahead and cut Highway 7 between Velletri and Cisterna, virtually isolating the latter town, now a rubble and dust pile. The stubborn German defenders there continued to hold out against heavy attacks by the 7th Infantry Regiment, but other 3rd Division units had bypassed Cisterna on each side and the First Special Service Force on the right also plunged ahead. The German resistance center was hemmed in on three sides.

Meanwhile General von Mackensen had belatedly reacted to the threatened breakthrough at Cisterna. That evening the American attackers became bogged down in fierce fighting with elements of the 4th Parachute Division which had been shifted over from the British sector. At sundown bitter fighting still raged along the entire front.

With the arrival of dawn on the twenty-fifth a long German

convoy of panzers, trucks and other vehicles, many loaded with troops, was edging along a road beyond Cisterna. These were elements fleeing before the advance of Fifth and Eighth Army from the south. Suddenly Germans in the convoy heard the frightening sound of airplane motors overhead and the cry *"Jabos! Jabos!"* (American fighter-bombers) swept through the column.

Vehicles careened off the road seeking cover, and grenadiers scrambled for the cover of roadside ditches. Moments later swarms of P-47 Thunderbolts and P-51 Mustangs, loaded with 500-pound bombs under each wing, swooped down on the trapped column like prairie hawks pouncing on chickens. For a half-hour the fighter-bombers strafed and bombed the German vehicles, which stretched along the road as far as the eye could see.

The carnage and slaughter was as great as any encountered in the savage Italian campaign. Fourteen German panzers lay mute, now only burning, blackened hulks. For miles trucks had been smashed. Dead horses, their entrails strewn over the road, were sprawled about by the score. Interspersed among the smoking vehicles and dead animals were the corpses of hundreds of Wehrmacht soldiers.

At Cisterna, the hard-pressed 3rd Division men of the 7th Infantry had fought their way into the smashed town reeking with the pungent odor of explosives and dead bodies. The dogfaces battled the German defenders from rubble pile to rubble pile, a fierce nose-to-nose encounter with bayonets, grenades and rifles. Only when the Americans reached the mounds of masonry which marked what had once been the town square did the final 226 Germans burrow out of their positions and surrender, their faces covered with dust.

In the huge, deep cellar under the palace, where the defenders had taken refuge from the holocaust-like bombardment, scores of German corpses intermingled with seriously wounded grenadiers were strewn about in heaps amid piles of soiled clothing and human excrement. The ugly odor was so intense that some Americans on entering gagged and vomited.

Earlier that morning, General Mark Clark was traveling through forward areas in his jeep. He felt a cautious inner optimism. Beachhead forces had at that point captured 9,018 Germans, perhaps twice that number were dead or wounded,

and the enemy's defensive positions had been penetrated at
numerous places. The recurring thought raced through the Fifth
Army commander's being: is this the time to make a bolt
directly to Rome?

Shortly after 10 A.M. the jeep's radio picked up word that
elements of the 48th Engineer Regiment and the 91st Reconnaissance Squadron were nearing a linkup with a task force
from the beachhead consisting of elements of the 36th Engineer
Regiment, members of a reconnaissance unit of the British 1st
Division, and a group of American tank-destroyers. General
Clark felt a strange thrill surge through his being. After four
months of excruciating agony at bloody Anzio, his beachhead
force and main body of Fifth Army were about to join hands.

Clark ordered his driver to race for the impending juncture
site. The general arrived just as the tired, grimy and dust-
covered American dogfaces from north and south were grinning and vigorously shaking hands on the Anzio-Terracina
road. The meeting took place about a mile northwest of Borga
Grappa, a village which had, perhaps symbolically, been
flattened by Allied air attacks. That concluded the brief,
impromptu ceremony.

Beleaguered Anzio beachhead no longer existed.

Driving back to the scene of the fighting to the north,
General Clark mentally reviewed the tactical situation. His five
American beachhead divisions were attacking toward the
northeast to seize Valmontone which sat astride Highway 6, the
route leading from Cassino to Rome. General Alexander felt
that capturing Valmontone would trap a major portion of
General von Vietinghoff's Tenth Army, which was fleeing
northward in front of the British Eighth Army.

Clark disagreed that this would trap the Tenth Army. The
German force could withdraw toward Rome along other roads
to the east. The Eighth Army, moving methodically up the Liri
Valley on Highway 6, did not need the full weight of VI Corps
to assist it forward, Clark concluded, as the British had already
smashed the final German positions below Valmontone. The
Fifth Army commander was far from anxious to "draw Eighth
Army along like a rope" and permit the British to become full
partners in the race for Rome.

Clark concluded that even if Truscott were to fight his way
through to Valmontone and seize the town, VI Corps would

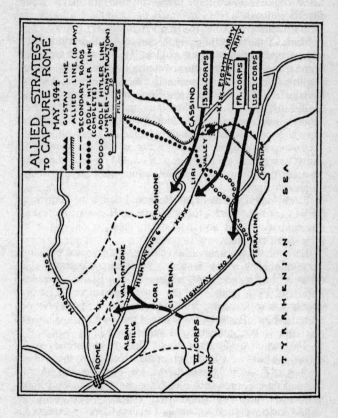

ALLIED STRATEGY
TO CAPTURE ROME
MAY 1944

Gustav Line
Allied Line (10 May)
Secondary Roads
Adolf Hitler Line
(Complete)
Adolf Hitler Line
(Under Construction)
Miles
0   10   20   30

CASSINO
LIRI
VALLEY
FORMIA
FROSINONE
HIGHWAY No 6
HIGHWAY No 5
VALMONTONE
CORI
CISTERNA
HIGHWAY No 7
TERRACINA
ALBAN HILLS
ROME
ANZIO
VI CORPS
TYRRHENIAN SEA

13 BR CORPS
EIGHTH ARMY
FR CORPS
FIFTH ARMY
US II CORPS

have an extremely difficult time in conducting a complicated 90-degree turn to the left to advance toward Rome up Highway 6. It would be much more expedient, the Fifth Army leader decided, to switch VI Corps' main thrust to the northwest and take the shorter route to Rome up Highway 7.

Mark Clark had another significant reason to question if the current operational plan was prudent. He knew that the Allies were going to launch a massive cross-Channel attack against northwest France on June 6 and that Clark's boss, General George Marshall, and President Roosevelt had stressed to him in his mid-April visit to the States that great psychological value would accrue to the Allies if Rome could be captured before the assault on Normandy. Slugging his way through the mountains to Valmontone, a direction which was taking Fifth Army *away* from the Italian capital, would make it impossible to seize the Italian crown jewel before the fast-approaching D-Day in France.

Clark's mind was made up. He would switch the main thrust of VI Corps and head it toward Rome up Highway 7—and tell his immediate superior, Alexander, about it only after the new-direction attack was in progress.

Early on the morning of May 26, as VI Corps was preparing to continue its attack toward Valmontone, General Lucian Truscott had a caller. Major General Don Brann, operations officer of Fifth Army, told the corps commander: "The boss wants you to leave the 3rd Division and the Special Service Force to block Highway 6 and mount the assault you discussed with him to the northwest as soon as you can."

The switch in direction would send the main body of VI Corps over the western portion of the Alban Hills, the gateway to Rome. Truscott doubted the wisdom of the switch. He told Brann that his corps should continue the attack toward Valmontone to "trap" the withdrawing German Tenth Army. He asked for permission to contact General Clark to express his objections.

"Can't be done," Brann responded. "The boss is on his way to his rear CP." The Fifth Army operations chief added that "there's no use in arguing about it," the decision was irrevocable.

That evening General Clark conferred with Lucian Truscott at Anzio and plans were worked out for the VI Corps' change

"My God! Here they wuz an' there we wuz."

Bill Mauldin's famed infantry dogfaces Willie and Joe are shocked on breaking out of the beachhead and getting the view the Germans had of American movements for nearly four months. (COPYRIGHT 1944-45 BY BILL MAULDIN. USED WITH PERMISSION OF BILL MAULDIN.)

of direction. Clark radioed Gruenther that he was launching this "new attack with all speed possible . . . in order to overwhelm the enemy in what may be a demoralized condition at the present time."

Clark added: "You can assure General Alexander this is an all-out attack. We are shooting the works."

That night Truscott summoned his divisional commanders. He presented the new plan as his own and waxed enthusiastic over its potential. The 3rd Division, First Special Service Force and part of the 1st Armored Division would continue to attack toward the northeast to Valmontone, the corps leader pointed out. At the same time, the 34th and 45th Infantry Divisions would face to the north, directly toward Rome. The balance of the 1st Armored and the 36th Infantry Division would be held in reserve to dash for the Eternal City across the Alban Hills should the opportunity arise.

Truscott told his division leaders, "The Boche is badly disorganized, has a hodge-podge of units, and if we can drive as hard tomorrow as we have done the last three days, a great victory is in our grasp!"

As customary when opposed by first-rate German divisions, the assault across the Alban Hills would be difficult. Arrayed in front of the land mass were the battle-tested 3rd Panzer Grenadier, 4th Parachute and 65th Divisions.

On May 28, another dispute broke out between Clark and Alexander. Tempers, already short-fused under months of grueling pressure, now reached the boiling point. Clark was furious on learning that General Alphonse Juin's French force was being shunted aside due to the fact that Eighth Army's line of advance up Highway 6 would eventually intersect that of the beachhead divisions attacking toward Rome, leaving no road for the French to move supplies and vehicles forward.

"The French Expeditionary Corps, which actually sparked the whole drive toward Rome, is being squeezed out of our front and left dangling in the mountains south of the Liri (Valley)," Clark wrote in his diary.

General Clark promptly took up the matter with Alexander. He proposed that the French advance toward Valmontone up Highway 6, previously designated as the private preserve of the British Eighth Army, which was lagging many miles behind forward Fifth Army elements. Alexander agreed to this arrangement.

A few hours later the 15th Army Group commander's chief of staff, General John Harding, called Clark's chief of staff. Alexander wanted to make certain Highway 6 was kept open for the British, Harding told General Gruenther. The American told Harding that this would contradict an earlier agreement between Clark and Alexander.

"That's not true," General Harding snapped. "He (Alexander) will be glad to have the French advance . . . but he insists that the road to Valmontone remain clear for Eighth Army."

Harding added a remark which again rang a bell of suspicion in Gruenther's mind: "Otherwise, it might be impossible to bring the Eighth Army to bear in the battle for Rome."

There. It's out in the open, Clark and Gruenther thought. Their simmering suspicions were confirmed. The Eighth Army indeed considered itself as a contestant for the glory of being the first conqueror of Rome from the south in 15 centuries.

Clark discussed Alexander's viewpoint with General Juin, who was deeply disappointed. But the French leader insisted on attacking. He said his men, paced by knife-wielding Goumiers, would push ahead over the mountains toward Valmontone.

General Clark was thoroughly angry over this latest development. He told Juin, "From here on I will, by hook or by crook, arrange to have your forces (take part in) the attack toward Rome!"

Meanwhile, battered Anzio town continued to be bombarded by big German guns, even though the coastal port had lost its significance since the beachhead linkup. With the German Fourteenth and Tenth Armies in full retreat, it was time for the dreaded (by the Allied fighting men) Anzio Express to pull back also. But not before the huge gun with its 700-pound shells took one more whack at the inanimate object that was now only a symbol of Allied strength—Anzio.

On May 29 the Anzio Express was rolled out of its tunnel near the Pope's summer residence at Castel Gandolfo and fired its remaining projectiles into Anzio town. It was joined by other German big guns in the hills. Altogether that day, in a final burst of vengeance and frustration, the enemy guns plastered Anzio with 609 shells. The one difference this time was that instead of firing and trundling back into the tunnel, out of sight of Allied aircraft, Anzio Express moved northward. The big gun and the Allies would meet again—soon.

Efforts by VI Corps to fight its way up Highway 6 and over the Alban Hills were met by fierce resistance from the veteran German divisions. General Ernie Harmon's tankers and General William Eagles' 45th Division infantrymen fought bitterly for two days and made no progress. The 34th Division under Major General Charles Ryder was stopped cold in front of Lanuvio. Iron Mike O'Daniel's dogfaces of the 3rd Division found themselves on the defensive, beating off savage attacks near Valmontone by panzers of the Hermann Goering Division.

Fifth Army may have been banging on the gates of Rome— but the gates were refusing to budge.

On May 30, patrols of the 36th Infantry Division, probing toward Velletri, discovered that the Germans had left unguarded the slopes of Mount Artemisio in the Alban Hills. That night General Fred Walker of the 36th sent two regiments, totaling some 8,000 men, in a daring bolt through the yawning hole in the enemy line. Warned to maintain absolute silence, the men from the Texas National Guard outfit huffed and puffed up the steep elevation. They marched all night and by dawn had seized the peak of the towering mountain as well as a German observation post there—without firing a shot. Surprise had been so complete that one enemy officer was captured while taking an early morning dip in a bathtub.

Progress on May 31 was slight. The beachhead force had been attacking almost continuously for eight days and nights and was near exhaustion. But the British leaped forward along Highway 7. The following day General Leese, commander of Eighth Army, sent an aide to Mark Clark with a message from his boss: if Fifth Army was able to capture Rome without the assistance of Eighth Army, Leese would continue to attack in a direction north of Rome. Clark promptly agreed to this proposal.

The final attack by Fifth Army to drive into Rome opened on June 2. When results were still hanging in the balance, General Alexander called on Clark. The Army Group commander said that if Fifth Army could not break through to the Eternal City,

Alexander would "bring in the whole Eighth Army to assure success."

However well meaning Alexander's remark may have been, it rankled Clark. He replied that "our attack is *going* (to break) through!" The implication, the American general believed, was that the British might have to "ride to the rescue" of Fifth Army.

Early on the morning of June 4, General Harmon's tanks and elements of the First Special Service Force edged into the southern outskirts of Rome. A 60-man SSF patrol led by Captain Taylor Radcliffe slipped into the city at 6 A.M. but met with heavy machine gun fire and were forced back. Several jeep-loads of correspondents and photographers accompanying the patrol scattered for the ditches and buildings when the Germans opened fire.

A few hours later General Clark was jeeping toward Rome along Highway 6. At a point five miles from the capital, he halted on spotting his II Corps commander, General Keyes, and General Bob Frederick of the Special Service Force. The pair told Clark that SSF and several tank-infantry "flying columns" had penetrated Rome. Clark promptly decided to push on into the city.

As Americans entered Rome from the south and east, German forces were leaving along deserted streets in the north and west. The arrival of Clark's soldiers set off the most tumultuous celebration in Rome in several hundred years. Frenzied, wildly cheering natives poured into the streets by the hundreds of thousands, engulfing the perspiring, dust-covered and grinning Fifth Army fighting men in a sea of humanity.

While Romans were wildly rejoicing in the streets, Generals Truscott and Harmon were studying a map beside a factory on the southern outskirts. Suddenly a concealed machine gun opened up on the pair, and they flopped to the ground. Harmon peered from under the rim of his helmet and saw that the automatic weapon was being fired from an Italian outhouse. At that point an American tank rolled by. Harmon shouted and pointed toward the machine gun and with one shell the Sherman blew the building, and its occupants, into tiny pieces.

As the two generals regained their feet, Harmon observed that with all the two had been through during the war it would have been an inglorious ending to be killed by fire from an Italian privy.

Despite the wild civilian celebration raging in the city, German die-hard rear-guards, left behind to slow up the Fifth Army advance, continued to resist. When General Clark arrived on the outskirts there was much firing going on. He took cover at the bottom of a hill, and at the top he could see a large road sign which sent a thrill through his being—*ROMA*.

Clark was joined by General Keyes and Frederick and the three commanders began crawling up the hill on their hands and knees along a drainage ditch. As they reached the top, firing had tapered off. Several news photographers arrived, and they asked the generals to stand over by the *Roma* sign for pictures. Camera shutters were snapping furiously as a German sniper cut loose at the shining galaxy of generals' stars. The first bullet seemed to explode as it zipped through the *Roma* sign. Clark, Keyes and Frederick dropped to the ground, as did all others present.

Fifth Army troops were all over Rome that day and engaged in short, bitter fights at many locales. Clark's aides insisted that he wait a day to enter the city proper. Early on June 5, with a few Fifth Army generals and aides, the commander of Fifth Army drove into the heart of the historic center of Christendom. His jeep inched through throngs of cheering civilians who seemed on the verge of hysteria.

Clark hoped to reach the Town Hall on Capitoline Hill where he would confer with his commanders on plans to drive on north of Rome. The little convoy of jeeps wandered through the maze of streets looking for Capitoline Hill. None aboard wanted to admit it—but they were lost.

Eventually the group of jeeps meandered into St. Peter's Square, jam-packed with cheering humanity. As the convoy halted and Clark and the others stared up in wide-eyed awe at the dome of St. Peter's, a priest approached and said in English, "Welcome to Rome. Is there any way I can help you?"

"Well," a smiling Clark replied, "we'd like to get to Capitoline Hill."

The priest gave directions, then added, "We're certainly proud of the American Fifth Army. May I introduce myself?" He gave his name and said he was from Detroit.

"My name's Clark," the army leader responded.

Priest and general expressed mutual pleasure over the meeting, and as the cleric turned to leave he stopped and took another long look at the angular Fifth Army commander. "What did you say your name is?" he asked pleasantly.

By now the jeeps were nearly inundated by the surging throngs. When the priest called out that "this is the commander of the American army" and pointed to Clark, a mighty roar erupted. A mouth on a bicycle yelled that he would lead the jeep convoy to Capitoline Hill, and the vehicles followed the boy. Basking in his unexpected sudden pre-eminence, the boy pedaled furiously and shouted repeatedly for the frenzied Romans to get out of his way, that he was escorting the American Fifth Army commander.

Clark, with one long leg stretching out of his jeep and the foot resting on the fender, briefly reflected as to whether any other general in history had ever been led through a captured capital by a shouting boy on a bicycle.

When the tiny jeep convoy reached the Town Hall, the cheering masses had been left behind and the street was deserted. Clark hopped out of his jeep and briskly strode toward the building. The massive door was locked, and he banged his fist against it several times. There was no response. He struck it a few more blows, feeling less and less like the Conqueror of Rome. Still no answer.

To Mark Clark, the locked door to which there was no key available seemed symbolic of Fifth Army's bitter fight to reach the Eternal City. For months the men of Fifth Army had suffered frustration, danger, agony, pain and death while battling up the boot of Italy, fiercely resisted every step of the way by a skilled and deeply entrenched enemy and hampered by treacherous, towering mountains and abominable weather.

Now, to General Clark, even the doors of Roman buildings were conspiring to bar Fifth Army's path.

EPILOGUE

Controversy over the battle of Anzio beachhead will rage as long as men and women read military history, and tactics are dissected and analyzed in the classrooms of West Point and Great Britain's Sandhurst. The questions, the doubts, go on and on. Was Anzio a militarily sound operation? Did the Allies miss a golden opportunity to inflict a monumental disaster on the German Wehrmacht? If so, who was responsible for this failure? Were the heavy casualties justified? Why did the Allies not dash the 30 miles into a virtually unguarded Rome and achieve an enormous psychological victory? Was the sacking of the VI Corps commander at the beachhead fully justified, or was he cold-bloodedly sacrificed to fill the need for a scapegoat?

For years after World War II military historians fought and refought the battle of Anzio. So did top commanders—American, British and German. Much of what had been written and said was either self-deserving, based on error, or theory which can never be tested. Armchair generals found it easy to isolate what went wrong at Anzio and offer magical tactical solutions—with the aid of infallible hindsight.

The real failure at Anzio was pinpointed by Field Marshal Albrecht Kesselring, one of the war's most able commanders and tacticians. After the war he said:

"The (Allied) landing force was initially weak, only a

division or so of infantry, and without armor. It was a half-way measure as an offensive that was your (the Allies') basic error."

Another cause for Allied difficulties at Anzio was a major false assumption by Prime Minister Winston Churchill, whose "special baby" the landing operation was: that as soon as the Allies landed 60 miles to the rear of German forces arrayed along the Gustav Line, Kesselring would panic and order an immediate withdrawal of his Tenth Army in front of Cassino. Instead, moving with customary alacrity, the German commander in Italy began rushing thousands of first-rate troops and swarms of panzers toward Anzio—far faster than any Allied leader had anticipated.

Much of the Anzio controversy had swirled around the unfortunate General John Porter Lucas, the initial beachhead commander. In its simplest form, the case against Lucas has been that the landing caught the Germans by total surprise and that a golden opportunity was present for a brilliant victory. A "bold" general would have sent a "flying column" racing for the Alban Hills and onward to Rome. Instead, the critics held (and hold), Lucas twiddled his thumbs, let the Germans build up in front of him, and soon was hemmed in a pocket and fighting for VI Corps' life.

In reality, it was not all that simple. Battles never are.

Authoritative evidence has mounted over the years that General Lucas acted with tactical prudence and in compliance with the operational order he had received from General Mark Clark of Fifth Army: "Seize and secure a beachhead in the Anzio area and advance *toward* the Alban Hills." There was no mention of a "bold thrust to Rome," a catchy phrase divorced from battlefield reality and often bandied about by critics at the time of Anzio and in succeeding decades.

Qualified military authorities have agreed that elements of the Anzio force could have reached Rome in the first two or three days. Reaching an objective and holding it are two different matters. The wily and experienced German commanders were past-masters at cutting off and chewing up "flying columns."

General Ernest Harmon, leader of the U.S. 1st Armored Division and a fighter if there ever was one, years later dismantled the critics' "bold thrust" theory:

"To be sure, Allied armor could have swept up into (the

Alban Hills) the first day and plunged into Rome the second day. At staff meetings in Naples I had proposed doing it. Now I am glad I was overruled. The fast assembling Germans would have sliced our supply lines and chewed us up at their leisure. The Allies would have had Rome for 24 hours. After that the Germans would have had us."

General Gerald Templer, the energetic commander of the British 56th Division on the beachhead, was equally emphatic concerning a "bold thrust" to Rome. He later declared that had an Allied force been sent to Rome promptly, "there would not have been a single Allied soldier left in the bridgehead within a week. Every one would have been killed, wounded or captured."

General Lucian Truscott, who lived through every second of the Anzio operation, was widely regarded as a resolute, bold and determined leader. Years later he had this to say:

"I suppose that armchair strategists will always labor under the delusion that there was a 'fleeting opportunity' at Anzio during which some Napoleonic figure would have charged over the (Alban Hills), played havoc with the German line of communications, and galloped on into Rome. Any such concept betrays lack of comprehension of the military problems involved."

Truscott added: "Any reckless advance (by VI Corps) without establishing a firm base to protect our beaches would have been sheer madness."

Since the war, military historians have tended to side with the tactics of the beleaguered and mild-mannered Lucas, maintaining that his actions were militarily sound and proper with the limited forces available. General George Marshall, U.S. Army Chief of Staff, defended General Lucas after the war:

"Every mile of advance made at Anzio in the early days would have added seven miles to the perimeter. This would have required at least an added division for each mile gained. And we had no more troops to send in."

So if General Lucas acted with military prudence, why was he sacked?

Anzio had always been Winston Churchill's "special baby." He had conceived it, nurtured it and took deep pride in what he considered its tactical brilliance. Beginning with D-Day, the

British Bulldog in far off London waited in vain for word that Kesselring had pulled back from the Cassino front and that one or more Allied "flying columns" had raced into Rome from Anzio. In his assumed role as a super supreme commander for the Mediterranean, Churchill could conceive only one reason for the failure to achieve either goal—timidity in the Allied commander on the beachhead.

Lucas, the prime minister decided, had to go. What was needed was a "bold thruster." General Alexander, Churchill's protege, concurred. Behind-the-scenes pressure to sack Lucas mounted. General Jacob Devers, American deputy to British General Maitland Wilson at Mediterranean headquarters, joined the chorus. Even Army Chief of Staff Marshall gave his tacit approval to a command change.

In its simplest form, Johnny Lucas had lost the confidence of his superiors and of his subordinates at Anzio. Clark, who had been defending old friend Lucas from outside attacks, privately had become increasingly concerned that the VI Corps commander was suffering from extreme mental and physical exhaustion, due to Lucas' long battle responsibility in Italy. General Clark reluctantly decided a change would have to be made.

Military historians, students and buffs will argue until the end of time on the Anzio operation—and never arrive at a consensus. But one thing was certain: Anzio beachhead was one of the bloodiest, strangest and most controversial actions of the war. "Worse than Stalingrad!" captured Germans declared. "Absolutely the worst!" exclaimed American paratroopers, Rangers and Special Service Forcemen after the war. Those who fought at Anzio would forever have the imprint of that unending nightmare seared into their beings.

Heroes were legion at Anzio beachhead—on both sides of the lines. None more so than the American doctors, nurses and medical orderlies in the tented hospitals. Living and working under the most primitive conditions, the medical people were under constant threat of sudden death from artillery or air. Often toiling around the clock, they treated 33,128 patients. Ninety-two medical personnel were killed and 387 wounded. Among those killed were six lady nurses who refused to leave their patients while under heavy fire. Four nurses received the Silver Star for gallantry, the first women ever to be so honored.

Perhaps the best indicator of the danger these Anzio angels of mercy existed under was the fact that tough paratroopers, Rangers, Special Service Forcemen and other front-line troops often concealed minor wounds so they would not have to go back to what they called Hell's Half-Acre, the beachhead hospitals.

Two days after Rome fell, the Anzio Express was captured, to the great glee and inner satisfaction of thousands of Anzio veterans. The railroad gun with the 70-foot barrel and the 700-pound shells was found abandoned by the Germans at Civitavecchia, due to bomb destruction of tracks to the north which prevented its removal. Actually, the Anzio Express was two monsters, but beachhead survivors long tormented by the huge projectiles liked to think of the weapon as singular.

The savagery of the fighting at Anzio was starkly dramatized on the first day of the breakout in the 3rd Infantry Division assault on Cisterna. Not only did Iron Mike O'Daniel's outfit suffer 995 casualties (perhaps the highest one-day toll by any division in the war) but four men were later awarded Medals of Honor.

A few weeks after Rome was liberated, General Ernest Harmon had an audience with Pope Pius XII. The American apologized for the fact that on liberation night the hundreds of tanks, armored cars and vehicles of the 1st Armored Division roared and clattered past the Vatican all night.

The Pope smiled and remarked, "Anytime you liberate Rome you can make all the noise you want."

Thousands of those who fought and endured the sufferings at Anzio failed to survive the war. One of these, Colonel William Darby, whose three Ranger battalions were wiped out in the first effort to capture Cisterna, was killed in northern Italy while leading a combat patrol. He was assistant commander of the Tenth Mountain Division at the time. Two days later Wehrmacht forces in Italy surrendered. The 34-year-old Darby was promoted to brigadier general posthumously.

Curly haired, baby faced Ted Bachenheimer, the incomparable master scout of the 504th Parachute Infantry Regiment whose regular forays behind German lines made him a legend in the 82nd Airborne Division, was captured and killed in Holland later in 1944—while, typically, behind German lines. Decades later, whenever two or more 82nd Airborne veterans gather, the subject of Ted Bachenheimer and his exploits always surfaces. His legend lives on.

Many years after the war, General Mark Clark was attending a formal dinner in Los Angeles and a waiter was introduced as the minesweeper gunner who had fired on Clark's PT boat off Anzio and nearly killed the Fifth Army commander. The story appeared in the newspapers and a short time later Clark received letters from two indignant former Navy men. The waiter, they declared, was a "damned liar," that it was they who should receive the "honor" of almost killing the general.

Was Anzio worth the substantial cost in Allied bloodshed and agony? Just before the Anzio landing the Oberkommando der Wehrmacht had planned to send five of its crack parachute and panzer divisions from Italy to the English Channel coast to meet the powerful looming Allied threat. When the Anglo-Americans struck at Anzio, the procedure reversed—Hitler started pouring divisions from France into Italy.

Two months after the Allied beachhead was carved out only 30 miles south of the Eternal City, the fuehrer, determined to hold onto the psychological prize that was Rome, had 24 divisions in Italy, three times the number in his Seventh Army which was defending Normandy in France.

The number of German paratroop, panzer and panzer grenadier divisions—the elite of the Wehrmacht—in Italy at the time Rome fell, only two days before the massive Allied cross-Channel smash into Normandy, was of especial significance. Hitler had nine of these crack divisions in Italy, as many as were in all of France.

Had only one or two of these paratrooper or panzer divisions fighting in Italy been positioned along the coast of Normandy on June 6, the Allied invasion there most likely would have been bloodily repulsed.

BIBLIOGRAPHY

Adleman, Robert H. and Walton, George, *The Devil's Brigade*. Philadelphia: Chilton, 1966.

Altieri, James, *The Spearheaders*. New York: Bobbs-Merrill, 1960.

Ambrose, Stephen E., *The Supreme Commander: The War Years of General Dwight D. Eisenhower*. New York: Doubleday, 1970.

Bauer, Eddy, *Encyclopedia of World War II*. New York: Marshall Cavendish Corp., 1970.

Bekkar, Cajus, *The Luftwaffe War Diaries*. New York: Doubleday, 1969.

Blumenson, Martin, *Anzio*. New York: J. B. Lippincott, 1963.

Blumenson, Martin, *Salerno to Cassino*. Washington: United States Army, 1969.

Brown, Anthony Cave, *Bodyguard of Lies*. New York: Harper & Row, 1975.

Butcher, Harry C., *My Three Years With Eisenhower*. New York: Simon & Schuster, 1946.

Churchill, Winston S., *Closing the Ring*. Boston: Houghton Mifflin, 1951.

Clark, Mark W., *Calculated Risk*. New York: Harper & Row, 1951.

Eisenhower, Dwight D., *Crusade in Europe*. New York: Doubleday, 1948.

Fehrenbach, T. R., *The Battle of Anzio*. Darby, CT: Monarch, 1962.

Harmon, General Ernest N., *Combat Commander*. New York: Prentice-Hall, 1964.

Keitel, Wilhelm, *The Memoirs of Field Marshal Keitel*. New York: Stein & Day, 1965.

Kesselring, Field Marshal Albrecht, *A Soldier's Record*. New York: William Morrow Co., 1954.

Killen, John, *A History of the Luftwaffe*. New York: Doubleday, 1968.

Kurzman, Dan, *The Race for Rome*. New York: Doubleday, 1975.

Lewin, Ronald, *Ultra Goes to War*. New York: McGraw-Hill, 1978.

Liddell Hart, B. H., *History of the Second World War*. New York: Putnam's Sons, 1971.

Morison, Samuel Elliott, *History of Naval Operations in World War II (Sicily—Salerno—Anzio)*. Boston: Little Brown & Co., 1954.

Routhier, Ray, *The Black Devils*. Great Falls, Montana: Privately Printed, 1982.

Senger und Etterlin, General Fridolin von, *Neither Fear Nor Hope*. New York: Putnam's Sons, 1964.

Summersby, Kay, *Eisenhower Was My Boss*. New York: Prentice-Hall, 1948.

Taggart, Donald G., *History of the 3rd Infantry Division*. Washington: Infantry Journal Press, 1947.

Toland, John, *Adolf Hitler*. New York: Ballantine Books, 1972.

Tompkins, Peter, *A Spy in Rome*. New York: Simon & Schuster, 1962.

Truscott, General Lucian K., *Command Missions*. New York: E.P. Dutton, 1960.

Vaughan-Thomas, Wynford, *Anzio*. New York: Holt, Rhinehart & Winston, 1961.

Wallace, Robert, *The Italian Campaign*. Alexandria, VA: Time-Life Books, 1978.

Westphal, General Siegfried, *The German Army in the West*. London: Cassell, 1951.

Winterbotham, F. W., *The Ultra Secret*. New York: Harper & Row, 1974.

INDEX

THE BEST IN WAR BOOKS

__DEVIL BOATS: THE PT WAR AGAINST JAPAN
William Breuer 0-515-09367-X/$3.95
A dramatic true-life account of the daring PT
sailors who crewed the Devil Boats—outwitting
the Japanese.

__PORK CHOP HILL S.L.A. Marshall
0-515-08732-7/$3.95
A hard-hitting look at the Korean War and the
handful of U.S. riflemen who fought back the
Red Chinese Troops.
"A distinguished contribution to the literature
of war."—New York Times

__THREE WAR MARINE Colonel Francis Fox Parry
0-515-09872-8/$3.95
A rare and dramatic look at three decades
of war—World War II, the Korean War, and
Vietnam. Francis Fox Parry shares the
heroism, fears and harrowing challenges of
his thirty action-packed years in an
astounding military career.

234